Franklin and Galloway: A Political Partnership

Franklin and Galloway: A Political Partnership

by Benjamin H. Newcomb

New Haven and London: Yale University Press

1972

Designed by John O. C. McCrillis
and set in Baskerville type.
Printed in the United States of America by
The Vail-Ballou Press, Binghamton, N.Y.

Published in Great Britain, Europe, and Africa by
Yale University Press, Ltd., London.
Distributed in Canada by McGill-Queen's University
Press, Montreal; in Latin America by Kaiman & Polon,
Inc., New York City; in Australasia and Southeast
Asia by John Wiley & Sons Australasia Pty. Ltd.,
Sydney; in India by UBS Publishers' Distributors Pvt.,
Ltd., Delhi; in Japan by John Weatherhill, Inc., Tokyo.

For L. B. N. and M. G. N.

Contents

Acknowledgments

The courteous and efficient aid of the staffs of the library of the American Philosophical Society, the Historical Society of Pennsylvania, Yale University Library, and the manuscript division of the Library of Congress made the task of reading the papers of Franklin, Galloway, and their contemporaries much easier. The William L. Clements Library, University of Michigan, kindly permitted me to quote from microfilm copies of Franklin letters which were consulted at the Princeton University Library. Leonard W. Labaree of the Papers of Benjamin Franklin permitted me to use that project's card index of the Franklin papers. The *William and Mary Quarterly* permitted me to use material that was previously published in that journal.

Richard S. Dunn of the University of Pennsylvania guided this study through the dissertation stage and read a later draft. His advice and criticisms were very helpful. Robert Zangrando and Edward Tripp of Yale University Press were most patient and encouraging. Finally, a very special person aided me in a very menial task: Sara P. Newcomb helped review proof.

B. H. N.

Abbreviations

Full bibliographical information can be found in the
Note on Sources.

APS	American Philosophical Society, Philadelphia
Evans	Charles Evans, *American Bibliography*
Franklin Papers	*The Papers of Benjamin Franklin* (Yale edition)
HSP	Historical Society of Pennsylvania. Philadelphia
Pa. Arch.	*Pennsylvania Archives*
PMHB	*Pennsylvania Magazine of History and Biography*
Votes	*Votes and Proceedings of the House of Representatives of the Province of Pennsylvania, Pennsylvania Archives,* 8th ser.
WMQ	*William and Mary Quarterly*

Introduction

A political partnership between Benjamin Franklin, one of the most revered men in American history, and Joseph Galloway, half-forgotten Loyalist, seems at first glance as plausible as an alliance between God and the Devil. Everyone knows of the scientist, statesman, and Founding Father. Few remember the man for many years considered a despicable traitor and erroneously classed with historical villains like Benedict Arnold.[1] Clio loveth not a loser; the result of the American Revolution has all but erased Galloway from the list of important leaders of the prerevolutionary period. Vaguely recalled by some is his plan of union, but its failure of adoption is regarded as symbolic of the failure of Galloway and other American Tories to promote loyalty and monarchy when confronted by overwhelming revolution and republicanism. Yet before the Revolution, Franklin and Galloway were ranked together as the most eminent men in Pennsylvania, and as among the most important in America. They collaborated as partners to achieve specific political goals in colonial Pennsylvania: control of the legislature, supremacy over the proprietors, and appropriate responses to British imperial policy. Franklin, twenty-four years older, more experienced, and widely recognized by his contemporaries for his scientific and civic achievements, was the senior partner. Galloway was

1. The works on Franklin are legion. Galloway, as a single subject, has been deemed worthy of only three complete treatments: a series of articles and two dissertations. His plans of union have been discussed at length, and he also has been contrasted with his chief political enemy, John Dickinson. Lorenzo Sabine, in his *Biographical Sketches of the Loyalists of the American Revolution with an Historical Essay*, 2d ed. (Boston, 1864), 1 : 457, has little sympathy for Galloway or his motives, although Sabine was the most charitable of early commentators on the Loyalists.

1

disciple, protégé, confidant, and invaluable aide. From 1755 to 1775 these two politicians attempted to change Pennsylvania to fit their conceptions of how the colony and the British Empire should be governed. The challenges of Pennsylvania's proprietary governors and of Britain's imperial policy confronted them throughout this period. When imperial crisis became battlefield conflict, the partners chose different sides. The outcome of the conflict caused one to be deified and the other damned.

It is principally with the political relationship between Franklin and Galloway and with their activities in politics that this study is concerned. Much has already been written about the "polygonic" Franklin, recounting his scientific achievements, his political thought, his diplomatic activities, and his general character. Comparatively little has been written about Galloway, who left fewer personal records dating from the prerevolutionary period. The surviving Galloway material is almost entirely concerned with his political activities, especially those undertaken jointly with Franklin, and contains very little about his private affairs. Therefore, this study has been limited to an analysis of these two men in politics, rather than broadened to paint a complete human portrait. The political story deserves telling in order to fill out the history of Franklin's career, to bring to light Galloway's achievements and failures, to explain Pennsylvania politics in this crucial period, and to suggest how patriot and Loyalist positions developed.

The particular historical questions raised by the closely intertwined careers of Franklin and Galloway are those about the nature, the achievements, and the final dissolution of this political partnership. Why did Franklin and Galloway join forces in politics and remain allied for twenty years? Their friendship has been mentioned but not explained by their biographers.[2] What common ideas and ambitions propelled

2. Carl Van Doren, *Benjamin Franklin* (New York, 1938), and Verner W. Crane, *Benjamin Franklin and a Rising People* (Boston, 1954), rank Galloway as Franklin's lieutenant—"more or less," as Van Doren puts it (p.

them through Pennsylvania's violent political storms? Galloway has been generally seen as acting according to honorable, although mistaken, principles of conservatism. In the view of one biographer, he "lacked that faith in the common people which gave courage to the patriots and enabled them to persevere in what at times seemed a lost cause." [3] Most investigators of Franklin's career find him the apostle of a new American order, the advocate of freedom and democracy.[4] A minority report criticizes Franklin as vengeful, overambitious for power and profit, and, before 1776, insensitive to the stirrings of liberalism in Pennsylvania.[5] A clearer interpretation of the political ideas and aims of both men, as these were manifested during their long association, seems required.

The political methods that Franklin and Galloway used to gain and retain power also demand investigation. Franklin's career in Pennsylvania politics has been termed a disaster because he failed to oust the proprietary government and because, supposedly, after 1766 he lost most of his political influence in the colony.[6] Galloway's failure at the First Continental Congress has indicated to historians that he lacked practical political ability.[7] More investigation is required to explain how, during their long tenure in office together,

---

314). Galloway's biographers have not clearly shown how important to Franklin, and how close to Franklin, he was.

3. Ernest H. Baldwin, "Joseph Galloway, the Loyalist Politician," *PMHB* 26 (1902) : 442.

4. Theodore Thayer, *Pennsylvania Politics and the Growth of Democracy, 1740–1776* (Harrisburg, 1953), pp. 22–23, 40, 59, presents this view of Franklin. Clinton Rossiter, *Six Characters in Search of a Republic: Studies in the Political Thought of the American Colonies* (New York, 1964), pp. 220–32, finds Franklin with strong principles but without real political theory. Paul W. Connor, *Poor Richard's Politicks: Benjamin Franklin and His New American Order* (New York, 1965), sees both consistency and principle in Franklin's political thought.

5. William S. Hanna, *Benjamin Franklin and Pennsylvania Politics* (Stanford, 1964), p. 204. This book presents an unfavorable description of Franklin, based on the views of his political enemies.

6. Ibid., pp. 197, 204.

7. William H. Nelson, *The American Tory* (Oxford, 1961), pp. 54–55.

they attempted to cope with the problems that all politicians face. These two men of vision and initiative felt compelled to implement new programs in Pennsylvania, and consequently had to gain the support of both the populace and their colleagues in the government. They also at the same time had to conform to the conservative inclinations of their constituents, who desired preservation of their charter rights, who saw little need for change in traditional practices, and who were generally apathetic toward the processes of politics except when their daily lives were directly touched. To retain power and gain acceptance of their policies, Franklin and Galloway had to play what one might regard as the dirty political game. They had to build and sustain a party by rewarding their adherents, punishing their enemies, and manipulating voters.

As political leaders during the critical prerevolutionary years, Franklin and Galloway were forced to take positions on the growing Anglo-American conflict. How did their partnership meet the series of progressively graver crises that were splitting the empire apart? How did their stands on imperial issues affect their political positions? Certainly the most puzzling question of all, as Julian P. Boyd asserts, is why Galloway, in 1775–76, repudiated Franklin's friendship, partnership, and "deeply concerned solicitations." [8] Franklin's and Galloway's responses to the challenges of local political conflict in Pennsylvania and of new, oppressive imperial measures first joined them as partners and cemented their alliance more firmly, but later drove them to part. These important colonial leaders were political allies and friends for about twenty years. Their partnership, weakened by the growing split between Britain and America, was finally torn asunder by the Revolution. Friendship turned to enmity. The story of their careers is in many ways parallel to the history of the separation of Britain and America.

8. Julian P. Boyd, *Anglo-American Union: Joseph Galloway's Plans to Preserve the British Empire, 1774–1788* (Philadelphia, 1941), p. 16.

1 The Unequal Partners

Benjamin Franklin, with infinite interests and abilities almost as boundless, was nevertheless perceptive of his human limitations: he could not successfully devote his enormous energy to many different fields of endeavor at one time. For specific purposes he sometimes took others into partnership, managing jointly with them the particular concern at hand. A partnership, he well understood, would merge his powers with those of some other competent person to produce greater results than if they acted separately. In 1748, when Franklin determined to retire from full activity in his printing establishment in order to devote himself to "Philosophical Studies and Amusements," he chose his foreman, David Hall, as his business partner so that he would continue to receive income from his shop.[1] To aid him in his complex political ventures after 1755, Franklin selected as his political aide and partner Joseph Galloway.

Franklin's son William probably brought his father and Galloway together sometime around 1750. William Franklin was about the same age as Galloway, who was born in 1730.[2] Galloway had begun to practice law in Philadelphia in 1748, and William chose law as his career. In 1753 the younger

1. Benjamin Franklin, *The Autobiography of Benjamin Franklin,* ed. Leonard W. Labaree et al. (New Haven, 1964), p. 196.

2. In October 1778 Galloway claimed that he was forty-eight years old. Joseph Galloway, *Examination of Joseph Galloway, Esq., Late Speaker of the House of Assembly of Pennsylvania, Before the House of Commons, in a Committee on the American Papers, with Explanatory Notes* (London, 1779), p. 1. Also see Baldwin, "Galloway," pp. 161–62, who gives the date as 1731; and Raymond C. Werner, "Joseph Galloway, His Life and Times" (Ph.D. dissertation, State University of Iowa, 1927), pp. 1–2.

Franklin undertook the study of law in Galloway's office.[3] Perhaps the contrast between Galloway and William Franklin attracted William's father to the young Galloway, for the lawyer was beginning to make his mark in Philadelphia in the early 1750s, while the younger Franklin, his father noted in 1750, had "imagin'd his Father had got enough for him." [4] Galloway's success, Franklin probably believed, would provide a needed example for his son. No doubt the two younger men often sat at the feet of the philosopher, entranced by his personal charm, his wide experience, his scientific knowledge, and and his prescriptions for a useful and virtuous life.

A major topic of their discussions was certain local politics; each had his reasons for interest in it. Franklin had entered the Pennsylvania House of Representatives (also termed the Assembly) in 1751, although in the first years of the decade he was not a legislative leader.[5] William Franklin had assumed his father's old post, the clerkship of the House. Galloway's legal career brought him into close contact with Pennsylvania's political chiefs. Franklin's success as initiator of many public service enterprises in Philadelphia must have forecast to Galloway that Franklin's political involvement would increase. Galloway was thus probably inspired by Franklin to devote himself to public service as well. If Franklin, the self-trained son of a Boston candle maker, could achieve prominence, could not Galloway, the educated son of a wealthy landowner, follow his path to greatness?

In many respects Galloway does not appear to have been on the same path. Franklin's and Galloway's intellectual interests, abilities, and personalities, as seen in their writings and actions, seem to have made them very different persons.

3. Edward Shippen to Joseph Shippen, January 17, 1753, Shippen Papers, APS.

4. Franklin to Abiah Franklin, April 12, 1750, *Franklin Papers*, 3 : 474–75.

5. Contemporaries employed the terms "House" and "Assembly" interchangeably to refer to the House of Representatives; this book will do likewise.

One obvious difference, their twenty-four-year age gap, represented mainly a great difference in experience. Franklin had become a man of the world who had traveled to England and to many other American colonies. He possessed a cosmopolitan air—a self-assurance that comes from having been in many places and done many things. As a newspaperman, Franklin had to be familiar with happenings in remote parts of the world and to understand events from a broad viewpoint. His contacts with the mother country and with other colonies provided him with a well-informed outlook that few other colonials could boast. Galloway, in contrast, was a true provincial who seems never to have ventured outside the Pennsylvania-Maryland-Delaware environs, at least not before 1755.

Franklin's manifold interests show that he possessed the natural curiosity of the scientist. He desperately wanted to understand how things worked—things physical and things social. He craved to master mysterious processes. Curiosity begat in Franklin an unchainable passion for inventing, organizing, and directing. In comparison, Galloway's intellectual interests seem bland and sterile. He never took an interest in the scientific problems which aroused intellects in this Age of Enlightenment. He was not concerned with the scientific discoveries that were the products of Franklin's potent imagination. His letters to Franklin exhibited none of the curiosity about natural phenomena which Franklin displayed in his correspondence. He never joined the Library Company.[6] While wide travel and scientific curiosity had broadened Franklin's outlook, legal training had apparently narrowed Galloway's. The latter was much more interested in the lawyer's analytic tasks of defining terms and disputing over words and phrases. Franklin's writings show that he could synthesize much better than Galloway. The philosopher attempted to understand the world as a whole and bring it into

6. Galloway later served as vice-president of the American Philosophical Society, but the position was honorary. He had a practical interest in husbandry, as indicated by a letter from William Franklin to Galloway, December 28, 1759, Yale University Library.

scientific focus to permit his intellect to operate on complex problems. He tried to comprehend the natural laws that governed all the actions of physical bodies. Galloway was much more adept at tearing off segments of experience and closely scrutinizing them under the cold light of legal reasoning than at undertaking the kind of intellectual process that Franklin employed. His narrow focus and less creative mind never permitted him to understand his surroundings in the same way Franklin did.

The religious views of the two men provide further evidence of their intellectual differences. Franklin's critical and imaginative approach made him a freethinker. Galloway was not much given to religious speculation. The tone of his writings shows him to have had a somewhat more orthodox attitude toward religion than did Franklin. Probably he was most in sympathy with Anglicanism. His family and his wife's family were Friends, and he may have occasionally attended Meeting. Galloway's religious beliefs apparently paralleled his attitude toward science; he was not much drawn to the intellectual speculation on which Franklin's fertile mind thrived.[7]

Not only did Franklin and Galloway possess different intellectual and religious outlooks and interests, but they appear, from their writings and from the views of their contemporaries, to have been quite different in personality. Franklin's greatest personal asset, after his intellectual abilities, was his winning appeal to others. His warmth, liveliness, and charm sprang from his genuine interest in other people. In part, curiosity led Franklin to cultivate acquaintances, to learn what people thought and how they acted. He made friends easily and eagerly. His respect for others made him generally

7. Some commentators have erroneously thought Galloway a deist. Baldwin, "Galloway," p. 167, n. 2, suggests that he occasionally attended Quaker meeting. He is not listed in "A Directory of Friends in Philadelphia, 1757–60," *PMHB* 16 (1892) : 219–38. Galloway was married in Christ Church, but he held no pew there. In England after the Revolution he wrote religious tracts.

tolerant of other opinions and willing to listen to other points of view, even those much opposed to his own.[8] Galloway appears to have been more cold and unbending than Franklin. His sociability was founded on his handsome appearance, his upper-class family ties, and his wealth. Outside his political and business connections, he apparently had few close friends.

Another of Franklin's assets was his sense of humor. Contemporaries termed him droll; modern readers usually find him delightful. Not only did this attribute help win him friends, but it also buoyed him when he suffered reverses. Galloway apparently had no sense of humor at all. He took himself and the world very seriously, never making light of any occurrence.[9]

Franklin acknowledged that he calculated how his actions would look to others. He avoided appearances of vanity. He tried to make himself seem virtuous and industrious to other Philadelphians. He was careful not to assume credit for too many of his ideas, and he refrained from bragging about them; he was content to make others aware of his abilities by actions rather than words. He went out of his way to conciliate those who opposed him, for modesty and conciliation, he calculated, would win him friends and respect. Franklin consciously sought appreciation, but Galloway expected deference as a matter of course. He demanded attention because of his wealth, social position, and family connections. Consequently, he acted as if he did not need to flatter or conciliate others; he felt they should press their attentions on him. When Galloway was not accorded the deference which he thought he deserved, or when he was challenged or defeated on an important matter, he frequently lost his temper. In adversity,

8. Good examples are in Franklin, *Autobiography*, pp. 171–72, 178–79, 213.

9. George Vaux, "Extracts from the Diary of Hannah Callender," *PMHB* 12 (1888) : 434, gives a contemporary's view of Franklin's conversational humor. There seems to be no humor in Galloway's personal letters.

Franklin was much more patient and stoical, for he had great confidence in his ability to survive all blows.[10]

Consequently, Franklin cast an almost magic spell over supporters, friends, and acquaintances, getting them to do as he wished by pleasant persuasion. He could not resist a bit of bragging, however, after the first triumphs of his political career in November 1756; he said, "the People happen to love me. Perhaps that's my Fault." Galloway's associates respected him for his abilities, but even his friends thought that he was somewhat arrogant, overbearing, and hot-tempered. His enemies were to hate him for these traits, and the people never really loved him.[11] Galloway's abilities, not his personality, attracted Franklin to him. Franklin's personality, breadth of activity, and real concern for others charmed Galloway. Franklin was and is a very appealing character; Galloway was much more ordinary and much less attractive.

These two very different men never explained why they became friends and partners. Though their differences would seem to have kept them apart, a general overview of their ideas and activities shows that Galloway's capabilities in many respects complemented Franklin's and that they had common political ideas and interests. Political alliances are sometimes formed because the allies possess different and complementary abilities. If they were to act separately their inadequacies might hamper them; acting together, their respective characteristics mesh like well-oiled gears, and they can cooperate in

10. Franklin, *Autobiography*, pp. 158–60. Important descriptions of Galloway's personality are in William Goddard, *The Partnership: or the History of the Rise and Progress of the Pennsylvania Chronicle* (Philadelphia, 1770 [Evans no. 11669]), pp. 6–16; and [Rev. John Vardill] to [William Eden], April 11, 1778, in *Facsimiles of Manuscripts in European Archives Relating to America, 1773–1783*, ed. B. F. Stevens, reprint (Wilmington, Del., 1970), 4, no. 438.

11. Franklin to Peter Collinson, November 5, 1756, *Franklin Papers*, 7 : 13. Thomas Livezey to Galloway, December 14, 1765, printed in *PMHB* 12 (1888) : 367. During his political career, numerous broadsides and newspaper pieces appeared attacking Galloway with charges concerning his personal traits.

harmony, one supplying what the other lacks. The partnership of Franklin and Galloway was no misfit. Galloway possessed endowments and capabilities important in Pennsylvania politics, and these worked in tandem with Franklin's talents. Born into a wealthy family of Delaware and Maryland, Galloway had the social background and breeding necessary to penetrate the upper circles of Philadelphia society.[12] Franklin, a social nobody, was barred at many doors open to Galloway.[13] The younger man's success in moving among the social elite of Philadelphia, as well as his handsome looks and career prospects, proved of great personal, professional, and political benefit. In 1753 he captured the prize belle of the colony, Grace Growden. Her father, Lawrence Growden, was a justice of the Supreme Court and reputedly the wealthiest man in Pennsylvania.[14] In contrast, Franklin's wife, Deborah Read, was "a good and faithful helpmate" but intellectually inferior and socially perhaps a burden to her husband. Galloway's exalted marriage allied him more closely with the best of Pennsylvania society. In politics, where social distinctions played an important part, Galloway could give Franklin's cause a modicum of upper-class respectability.

Franklin described himself as a "bad Speaker, never eloquent, subject to much Hesitation in my choice of Words, hardly correct in Language, and yet I generally carried my Points." Galloway was a talented orator, the "Demosthenes of Pennsylvania." [15] No matter what Franklin's success, Galloway was evidently more expert at pleading a case before the courts, before the Assembly, and before the electorate. He could vocalize Franklin's ideas and present them more effec-

12. Werner, "Galloway," p. 2.

13. Connor, Poor Richard's Politicks, pp. 212–13, makes the stimulating point that Franklin's numerous activities grew out of feelings of social guilt and the need to prove himself.

14. Pa. Arch., 2d ser. 8 : 97.

15. Franklin, Autobiography, p. 160; North Carolina Magazine and Universal Intelligencer, November 10–23, 1764, p. 198, in American Periodical Series—18th Century.

tively than could the originator. A stirring orator would be invaluable in persuading voters or assemblymen to follow Franklin's lead.

Galloway understood the complexities of colonial Pennsylvania law and the esoteric legal terms which baffled laymen. Franklin admitted that he was not very knowledgeable in law and had little interest in legal proceedings.[16] The law was too narrow a field for his wide-ranging mind. Yet, effecting a political program required legal knowledge and the competence to draft clear and precise legislation. Franklin must have become aware of Galloway's talent when the young lawyer undertook the training of William Franklin, and he presumably saw that Galloway's legal skill might make him a useful advisor in his political activity. In social position, oratorical competence, and legal training, Galloway, although young and inexperienced in politics prior to 1755, complemented Franklin's few deficiencies.

These complementary abilities helped bring about the Franklin-Galloway alliance; their similar character traits and interests, as revealed in their careers and writings, were also instrumental in creating a harmonious partnership. One prominent similar trait was ambition. Both Franklin and Galloway were attracted to politics because it offered them a chance to attain positions higher than those which they could reach in their respective professions. Both had come to Philadelphia from other parts of America, and they remained there probably because they realized that their best opportunities for advancement lay in this rapidly growing city. By 1755 Franklin had made himself a success at printing, scientific experiments, and public service, and he appeared to be on his way to a noteworthy public career. Galloway's profession and marriage also led him toward political activity, although from a far different starting point. Franklin apparently was not satisfied with being a mere printer, with a minor role in the Assembly, or with only the civic projects which he had initiated in the late 1740s and early 1750s. Nor did Galloway

16. Franklin, *Autobiography*, p. 197.

remain content with merely a lucrative legal career. Politics
to eighteenth-century Pennsylvanians was a legitimate means
of social fulfillment—the honorable way for a gentleman to
advance and prove his worth to his peers and to the lower
ranks of society. This desire to succeed in the public eye impelled both men.

Secondly, both Franklin and Galloway viewed political activity as a public service. By entering the Pennsylvania Assembly, Franklin believed that he could "enlarge [his] Power
of doing Good." Galloway had a narrower view of benevo-
lence. He believed that he had an obligation to his business
and political allies to "serve ye public"; but this was not a
selfish interest, for to this cause "his life and fortune were entirely devoted," he claimed in 1766.[17] The able individual was
expected by his friends and supporters to use his abilities
on behalf of the community by taking an active part in the
political system. Efficient and effective government would,
both men probably hoped, be the practical result of their
political activity.

Thirdly, the abilities of Franklin and Galloway were well
suited to political activity. Both men were masters of persuasion. Franklin was particularly successful on the personal, individual level; both were very able with the pen. Franklin
had been contributing to newspapers since his youth in Boston. Through diligent practice he had acquired a distinctive
and pleasing style. Galloway's legal training had imparted to
his prose a logical and detailed form. Franklin wrote dialogues,
impassioned pleas, cool and conciliatory expositions, and sarcastic blasts. Galloway was more adept at drawing up clear,
concise pamphlets, replete with legal arguments, and at preparing broadsides full of invective. Other skills of politics—
organization and the planning of strategy—they would have to
acquire. Franklin had already successfully planned and organized the Library, the Association of 1747, and the Acad-

17. Ibid.; Hanna, *Franklin*, pp. 29–30; and Connor, *Poor Richard's
Politicks*, pp. 22–25. Goddard, *The Partnership*, p. 6; Galloway to Franklin, September 27, 1770, Franklin Papers, 3 : 28, APS.

emy. Galloway shows in his writings an instinct for capitalizing on the weaknesses of his opponents, probably sharpened in the courtroom. Both men were well equipped for a foray into the political jungles.

Fourthly, and of greatest importance, Galloway and Franklin both had a deep commitment to the principles of representative government as they understood the British constitution to exemplify them. The British constitution, nearly all eighteenth-century Englishmen agreed, established a "mixed" government, combining monarchical, aristocratic, and democratic elements (king, Lords, Commons). For Franklin and Galloway, as for many other political practitioners, the mixture had to be in certain proportions; they believed that the democratic part of the government should be more powerful than the other two parts. In matters of legislation, the democratic part should have the means to obtain at least a substantial portion of what it wanted. The monarchical and aristocratic elements constituted a rightful check—but never an absolute one. Certainly the representatives of the people should have the most voice in matters of taxation and appropriation, for it was the citizens' money that the representatives collected and spent. The democratic part of the government also bore the responsibility for protecting and asserting the traditional rights of Englishmen. It had to be able to resist encroachments on these rights by other parts of the government.

The intellectual attitudes of Franklin and Galloway, their familiarity with British history, and their interpretation of the writings of British political thinkers influenced their adherence to these principles. Franklin's scientific experiments and his knowledge of science demonstrated to him that nature was ordered by certain laws and principles. In the same way, he believed, the ordering of human society rested on fundamental principles; for Franklin, the principles of politics were as real as scientific laws. He often drew scientific analogies to illustrate a political point. Science not only led Franklin to the conclusion that certain principles guided men politically, but it also gave clues to what these principles were. Balance and order existed in nature and also in the best of human political constitutions. Galloway appreciated the same balance from the point of view of the lawyer. For him, the British constitution best protected the individual and his property.[18]

Recent British history provided further confirmation of the truth of the principles of representative government. Franklin and Galloway were steeped in the Whig tradition of British history. The victory of Parliament over the Crown in 1689, really the victory of the magnates over the abuse of the royal prerogative by James II, provided for the colonials proof that British freedom and the British constitution could be preserved only by preserving the supremacy of the popular branch of the government. The writings of British "radicals," who in the first half of the eighteenth century vigorously argued against the extension of ministerial power and for more privileges for the House of Commons, also convinced the colonials that the principles of representative government had to be upheld. Throughout the American colonies the voices raised in opposition to ministerial power and corruption—the voices of John Trenchard and Thomas Gordon, James Burgh, and Lord Bolingbroke—were heard clearly, known widely, and admired greatly. Franklin had been familiar with the works of these writers ever since his brother had reprinted *Cato's Letters* in Boston in 1721.[19] Galloway's political pamphlets show that he, too, subscribed to the Whig view of British history and to the radical view of the dangers in the

18. Connor, *Poor Richard's Politicks*, pp. 13–14, 56–57, discusses Franklin's admiration for order. Galloway stated his admiration for the British constitution in his writings and in the First Continental Congress as recorded by John Adams, *Diary and Autobiography*, ed. L. H. Butterfield et al., vol. 2 (Cambridge, Mass., 1961), p. 130.

19. James H. Hutson, "Benjamin Franklin and Pennsylvania Politics, 1751–1755: A Reappraisal," *PMHB* 93 (1969) : 305, 309–10. Bernard Bailyn, *The Origins of American Politics* (New York, 1968), pp. 52–58, discusses the influences of these writers on the colonists. Also see H. Trevor Colburne, *The Lamp of Experience: Whig History and the Intellectual Origins of the American Revolution* (Chapel Hill, N.C., 1965), pp. 127–28.

increase of ministerial and monarchical power. The writings and careers of both men demonstrate that they adhered firmly to the aims of limiting executive authority and strengthening the power of the legislature.

Putting the principles of representative government into practice in America was an ideal to be realized, not an accomplished fact to be preserved. Colonials believed that, in theory, the British constitution was intentionally duplicated in the colonies and that the House of Commons was the model for the colonial lower houses of assembly. As Galloway wrote in 1759, the Pennsylvania constitution was "a lively *Resemblance* of its Parent *Constitution*," and the Pennsylvania Assembly was entitled to all the powers of the House of Commons.[20] The colonials were familiar with the practical defects in the British constitution as outlined by British radical writers, and they applied the germane parts of these radical analyses to their own situations. In America, it appeared that the prerogatives of the monarchical part of the government were not substantially diminished after 1689; colonial America had not reaped the full benefits of the revolutionary settlement in England. In the proprietary and royal colonies the prerogatives of the governors—veto, prorogation, dissolution, control of elections, dismissal of judges—and the review of legislation by the King in Council prevented assemblies from (1) exercising powers equivalent to those of the House of Commons and (2) gaining the prominence over the executive that the Commons had gained over the Crown. Colonials saw the solution to be, in principle, the same as that advocated by British radicals; the latter wanted to purge the representative branch of monarchical influence and corruption by electoral reforms, while the colonial political leaders wished to limit the prerogatives of the executive directly by assuming some of them to the legislative branch and by countering executive power with unassailable parliamentary privileges asserted by the assem-

20. Galloway, *A True and Impartial State of the Province of Pennsylvania* (Philadelphia, 1759 [Evans no. 8349]), pp. 9, 36; Bailyn, *Origins*, pp. 61–63.

blies. Generally, colonial assemblies strove to gain privileges akin to those of the House of Commons—that is, more voice in the appointment of officials, control of officials' salaries, and control of monetary policy.[21]

The circumstances familiar to Franklin and Galloway in 1755—the facts of Pennsylvania's political history of the preceding fifteen years—were different in degree, but not in kind, from general American political conditions. William Penn's Charter of Privileges of 1701 had been interpreted by the House of Representatives to give that body extraordinary powers. In the early years of the century, the House, ably led by David Lloyd, won for itself the right to sit on its own adjournments over long periods of time, prevented the council from exercising any legislative authority, and obtained various other concessions. But the representative body was not satisfied, for defects in the constitution remained. Much of its dissatisfaction was with the activities and the suspected intentions of the proprietary heirs of William Penn. The title borne by Thomas and Richard Penn, True and Absolute Proprietaries, had an ominous ring in the colony. The sons of William Penn were thought to be attempting to make their absolute proprietorship include control of the popular branch of the government. The proprietors distributed patronage to attract a faction to support them; they appeared to interfere in elections, especially in 1742 when sailors allegedly were hired to terrorize supporters of the Assembly; and, most reprehensibly in the views of the House, they issued to their lieutenant governor ironclad instructions not to admit bills with certain objectionable provisions. The Assembly conceded the proprietary power to veto legislation through the ap-

21. Jack P. Greene, *The Quest for Power: The Lower Houses of Assembly in the Southern Royal Colonies, 1689–1776* (Chapel Hill, N.C., 1963), pp. 249, 298, 357–61, comments on the efforts of some southern colonies' assemblies to gain more privileges than Parliament possessed. The "quest" in the American colonies seems not to have been aimed at a strict imitation of the House of Commons, but at gaining at least as much power as the model.

pointed governor but argued that the governor should be able to deviate from his instructions when necessary. The process of legislation in colonial America was not that of Parliament, ministry, and Crown. When governor and assembly differed greatly on a specific measure, bargaining had to take place. In the case of Pennsylvania, the Assembly's control of the governor's salary gave that body an important bargaining point. But it was of little use if the governor was in no position to bargain, owing to his instructions. Nor was it feasible to bargain with the proprietors, who were independent of support by the legislature. Thus the instructions of the Penns made difficult the compromising process necessary to have workable government. The instructions relegated the House to a limited sphere of action, inspired it to carp at the governors, and engendered determined efforts to increase its power.[22]

The peculiar position of the proprietors as both governors and landholders, having special property interests to protect and control of the executive power to do so, also aroused the opposition of the Assembly. The proprietors attempted to safeguard their property by issuing instructions against its taxation and against excessive issuances of bills of credit which might depreciate their revenues. The Assembly argued that as landowners the Penns had to accept the responsibility common to all—to support the government—not avoid this responsibility by placing limitations on the taxing and borrowing powers of the Assembly. The combined roles of chief executive and chief landowner gave to the proprietors a preponderance of power and special interests which, in the Assembly's view, upset the balance that was supposed to exist between the executive and the legislative parts.

22. Bailyn, *Origins*, p. 71, notes that governors were hampered in their dealings with assemblies by a lack of flexibility. But it must also be noted that assemblies had to be staunch enough to endure a long and persistent series of negatives in order to best the governors. Hutson, "Franklin," pp. 342–43, discusses the Pennsylvania Assembly's view that governors were obliged to enter into consultation and dialogue with the House. On the election of 1742, see Norman S. Cohen, "The Philadelphia Election Riot of 1742," *PMHB* 92 (1968) : 306–19.

The proprietors were likewise fearful that the balance of the Pennsylvania constitution would be upset—by the Assembly. The House's control over the salary of the governor; its insistence on making appointments to various offices, especially those concerned with disbursing funds; and its attacks on the instructions all smacked of a design to reduce or even eliminate the executive power. Unlike William Penn, who had often given way to "governmentish" leaders of his Council and Assembly because he could not in good conscience deny them the privileges which they demanded, his sons were determined to protect the prerogatives of their office.[23]

Judging by both theoretical and practical considerations, the case of the Assembly seems better founded than that of the Penns. It could not and would not renounce its inheritance of liberal privileges. As private individuals, the proprietors could not have reasonably expected the Assembly to be as subservient to them as Parliament was to the king's ministers, or to regard them with the same awe as legislatures of royal colonies were supposed to regard the king. Yet they dealt with the Assembly as if they possessed monarchical power, continually resisting measures which they thought might in any way infringe on their prerogatives. The Penns were neither theoretically nor practically equipped to govern their province to the satisfaction of the legislature; it would have required more skill than they appear to have possessed, more willingness on their part to compromise, and local management in Pennsylvania, not remote administration from England, to maintain good relations with the Assembly.[24]

Regardless of which side had the better case, the determina-

23. For a summary of the 1740–55 period, see Thayer, *Pennsylvania Politics*, pp. 19–33. Roy N. Lokken, *David Lloyd, Colonial Lawmaker* (Seattle, 1959), discusses the earlier struggles. Hanna, *Franklin*, pp. 35–76, and Hutson, "Franklin," deal with Franklin's 1751–55 period in the Assembly and the issues involved from opposite points of view. Bailyn, *Origins*, pp. 117–19, gives a succinct account.

24. For a summary of historical viewpoints concerning the Penns and the Assembly, see Joseph E. Illick, "The Writing of Colonial Pennsylvania History," *PMHB* 94 (1970): 20–21.

tion of the Assembly to gain for itself what it considered its rightful privileges, and the determination of the proprietors to resist, resulted in a government that operated smoothly only at intervals. When effective action was necessary in a period of crisis, disputes between the governor and Assembly often prevented it. In the fifteen years before 1755, House and governor were so much embroiled in conflict that government became ineffectual. The proprietors would not permit their governor to compromise; the entrenched Quaker oligarchy controlling the Assembly was nearly as stubborn. This latter group could afford to confront the governor; even though the Society of Friends was becoming more and more a minority religious group, Quaker leaders of the Assembly were traditionally reelected. A small group of voters, about 2,000 in Philadelphia County in 1750 and probably not proportionately more in the other counties, continually chose the Quaker leaders because in most years those leaders had no opposition and because the government had given the people peace and prosperity.[25] Negative government, which was generally honest and which had avoided war with the Indians or with Britain's European enemies—which, in short, let every man sit content under his vine and fig tree—seemed to suit Pennsylvanians admirably. Only one important positive program had been implemented—the loan office from which inhabitants borrowed bills of credit. Yet even the operation of this contributed to the negative character of government, for the revenue from the interest on loans paid government expenses and lightened the tax burden. Consequently, Quaker dominance, which resulted in strong opposition to the proprietors, remained quite secure.

Before 1755, the proprietors and their supporters were no match for the Quakers in politics. The proprietors had a

25. J. Thomas Scharf and Thompson Westcott, *History of Philadelphia* (Philadelphia, 1884), 1 : 218, gives an election tally for Philadelphia County for 1750. The population of Philadelphia County was perhaps about twice as large as that of the city, which at the time had about 20,000 inhabitants.

small group of adherents, led by proprietary place holders and supported by some Anglicans and Presbyterians who opposed the Quakers on religious grounds. The Quakers controlled the eastern counties with large representations in the House. The roots of the oligarchy were planted firmly in the Burlington-Philadelphia Yearly Meeting, where Quaker policies on political issues were decided. The Quaker oligarchy was composed of able and rather doctrinaire professional men, merchants, and prosperous farmers who closely adhered to Quaker peace principles and firmly resisted what they thought were proprietary encroachments. Its leaders caucused immediately before election day to determine the ticket, and they made efforts to garner support among non-Quakers, especially the Germans.[26] Philadelphia Quakers, notably John Kinsey, Speaker 1739–50, and Isaac Norris, who succeeded Kinsey as Speaker, dominated the Assembly. Proprietary supporters' efforts to oust the Quaker group and install assemblymen more sympathetic to the Penns' instructions were unsuccessful during this period.

Franklin and Galloway stood outside both Quaker and proprietary groups before 1755. Franklin had been in the Assembly since 1751, but he apparently had had little influence on politics or policy. His popularity won him election, but he did not have the ticket of admission to the inner councils of the leadership—membership in the Society of Friends. Franklin was on good terms with his colleagues, and his Whig view concerning the supremacy of the representative body generally accorded with the views and actions of the Quaker group. Since his first election, he had endorsed Quaker policies, and the House often employed his ability for the drafting of messages to the governors. Yet he rarely initiated policy successfully; the most ambitious scheme that he presented before 1755, the Albany Plan of Union, was not approved by the Pennsylvania Assembly nor by any other colonial legisla-

---

26. Hanna, *Franklin*, pp. 10–11; *Votes*, 4 : 2958, mentions one caucus of Quakers and Germans in 1742.

ture.[27] Galloway was originally a Quaker, but because he had left the Society of Friends he likewise was not eligible to join the governing clique.

Both men could have allied with the proprietary side, for the bonds of friendship, relationship, and religion were strong with that group. Two of Franklin's most important connections were proprietary partisans: Chief Justice William Allen and William Smith. Allen was a fellow Mason who had obtained the deputy postmaster general's office for Franklin.[28] Smith was provost of the college that Franklin had helped found.[29] Galloway's father-in-law, appointed to the Supreme Court by the Penns, could have obtained preferment for him. Franklin and Galloway were at least as closely connected with Anglicanism as with Quakerism. Franklin had a pew in Christ Church. Galloway was married there; perhaps he or his wife attended services. If personal considerations had influenced the political behavior of Franklin and Galloway, they would appear to have drawn both men in the direction of the proprietary camp.

The kind of factional battles which raged between governor and Assembly in the fifteen years before 1755 convinced Franklin that he could not fully join either group except on his own terms. The dominant problem of the period was preparation for war and for defense. The Quaker-led Assembly, maintaining the pacifist position, fought with Governor George Thomas throughout the early 1740s over the issue of support for the war effort. The body never prepared the province for defense, and it was left to Franklin to form the unofficial Association for voluntary defense in 1747. He could

27. Franklin, *Autobiography*, pp. 210–12; Hanna, *Franklin*, pp. 73–76.

28. William Smith, *An Answer to Mr. Franklin's Remarks on a Late Protest* (Philadelphia, 1764 [Evans no. 9841]), p. 15; Hanna, *Franklin*, p. 49.

29. Ralph Ketcham, "Benjamin Franklin and William Smith: New Light on an Old Philadelphia Quarrel," *PMHB* 88 (1964): 143. G. B. Warden, "The Proprietary Group in Pennsylvania, 1754–1764," *WMQ*, 3d ser. 21 (1964): 371–80, shows the close connections among the proprietary group and discusses the wealth of its members.

not fully follow the Quaker leadership clique while it deferred to Quaker ideals. Yet the proprietary position in the early 1750s, as stated most forcefully by Governors James Hamilton and Robert Hunter Morris, was even less agreeable to Franklin. The governors opposed increased issues of paper money, the Assembly's claim to the power to appoint loan office commissioners, and the Assembly's right to appropriate the loan office interest revenue. Proprietary instructions required the governor's approval for appointments, his consent in the disbursement of the interest revenue, the speedy retirement of bills of credit, and a suspending clause in bills authorizing paper money issues to give the Penns and the Privy Council the opportunity to evaluate them before they took effect. None of these terms was the House willing to meet; Franklin agreed with the Quaker leadership that the proprietary instructions in this regard were abridgments of the power of the representative body and infringements on privileges already established by the Assembly. Since 1751 Franklin had written the messages of the House to the governors; these were the main vehicles of the controversy.[30] Deadlock resulted, for in 1753, 1754, and early 1755 Governors Hamilton and Morris refused to agree to paper money legislation. The quarrel between the parts of the government produced an impasse that served neither the Assembly, the proprietors, nor the province.

To Franklin the impasse was intolerable. While the Assembly and the governor debated, the French industriously prepared for another war, forging alliances with the Indians in backcountry Pennsylvania. "I am heartily sick of our present Situation: I like neither the Governor's Conduct nor the

30. For especially querulous messages, see *Franklin Papers,* 4 : 273–74; 5 : 29–34, 281–82, 527–31. Hanna, *Franklin,* pp. 51–52, argues that Franklin was only the clerk of the committees of the Assembly, had little choice in writing antagonistic messages to the governors, and had not taken sides before 1755. Perhaps Franklin was less bitter toward the governors than were the Quaker leaders of the House; but, he substantially subscribed to their viewpoint—not to that of the proprietary group. He was not such a hypocrite that he could pen the Assembly's tirades without agreeing generally with the sentiments they contained.

Assembly's, and having some Share in the Confidence of both, I have endeavour'd to reconcile 'em, but in vain, and between 'em they make me very uneasy," Franklin wrote in June 1755. He accorded Governor Morris most of the blame, for he "spurs with both Heels, at the same time reins-in with both Hands, so that the Publick Business can never move forward." [31] Morris appealed to the House to adopt a defense posture, but at the same time he was unwilling to deviate from the proprietary instructions regarding paper money. The Assembly ignored any defense measures and refused to issue paper money on proprietary terms. The breakdown in constructive government at the very time when war against the French was planned, when Braddock's troops were marching on Fort Duquesne, caused Franklin to consider, presumably, how he could revitalize the political situation. A man ready to formulate plans of union for all America could not ignore the lack of imperial responsibility shown by Pennsylvania. A man of ambition and sincere concern for the welfare of his province and the British colonies would seize the opportunity to shape the crisis situation to his own desires. The solution was becoming obvious; a third force had to be formed in Pennsylvania politics, controlled neither by proprietary supporters nor by nonresisting Quakers.

Braddock's defeat in July 1755 determined Franklin's and Galloway's course of action in Pennsylvania politics. The Assembly, predictably, refused to supply defense forces because of the pacifism of Quaker leaders and because the proprietors refused to allow their estates to be taxed to help meet the emergency. Governor Morris insisted that the Assembly institute a militia under his command and drop its intentions to tax the Penns. The positions of both sides were completely opposed, and no reconciliation seemed possible. To save the frontier settlers from massacre and the political system from complete collapse, Franklin, in August 1755, apparently set about constructing a new group in the Assembly, a group that would take a fresh approach, siding neither with the proprietors nor with the nonresisting Quakers. To his friend

31. Franklin to Peter Collinson, June 26, 1755, *Franklin Papers*, 6 : 86.

Collinson, he hinted how he would accomplish his goal. He would continue battling the proprietary faction, confidently asserting that "it happens that I have the means of my full Defence and their effectual Defeat, in my Power, and shall use those means in due time." While breaking the power of the nonresisting Quakers, Franklin hoped to combine with those Quakers who were amenable to moderate defense measures. "To me, it seems that if *Quakerism* (as to the Matter of Defence) be excluded the House, there is no Necessity to exclude *Quakers,* who in other respects make good and useful Members." [32] Some leading Quakers, like Isaac Norris, the Speaker, had heretofore deferred to the nonresisting point of view but were not personally committed to it. Non-Quakers who supported the Assembly's position, such as Galloway, would comprise an important part of this new group. Franklin's new combination of nonpacifist Quakers and non-Quaker Assembly supporters would propose new measures and break the deadlock that endangered the province.

The prospective political leader, in November 1756, summed up the reasons for his decision to create a new political group. His attitude toward the Penns was a major influence. "I have some natural Dislike to Persons who so far *Love Money,* as to be *unjust* for its sake: I despise their *Meaness,* (as it appears to me) in several late Instances, most cordially, and am thankful that I never had any Connection with them, or Occasion to ask or receive a Favour at their hands." Franklin may have been annoyed at the proprietary neglect to recognize his services to General Braddock and at proprietary sympathizers' attempts to take control of the College of Philadelphia and the Philadelphia Common Council. But he disavowed any personal motive for his political activity. "For now I am persuaded that I do not oppose their Views from Pique, Disappointment, or personal Resentment, but, as I think, from a Regard to the Publick Good. I may be mistaken in what is that Publick Good; but at least I mean well." [33]

32. Franklin to Collinson, August 27, 1755, ibid., 6 : 171.

33. Franklin to Collinson, November 12, 1756, ibid., 7 : 14. Hanna, *Franklin,* pp. 84–87, argues that Franklin was motivated by personal con-

During and after the annual Assembly election in October 1755 Franklin, the evidence suggests, began to organize his antiproprietary, "Half-Quaker" third group. He recruited John Hughes, an Anglican landowner and baker; Hughes remained Franklin's aide for nine years. He also won over Quaker assemblymen who did not oppose defensive war; of twenty-six Quakers in the House, only four offered him strong resistance.[34] On November 19 he introduced a measure that would line up his third group against both the proprietary supporters and the "stiff" Quakers: a militia bill that provided for an organization of volunteers with elected officers. A voluntary militia was acceptable to the less strict Quakers, who feared that continued intransigence might result in an effort in Britain to bar Quakers from office. Under Franklin's leadership, the Assembly showed for the first time a willingness to meet a military emergency and to retreat from its uncompromising stand.

Governor Morris and the proprietary sympathizers did not regard Franklin's militia bill as conciliatory. Morris first opposed the bill because of its seemingly lax and unmilitary provisions; but, convinced that Franklin and the Assembly would never offer him anything better and that the militia therein established would be so unsuitable that the bill's passage would reflect on the House, he finally agreed to it on November 25.[35] In the passage of this Militia Act, Franklin's policy of defense of the province and resistance to the proprietors found its first success. The act became the keystone

---

siderations. Hutson, "Franklin," pp. 363–70, rebuts Hanna's contention, maintaining that Franklin's split with Penn was consummated by the dispute over taxing proprietary lands.

34. Robert L. D. Davidson, *War Comes to Quaker Pennsylvania, 1682–1756* (New York, 1957), p. 168; Thayer, *Pennsylvania Politics,* p. 46.

35. *Votes,* 5 : 4143. Robert Hunter Morris to Thomas Penn, November 28, 1755, Penn Papers, HSP. The Privy Council disallowed this act in April 1756. During the war, other acts were passed establishing military discipline, but the voluntary and elective principles were retained. *The Statutes at Large of Pennsylvania,* 5 (Harrisburg, 1898) : 197–201, 219–21, 281–83, 334–37, 540–41.

in Franklin's bid for support for non-Quaker and defense-minded Quaker groups in Pennsylvania, who would provide the major backing for his new faction.

The other aspect of Franklin's policy, the attack on the governor's adherence to the proprietary instructions, had no such favorable reception. Franklin's group continued the Assembly's demand that the Penns' located unimproved estates be taxed. Governor Morris accused the Assembly of allowing the French and Indians to rampage unmolested while it haggled over who would pay the expenses of the war; the Assembly in reply claimed that it had done all it could by providing arms and ammunition to settlers and that it could not spend more money unless the proprietors would agree to the taxation of their located lands. Franklin expressed the principle held by the Assembly majority when the wrote, in a message of the House to the governor, that the Assembly would provide more funds only if the governor would relent, for "those who would give up essential Liberty, to purchase a little temporary Safety, deserve neither Liberty nor Safety." [36] The Assembly's steadfast position helped to persuade the Penns to acknowledge more responsibility for the defense of their province; in October 1755 the proprietors agreed to donate £5,000 toward the defense of the colony in lieu of the taxation of their estates. The Assembly accepted this offer but did not renounce its right to tax the Penns. Now that Franklin had broken the deadlock over the militia and the proprietors had made some contribution to the defense effort, agitation in the legislature quieted down. With some relief, Franklin reported in December 1755 that, at least in regard to military preparations, "good Agreement with the Governor" now prevailed.[37]

The supporters of the proprietary side would not be quiet; there was no "good agreement" between them and Franklin's

36. *Votes*, 5 : 4113.

37. Franklin to William Parsons, December 5, 1755, *Franklin Papers*, 6 : 290. Hanna, *Franklin*, pp. 94–95, notes that Penn's opposition to taxation of his estate aroused opinion against him in England.

group. Franklin's strategy appeared dangerous to their political aims because his group possessed none of the weaknesses ascribed to the "stiff" Quakers and yet assumed all the strengths of the traditional Quaker antiproprietary side. The task of combatting the threat that Franklin posed was undertaken by his old friend, William Smith. Probably by September 1755 Smith was aware of and very apprehensive about Franklin's political "scheme." [38] Earlier in the year Smith had tried to counter the Assembly's attacks on the governor and its refusal to defend the province. His *Brief State of the Province of Pennsylvania,* published in London probably in January 1755, had accused the political alliance of Quakers and Germans of preparing to deliver up the colony to the French and Indians. *Brief State* had important repercussions in Britain, where the government considered placing political disabilities on Quakers; in Pennsylvania it failed to help the proprietary cause because Franklin's group was shaping a defense policy. In late 1755 Smith shifted his attack to bear more directly on Franklin. He castigated the founder of the militia as a "mighty Politician who expected that every Person would fall and Worship the Golden-Calf"—meaning the allegedly unworkable Militia Act. He attempted to discredit Franklin, accusing him of persuading non-Quakers to support the Militia Act because it would weaken the political hold of the Quakers, while at the same time mollifying the Quakers by arguing that the "scheme was wholly to support their society." [39]

Supporters of Franklin could not permit Smith to malign the Quakers, the militia, or the leader with impunity. Frank-

38. William Smith to Thomas Penn, [September, 1755?], Penn Papers, HSP, mentions that Franklin had some political scheme.

39. William Smith, *A Brief State of the Province of Pennsylvania* (London, 1755), pp. 15–16, 33. *Pennsylvania Journal*, April 15, 1756. William Peters wrote Thomas Penn, January 4, 1756, Penn Papers, HSP, that "many People think that their mighty Favourite Mr. F—— has a deep laid Design to dupe [the Quakers] as well as you," for Franklin was believed by the proprietary supporters to be planning to force the Quakers out of the House.

lin himself was somewhat reluctant to retaliate against his adversary because they had once been close friends and because he hoped that his new political group would lessen factional discord. Yet to the eighteenth-century politician, such charges as Smith levied demanded exact refutation; to allow them to stand unchallenged was tacitly to admit their truth. Convinced of the need to return Smith's fire, William Franklin, Joseph Galloway, and George Bryan made their first entrance into politics as polemicists. This triumvirate of young Turks began in December 1755 by blasting Smith and the proprietary faction in a piece called *Tit for Tat, or the Score wip'd off*, by "Humphrey Scourge." [40] It paid Smith off in his own coin by claiming that not the Quakers but the proprietary sympathizers were in league with the French, and that to boot Smith was really an arch Jesuit who deserved canonization.[41] *Tit for Tat* was so venomous in its effort to make Smith appear foolish that even the Philadelphia Monthly Meeting, hardly sympathetic to Franklin's enemy, branded it as a "virulent, seditious, and scandalous Libel." [42] Popular notice of their first propaganda foray further confirmed Galloway, Bryan, and Franklin *fils* in their determination to defend Franklin's cause. Franklin apparently had kindled the enthusiasm of the younger men of Philadelphia for his way out of the political tangle, and they were ready to march behind him.[43]

40. The authors are identified in a letter of Joseph Shippen to Edward Shippen, Sr., December 5, 1755, Balch Papers, Shippen, HSP. It is quite likely that most people in Philadelphia knew who the authors were. Joseph Shippen was highly amused at the piece. Ketcham, "Franklin and Smith," pp. 145–46, comments on Franklin's reluctance to attack Smith.

41. "Humphrey Scourge," *Tit for Tat, or the Score wip'd off* (Philadelphia, 1755 [Evans no. 8256]), p. 3.

42. *Pennsylvania Gazette*, January 1, 1756. The Quakers claimed that they had nothing to do with the broadside.

43. There has been some uncertainty about Galloway's pamphleteering in this period. Thayer, *Pennsylvania Politics*, pp. 40–41, attributes to Galloway *An Answer to an invidious Pamphlet, intituled, A Brief State of the Province of Pennsylvania* (London, 1755). J. R. Pole, *Political*

As Smith continued to lash out at Franklin and the Militia Act through the early months of 1756, the propagandists replied with unflagging spirit. Franklin tried in his *Dialogue between X, Y, and Z,* to defend the act in a conciliatory manner. Because Smith refused to be polite and conciliatory in return, the Scourge threesome continued to hammer at his motives and character. They accused Smith of conspiring to become a bishop, although his conduct was unbecoming a cleric. His most endearing charms, according to an anonymous writer who was probably Galloway, were "inveterate Calumny, foulmouth'd Aspersion, shameless Falsehood, and insatiate Malice." [44] By June 1756, after weeks of charges and countercharges, the Franklin faction could claim a solid propaganda victory over Smith. Galloway, William Franklin, and Bryan had ably defended Franklin's platform and destroyed the credibility of his major opponent. Franklin had not ended the old factional debate by working for a realignment in politics, but he had created a group which was grounded more solidly on what Pennsylvania required—defense and opposition to the Penns—and which could, because of its programs

---

Representation in England and the Origins of the American Republic (New York, 1966), follows Thayer's attribution (p. 113) and refers to this pamphlet as an example of Quaker ideas about government (pp. 121–22). Thayer based this attribution on letters from Isaac Norris to Robert Charles, January 12 and January 19, 1757, Norris Papers, Copybook of Letters beginning June 16, 1756 (hereafter cited as Copybook), HSP, referring to material by a young member of the Assembly that Norris was at that time forwarding to Charles in Britain. It is not clear what this material was, who wrote it, or what became of it. It had nothing to do with *An Answer to . . . Brief State,* the authorship of which remains uncertain. The pamphlet seems to have been written by someone in Britain who was familiar with Pennsylvania and sympathetic to Quakerism. Galloway did answer Smith in 1759 in *A True and Impartial State of the Province of Pennsylvania.* In *True State,* p. 3, he wrote of Smith's *Brief State* that when it was published "none thought it worthy a Remark, much less a formal Refutation."

44. *Pennsylvania Journal,* April 22, 1756. Also see ibid., March 25, June 17, 1756. Ketcham, "Franklin and Smith," p. 150, n. 20, suggests that Galloway was the author of the scurrilous attack cited.

and its propaganda, gain more support from the electorate than could the proprietary side.

Proprietary sympathizers groaned in despair that "two thirds of the Church are gone off from Church Principles & Church Politicks in favor of [Franklin] & his Politicks & will at ye next Election join the Quakers & chuse for him a Set that he may turn & twist as he pleases." [45] Anglican voters, normally supporters of the Anglican proprietors, were "so poysoned by Franklin that they may prove even worse Enemies to the Proprietaries than the Quakers." [46] Anglicans and some Presbyterians like George Bryan supported Franklin because of his Militia Act and his opposition to the proprietors. Quakers supported him because he stood for the supremacy of the Assembly. The large German group, more than one-third of the total population of the province, swung to Franklin because he had negotiated good contracts for the thrifty "Dutch" to supply the ill-fated Braddock expedition.[47] Franklin had very neatly welded together a group of supporters that transcended religious and ethnic lines to a degree greater than ever before seen in Pennsylvania. By breaking down the Quaker exclusiveness of the old antiproprietary fac-

45. Richard Peters to Thomas Penn, April 29, 1756, Penn Papers, HSP.

46. Richard Peters to Thomas Penn, April 25, 1756, ibid.

47. Franklin estimated the German population of the province at one-third the total. See *The Examination of Doctor Benjamin Franklin, &c., in the British House of Commons, Relative to the Repeal of the American Stamp Act, in 1766,* in *Franklin Papers,* 13 : 132. This is low compared to the estimates of Galloway, *True State,* p. 168, who calculated it at about 50–55 percent; and Smith, *Brief State,* p. 4, who placed it at one-half. David Hawke, *In the Midst of a Revolution* (Philadelphia, 1961), p. 64, estimates that in the backcountry, Germans numbered close to one-half the population. Franklin's attitude toward the Germans before 1755 was antagonistic; he had tried briefly to split the Quaker-German alliance. By 1755, however, Franklin realized that the Germans would throw strong support to him in return for favors. See Glenn Weaver, "Benjamin Franklin and the Pennsylvania Germans," *WMQ,* 3d ser. 14 (1957) : 536–59; and, for corrections, Dietmar Rothermund, *The Layman's Progress: Religious and Political Experience in Colonial Pennsylvania 1740–1770* (Philadelphia, 1961), pp. 86–87.

tion, he opened up political activity to ambitious and able
men such as Galloway, who were attracted to Franklin by
great personal respect, by his program, and by his effective
leadership. When three of Franklin's adherents were elected to
the Assembly in June 1756, on the resignation of nonresisting
Quakers, it was obvious to proprietary sympathizers that
Franklin had won control of Philadelphia County.[48] Because
the Philadelphia members invariably led the Assembly, Franklin's control of this delegation also meant his direction of the
battle against the governor. The successful party leader was
much pleased, for these changes "promise us some fair
Weather, which I have long sigh'd for." [49]

The proprietary group also wanted to calm the political
storms by reaching some agreement with Franklin. Smith's
blasts, threats to get Franklin removed from his post office
job, and the tempting offer of "any Service in his Power"
made to Franklin by Governor William Denny, who replaced
Morris in August 1756, all failed to dissuade him from his
political goals.[50] Franklin and the proprietary leaders were
in accord that further political strife should be avoided in
the October 1756 election. Allen, James Hamilton, and Benjamin Chew, Penn supporters with whom Franklin was on
fairly good terms, met with him to agree on a joint ticket
for Philadelphia County. For the eight seats at stake, Franklin picked five nominees from his supporters, and the proprietary leaders nominated three from their side.[51] Franklin

48. The Franklin men were Thomas Leech, Daniel Roberdeau, "a most
violent Partisan & Creature of Mr. Franklins . . . and Coll. [William]
Masters, another Minion of Franklins," as Richard Peters described them
to Thomas Penn, June 26, 1756, Penn Papers, HSP.

49. Franklin to Peter Collinson, June 15, 1756, *Franklin Papers*, 6 : 456–
57.

50. Franklin to William Shirley, [July, 1756], ibid., 6 : 478–79; Franklin
to Collinson, November 5, 1756, ibid., 7 : 10.

51. Isaac Norris, Joseph Fox, John Hughes, Daniel Roberdeau, and
Jacob Duché were Franklin's nominees. The proprietary leaders chose
Phineas Bond, Henry Pawling, and William Coleman. Richard Peters to
Penn, September 16, September 22, 1756, Penn Papers, HSP.

gave all appearances of willingness to compromise. The proprietary leaders apparently believed that they had won Franklin over by promising to agree on a militia bill; moreover, they felt that Franklin found further factional discord distasteful. If they could continue to do business with Franklin, they could outmaneuver the more intractable antiproprietary assemblymen.

However, it was the proprietary group that found itself outmaneuvered on election day, for Franklin had tricked them. He did not support the proprietary nominees on this compromise ticket. Both Thomas Leech, a Franklin supporter already in the Assembly, and Galloway, his staunch defender, had been omitted from the compromise ticket. Franklin apparently intended not to ignore these allies to conciliate his enemies, but rather to trick his enemies. Because Franklin's opponents thought the ticket was settled, they did not believe it necessary to mount a propaganda campaign at election time. Meanwhile, Franklin and his allies among the Quakers saw to it that no proprietary candidates were elected; the names of his supporters, particularly Galloway and Leech, were substituted on the ballots for those of the proprietary nominees. It was an able stratagem, at which moralistic Poor Richard did not stick. Franklin was, in his scientific activities, his post office management, and his public service enterprises, honest and fair; but, in politics he quickly discovered that deception was sometimes necessary. He was not reluctant to step out of character. The end, the defeat of the opposition, was right; consequently, a bit of chicanery, if necessary, was quite in order to achieve it.[52]

Franklin's strategy worked to perfection. No proprietary broadsides appeared on election day; the leaders of that group

52. Apparently Franklin agreed to have tickets made up and distributed to the voters on which would be written the compromise slate. But the tickets contained a slate of Franklin's supporters. For election methods, see "Statement of Benjamin Kite, 1828," *PMHB* 19 (1895) : 264–66; and Sister Joan de Lourdes Leonard, C.S.J., "Elections in Colonial Pennsylvania," *WMQ*, 3d ser. 11 (1954) : 385–402.

were confident that all was prearranged. Franklin's friends did not bother with broadsides but thoroughly canvassed the city for voters. "The Quakers were never more assiduous, nor more of their young People avowedly busy, tho a few serious & grave men did not show themselves." [53] The tickets or ballots that they handed out to the voters to drop in the ballot box did not contain the names of any proprietary supporters. Consequently, "a Set . . . of the Partisans against the propts." was elected, including Norris, Joseph Fox, Hughes, Daniel Roberdeau, Leech, John Baynton, Richard Pearn, and Galloway.[54] Franklin and William Masters were reelected as burgesses from the city of Philadelphia. The returns in counties outside Philadelphia closely paralleled the result in Franklin's home county. Sixteen Quakers who did not oppose defensive war remained in the Assembly. They joined with Franklin and most of the other nineteen non-Quakers to continue the struggle against the proprietors.[55]

Upon his election, Galloway was accorded some recognition by Secretary of the Council Richard Peters as a "noisy young Quaker lawyer." Peters was inaccurate on one count but not on the others. Galloway had made a good deal of noise since the publication of *Tit for Tat,* and election to the Assembly

53. Richard Peters to Penn, October 2, 1756, Penn Papers, HSP.

54. Ibid. Duché, an Anglican merchant who supported Franklin, was dropped by the latter from the ticket perhaps because one of the other candidates was more acceptable to the Quaker bloc. This was apparently a minor concession that earned Franklin more Quaker support in the election. The proprietary supporters naively blamed the Quakers, not Franklin, for their defeat. Ralph Ketcham, "Conscience, War, and Politics in Pennsylvania, 1755–1757," *WMQ,* 3d ser. 20 (1963) : 432, follows Richard Peters's account in blaming the Quaker meeting for backing out of the agreement with the proprietary leaders. However, of those elected from Philadelphia, only Norris and Fox were Friends. The others were Franklin's followers from outside the Quaker clique. Clearly, it was Franklin who sabotaged the compromise with the proprietary leaders.

55. John J. Zimmerman, "Benjamin Franklin and the Quaker Party, 1755–1756," *WMQ,* 3d ser. 17 (1960) : 291–313, argues rightly that Franklin took over the old Quaker faction, but it does not deal very thoroughly with the election of 1756.

was his reward for being noisy in Franklin's behalf. Perhaps the invective and the deception which characterized the political strife of 1755–56 were not entirely to Franklin's liking, for he had written of "good agreement" and "fair weather." In 1731 he wrote disparagingly of parties, but he soon became aware, as other Americans were also becoming aware, that "there is no liberty without faction, for the latter cannot be suppressed without introducing slavery in the place of the former." [56] Galloway demonstrated his commitment to Franklin by entering the factional battles. The method was justified because it was the only way to deal with the calumnious proprietary writings. For continued success, Franklin and his allies would have to employ the kind of political weapons that Galloway was most adept at wielding.

Franklin had other important tasks in view for the young lawyer. Although Galloway was only a novice assemblyman, Franklin chose him as his chief legislative assistant soon after the House convened in October 1756. Speaker Norris, Hughes, Roberdeau, and Masters all were important aides to Franklin, but Galloway worked most closely with the leader on the major measures calculated to assert the Assembly's rights. By December, only a year after entering the political lists, Galloway was more important than any other assemblyman except Franklin and Norris.[57]

Events of the past two critical years, especially the war danger to Pennsylvania, had inspired Franklin, a man who excelled in other fields, to turn his talents to political leadership. With the aid of men like Galloway, he made a good beginning. The old, exclusive Quaker faction was now Franklin's party. He incorporated the Quaker organization into his group to win the 1756 election—which put non-Quakers in the Assembly. By bringing diverse interests into his group and

56. Franklin, *Autobiography*, pp. 161–62. *Pennsylvania Gazette*, March 21–30, 1737–38, quoted in Bailyn, *Origins*, p. 127. It seems likely that Franklin penned this anonymous piece. One might compare this idea with those of Madison's *Federalist No. 10*.

57. *Votes*, 6 : 4419, 4429, 4477.

by espousing principles and policies with broad appeal, he fashioned the group into a party. Franklin's party, dedicated to upholding the principle of the supremacy of the representative body and to defending the province from attack, was securely in power. Reasoned argument, invective, and shrewd political maneuvering helped put it there. It was not much like the "Party for Virtue" that Franklin dreamed of back in 1731; it was the product of necessity and apparently recognized as such by its founder and leader. The task remaining was to achieve the party's goal—to eliminate the special privileges of the proprietors. This fight would occupy the next ten years of the careers of Franklin and Galloway. During this time the political alliance of the Assembly's new chief and his devoted follower would be transformed into a real partnership of more nearly equal political leaders.

2 The Partnership Matures

In October 1756 Franklin decided, according to reports, to shift the focus of his campaign against the proprietors to England.[1] Political victory in Pennsylvania permitted him to leave the colony; the obstinance of the Penns and their governor made it necessary. The Assembly was now securely under his control. As one proprietary observer noted, the country representatives were not clever enough to oppose Franklin, and "those of the City, [were] clamorous & malicious Dupes." [2] With loyal supporters, particularly Galloway, prepared to manage the Assembly competently, Franklin did not hesitate to leave Pennsylvania politics in their charge while he attempted to beard the mighty Penns in their own lair.

Basing his reasoning on past experience, Franklin must have thought it doubtful that he could achieve an alteration of the instructions by merely agitating against the governor in Pennsylvania. By presenting his case in person in England, he apparently believed he would be more likely to persuade the British government, through rational and cordial discourse, to force the proprietors to revoke the oppressive instructions. Had he not already demonstrated his persuasive powers over Quakers, Anglicans, merchants, artisans, and Germans in Pennsylvania? Why would not the British ministry also act at his behest? Apparently he was dazzled by his rapid political success. His rise to power in 1755–56, his tremendous popularity in Philadelphia, and his belief in the self-evident justice of the case against the instructions probably made him more daring.

1. Richard Peters to Thomas Penn, October 30, 1756, Penn Papers, HSP.
2. Richard Peters to Penn, December 11, 1756, ibid.

Giving his adversaries every opportunity to surrender before he carried on with some drastic measure was a cardinal
point in Franklin's strategy. Governor William Denny appeared less obstinate than his predecessor, Morris; he had,
on the request of Franklin and Galloway, allowed the Assembly to inspect his instructions from the proprietors.
Franklin and Galloway, before proceeding further, attempted
to test whether Denny would adhere to these. In December
1756 the party leader and his young ally drew up a bill for
printing £100,000, to be "sunk" or redeemed by taxing all
estates including the heretofore untaxed located lands of the
proprietors. It was a fair test, for the Assembly needed the
money to support the war effort. Denny refused the bill, for
if he agreed to it he would violate his instructions, be dismissed
from office, and forfeit his bond. Then Franklin, in January
1757, attempted to raise the populace of Philadelphia against
the governor. The Assembly drew up a sharply worded
remonstrance, which Franklin planned "to be presented by
the Speaker and the whole House, who are to march in a
formal manner thro' the Streets to alarm every Body with the
Sight and Occasion." [3] The Assembly decided against this
bit of demagoguery and presented the remonstrance more
privately. Denny remained obstinate, for to him his instructions and the attendant financial liability in breaking them
were more persuasive than Franklin's threats. By his tactics,
Franklin demonstrated conclusively that Denny could not be
moved and that nothing more could be done against the
instructions in Pennsylvania. It was manifest to the assemblymen and to their constituents that Franklin would have to go
to England to obtain the relief they sought.[4]

3. Richard Peters to Penn, January 27, 1757, ibid.; *Votes*, 6 : 4498–4500.
4. On January 29, Franklin and Norris were both chosen as agents.
Norris begged off; Franklin replied that he would not go if Norris would.
The whole proceeding of December 1756–January 1757 bears the marks of
a neatly calculated plan to get Franklin chosen as agent, to get the agency
approved by the populace, and to prevent the feelings of Speaker Norris
from being injured. *Votes*, 6 : 4504–06; *Franklin Papers*, 7 : 9–11. Richard

On February 22, 1757, Galloway and six other colleagues of Franklin submitted to the House a list of grievances for Franklin to present to the British government. On these, Franklin's party built its case against the proprietors, who had, in the extravagant language of Galloway and Franklin's other colleagues, assumed "an arbitrary and tyrannical Power over the Liberties and Properties of his Majesty's Liege Subjects." The most important grievance was that the Penns had infringed on the rights of the legislature by refusing to allow the taxation of their located estates, except for a small tax on the proprietors' improved lands. The proprietors had thus denied the people's representatives the "original Right of Legislation inherent in them" and prevented the granting of funds for the war effort. The Assembly argued that the Crown lands in Britain were taxed; this constituted an important parliamentary limitation on the executive power. In Pennsylvania, however, the executive could not only determine whether it was to be taxed but also had "a Negative in the Disposition of the Monies" paid by the ordinary unprivileged citizens of the province. The proprietors could not have greater power than the king; the Assembly could not have less power than Parliament.[5]

A second important grievance, one which Galloway particularly felt, was that the proprietors appointed judges who held their commissions at the pleasure of the executive. Consequently, according to the report on grievances, laws were "wrested from their true Sense" by a subservient and pliable judiciary. Galloway and the committee demanded that judges hold their commissions *quam diu se bene gesserint* because judges in Britain held their commissions during good behavior. Pursuant to the Act of Settlement of 1701, only Parliament could effect the removal of a judge; the king could not dismiss a judge with whom he disagreed. Likewise, in

---

Peters to Penn, January 29, 1757, Penn Papers, HSP, comments on these events.

5. *Votes,* 6 : 4537–39.

Pennsylvania the proprietors should not have the exclusive power to remove judges. Here again, the Pennsylvania Assembly asked for the same privilege which belonged to Parliament. The grievance was exaggerated, for Pennsylvania's judges were not hopelessly corrupt, but the constitutional principle at stake was very real. In their quest for the redress of these grievances, Franklin, Galloway, and their party in the Assembly demonstrated their view that the curtailment of executive prerogative and the enlargement of legislative power were fundamental to the liberties of Englishmen on both sides of the Atlantic.[6]

Franklin set off for England, leaving Philadelphia on April 4, 1757, en route to New York. Probably he was optimistic that the Assembly's claim to equality with the House of Commons would be heard with sympathy. His willingness to leave Pennsylvania shows that he was confident that his colleagues in the Assembly would not in his absence deviate from the aims and programs he had developed in the last two years. Galloway he trusted most to keep his party steadfast in his absence. Before Franklin left, he chose Galloway as his alter ego in the Assembly. Despite his youth, Galloway was an excellent choice. He was not as popular as Speaker Norris, but Franklin did not completely trust the old Quaker, who may have been jealous of Franklin's new prestige. John Hughes, who had worked with Franklin in the Assembly longer than had Galloway, was of undoubted loyalty but of uncompromising and obstinate mind and had limited political ability. And Galloway's ambition, talent, and industry had in the five months since his election proved superior to that of Franklin's other colleagues. To reward the young man for his loyalty and service, Franklin had him appointed to the important committees of correspondence and grievances to fill the vacancies occasioned by his own departure for England.[7] These appointments demonstrate that Franklin wished Galloway to

6. Ibid., 4540. The Assembly also instructed Franklin to request more protection by the government for the merchants while the war lasted.
7. Ibid., 4557.

assume important responsibilities and to act in his place, so that his absence from Pennsylvania would not be detrimental to his cause.

Franklin had several important tasks for Galloway to undertake. "I leave some Enemies in Pensilvania, who will take every Opportunity of injuring me in my Absence," he warned his young ally. "However, as they are my Enemies, not on my own private Account but on that of the Publick, I seem to have some Right to ask the Care of my Friends, to watch 'em and guard my Reputation and Interest as much as may be from the Effects of their Malevolence." [8] Franklin promised reciprocation. "You may depend on my endeavouring to shield your Reputation wherever I find it attack'd, as I rely on the like Defence in the same Case from your Friendship." [9] Galloway, Franklin apparently believed, would be more than a match for William Smith and other proprietary scribblers. Secondly, Galloway had to continue to strengthen Franklin's party and concomitantly attempt to curtail the activities of the proprietary faction. Thirdly, Galloway had to support Franklin in building a case against the proprietors' instructions in England, by demonstrating that they were not competent governors. Fourthly, Galloway had to continue the attack against Governor Denny's insistent adherence to the instructions, which for the time being seemed to have the Assembly blocked.

Franklin's trust in Galloway to guard his reputation was not misplaced. From 1757 to 1762, while he was in England, Franklin was nominated as burgess in every election. His friends kept his name before the voters to preserve their own association with him and to reap the benefits of his vote-getting power. The name Franklin had almost magical effects on the electorate because of his rise from humble beginnings and his popular public service enterprises. Small merchants and mechanics supported Franklin as the mechanic who had made good and who was striking at the privilege and social

8. Franklin to Galloway, April 11, 1757, *Franklin Papers*, 7 : 179.
9. Franklin to Galloway, June 10, 1758, ibid., 8 : 97.

stratification represented by the proprietors and their allies. Quakers supported his antiproprietary stand; Anglicans and Presbyterians backed his defense policies; and the Germans remembered the contracts he had procured for them. These supporters chose Franklin and the whole Franklin ticket throughout the period he was in England. Loyalty to Franklin was so well maintained while he was absent that he was, in effect, still in Philadelphia. His election in absentia deprived his friends of a vote in the Assembly, but one vote meant nothing to their preponderant majority. Galloway, Hughes, Masters, and the others gained much more through their close association with Franklin's name than they lost by not having his vote. Franklin's name and reputation comprised the rock on which the church was built; the rock had to be displayed prominently and permanently.

Franklin, by transforming the old Quaker clique into a freely recruited party with broader support, had laid the foundation for an enduring and effective political group. Now, in Franklin's absence, Galloway had to build on this foundation. He planned to continue the policy, adopted by Franklin in 1755–56, of disregarding religious differences and concentrating on other issues. He hoped, he wrote to Franklin, that "Quaker Government and Quaker influence be Terms buried in Oblivion and no more remembered." [10] Franklin's group became known as the Assembly party. Its antiproprietary stand became, if anything, more intense during Franklin's London mission than it had been before. Galloway probably was responsible for the intensification. It apparently suited his personality to be on the attack, pursuing his political opponents with every fair and some unfair weapons. Galloway copied Franklin in his willingness not to balk at devious and deceitful practices to attain the ends toward which his principles drove him. In regard to strengthening the Assembly party, he had two ends in view: to make it dangerous for the "Small but violent Party" led by Allen and Smith to raise any resistance to the Assembly party's leaders

10. Galloway to Franklin, June 16, 1758, ibid., 107–08.

and aims; and to enhance the internal vitality of the party by building a patronage system that would benefit its adherents. Galloway wanted, in short, to make it profitable to join with Franklin and his party—and unprofitable to oppose them.

The proprietary leader whom the Assembly most desired to silence and punish was, of course, William Smith. The opportunity to attack Smith, in a roundabout way, soon presented itself. One William Moore, a proprietary-appointed justice of Chester County who had circulated a petition against Franklin's Militia Act of 1755, was denounced by petitions to the Assembly and consequently was accused of corruption by that body. Moore replied by publishing an *Address* to Governor Denny, which charged the House with slander, mishandling public funds, and other gross crimes. Smith had Moore's *Address* published in a German newspaper, thereby making himself an accessory to Moore's offensive against the Assembly.[11] On January 6, 1758, the House, probably led by Galloway, resolved that Moore's *Address* was "highly derogatory of, and destructive to, the Rights of the House, and the Privileges of Assembly," and that Smith was suspected of being "concerned in writing the aforesaid libellous Address of *William Moore,* or in some other Manner an Abettor of the same." [12] The legal basis of the intended prosecution was the claim of the Assembly to all the powers of the House of Commons, including that of convicting and punishing those accused of libeling it. The reason was purely political. Moore's real crime was opposition to Franklin and to the Militia Act; Smith's real libel was *Brief State,* as well as *A Brief View of the Province of Pennsylvania for the*

11. For Moore's *Address* to Governor Denny, see *Pennsylvania Gazette,* December 1, 1757. Moore's reply to the charges made against him as a judge is in William Moore, *A Preface to a Memorial Delivered in to the Assembly of the Province of Pennsylvania, September 22, 1757* (Philadelphia, 1757 [Evans no. 7958]).

12. *Votes,* 6 : 4677–78. The charge of breach of privilege was not formally raised against Moore and Smith.

Year 1755 (another anti-Quaker diatribe), for which the
Assembly believed *Tit for Tat* had not adequately chastised
him. The Assembly now would do so; Moore and Smith were
ordered into the custody of the sergeant at arms.[13]

It was apparently Galloway who directed the prosecution
when the trials began on January 11. That day Moore was
called into the House, and he admitted his authorship of the
Address. To dispose of his case quickly, Galloway drew up
a set of resolutions stating that the Assembly had the power
to punish libels on it and that Moore's *Address* was a libel.
The same day, Moore was committed to the "common
Goal" of Philadelphia County until he retracted.

The more important of the pair, Smith, was summoned
to the Assembly two days later. At his request, the Assembly
furnished him with a copy of the charge, appointed January
17 as his trial date, and permitted him counsel, but it refused
to release him from custody. On the appointed day the House
resolved that it would not permit Smith's counsel to dispute
its resolutions that the *Address* constituted a criminal act,
which it could punish. Four days were spent hearing witnesses
and listening to Smith's arguments, but apparently the outcome was a foregone conclusion. On January 24 the Assembly
resolved Smith's guilt in "promoting and publishing" Moore's
Address; the next day he was sentenced to join Moore in
jail. Thus, Galloway and Franklin's other allies brought their
leader's principal propaganda adversary to what they thought
was his just due.[14]

13. The intended prosecution of Moore and Smith was apparently too
extreme a step for Speaker Norris. He retired from the chair, pleading
illness, and was replaced by Thomas Leech, a Philadelphia representative and Anglican supporter of Franklin. Norris told Franklin, April 29,
1758, *Franklin Papers*, 8 : 57–58, that the odor from old books had made
him ill. He indicated to Thomas Pownall, January 29, 1758, Copybook,
HSP, that it was better that an Anglican, instead of a Quaker, preside
at the trial of an Anglican cleric.

14. *Votes*, 6 : 4686–90, 4691–4716. Smith protested that he had been un-
fairly singled out for punishment. His speech after receiving sentence
moved his friends in the audience to hiss his persecutors, stamp their

The trials were, under existing laws and practices, fair. They were open to the public and conducted by rules. Moore, by the standards of the time, was guilty of libel; in Smith's case, evidence to permit a modern judgment does not exist. But Galloway and Franklin, despite their claims to be guarding the privileges of the citizens of Pennsylvania, had no accurate conception of civil liberties. They later came to recognize that such legislative condemnations were unwise, if not unjust, and, even when more scurrilously slandered in succeeding years, never attempted to employ such a libel prosecution again. At the time, however, they saw no incongruity in the Assembly's course of action, for it was the power of the House, more than individual liberty, that they felt compelled to establish.[15]

The political effectiveness of the trials was as great as could be desired. Galloway's legal talents were well employed in frightening Franklin's opponents into believing that they had to act circumspectly or they might join Moore and Smith behind bars. Franklin's friend Hugh Roberts wrote him that "the proceedings of the Assembly therein has had this happy effect to make the Scots Clan who were very public in their Clamours against the Conduct of the House, now communicate their thoughts to each other in whispers under the Thistle." [16] For the next six years no direct attacks on the political policies of Franklin and Galloway appeared. During the same period the chief members of the Assembly party remained unchallenged at the polls.

---

feet, and clap their hands. These disrupters were forced by the House to make apologies.

15. William R. Riddell, "Libel on the Assembly: A Prerevolutionary Episode," *PMHB* 52 (1928): 176–92, 249–79, 342–60, comments on legal and constitutional aspects of the case. Leonard W. Levy, *Freedom of Speech and Press in Early American History: Legacy of Suppression* (New York, 1963), pp. 53–61, criticizes the Assembly's actions from a modern standpoint. The legal aspects of the trial were argued in the *Pennsylvania Journal*, February 9, February 23, March 2, March 9, March 16, and March 23, 1758.

16. Hugh Roberts to Franklin, July 1, 1758, *Franklin Papers*, 8: 81–82.

The trials made Galloway more widely respected both inside the Assembly and out. His avid and determined effort to punish Franklin's chief enemy made it obvious that he was the most able and loyal lieutenant in Franklin's party. More and more of the Assembly's activities fell to his management. By 1759 proprietor Thomas Penn recognized that Galloway was as troublesome as his mentor had been in 1755–57. "Has Mr. Growden no influence over Galloway?" he inquired.[17] Penn hoped that favors and personal appeals might silence the Assembly's young leader. But Galloway was tied securely to Franklin, whom he most admired, who had given him his start in politics, and who had put him in responsible posts. By his part in the Moore-Smith trials he had rewarded Franklin and made important political gains for himself.

Unchallenged by any opposition, Franklin's party began to put together a more effective political ring by 1758. At the top were Speaker Norris and Galloway; they were awarded reimbursements for "extraordinary expenses," a mysterious disbursement which was paid only in the years in which Galloway was in the Assembly.[18] Below them were the Philadelphia representatives: Hughes, Fox, Leech, Baynton, and Masters were the most significant. This group served on all the important committees and received patronage plums which gave them good jobs and the power to distribute employment and treats among the electorate.[19] We may con-

17. Thomas Penn to James Hamilton, September 21, 1759, Thomas Penn Letter Book, Penn Papers, HSP. Penn criticized Galloway for his part in the Moore-Smith trials in a letter to Richard Peters, July 20, 1759, ibid.

18. These "extraordinary expenses" arouse suspicion because they were always in round figures—£25 or £30—and because they were over and above the expenses that leaders of the House claimed for specific services. They may have been reimbursement for some political expense.

19. The House had plenty of opportunity during wartime to distribute plush contracts to members. Joseph Fox received £8,000 for building barracks in Philadelphia, and he was appointed barracksmaster. John Baynton received £4,500 for fitting out a warship for the colony. Galloway and the other Philadelphia delegates received fees for such services as superintending the issuance of paper money. It was traditional in

clude that the suppliers of materials and the workmen—
merchants, farmers, and mechanics—knew to which political
group they were indebted for their livelihoods. Patronage
and persecution of the opposition made Franklin's party,
inside the Assembly and outside, a solid and effective organization dominated by Galloway and the other Philadelphia
assemblymen, supported actively by members of various
religious and economic groups, and resisted very discreetly by
a small faction of proprietary placemen.

The two tasks of guarding Franklin's reputation and
achieving political supremacy were well in hand by the
middle of 1758. Now Galloway and his colleagues waited to
see what success Franklin would have in England, contributed
what they could to making a better case for him, and tried to
break down Governor Denny's adherence to the instructions.
Until the spring of 1758 the London agent was pretty much
on his own, probably because he, Galloway, and his other
supporters believed that his persuasive powers would soon
gain what they desired.

Before approaching the British government formally,
Franklin decided to test his abilities at conciliation on the
proprietors themselves.[20] In August 1757 the "tribune of the
people" and the "absolute Proprietaries" met at Thomas
Penn's Spring Garden town house in London. Franklin tried
conciliation. He claimed that he was no real enemy to proprietary authority justly exercised, disavowed any plot to
reduce the proprietors' quitrent receipts, and even admitted

Pennsylvania politics for the Philadelphia representatives to dominate
the less learned and less sophisticated "country" members of the Assembly. The financial arrangements and the organization of the committees
for 1757–63 can be followed in *Votes*, 6 : 4865–86, 4887, 5050–68, 5151–56,
5161, 5278–79, 5282, 5366–67, 5369–70, 5463–73, and 5476. The Assembly
could not distribute patronage equivalent in value to the proprietary
land grants that the Penns used to influence their supporters. But proprietary patronage was generally limited to the already wealthy landholders of the province.

20. This was apparently suggested by British Quakers.

that the Assembly might sometimes be in the wrong. But mutual distrust and animosity defeated all efforts at compromising their differences. Franklin believed the Penns pompous; the proprietors were certain even before they met the agent that he was a republican schemer. The "difference of opinion in regard to Powers and Privileges" precluded any agreement.[21] At the Penns' request, Franklin summarized the Assembly's grievances by drawing up a "Heads of Complaint"; he heard no more about this for over a year while the proprietors sought legal advice on the complaints. After several meetings marked by sharp disagreement, Franklin and the Penns grew more hostile. After Thomas Penn mocked the Assembly's claim to the powers of a House of Commons during a conference in January 1758, the Assembly's agent "conceived that Moment a more cordial and thorough Contempt for him that I ever before felt for any Man living." Franklin privately compared Thomas Penn to a "low Jockey," ready to swindle Pennsylvanians out of their birthright.[22] And Penn believed Franklin deserved equal contempt; he reported to Pennsylvania that Franklin looked and acted "like a malicious V[illain], as he always does." [23]

The Penns made no useful compromise proposals for the taxation of their located unimproved lands. They tried to get Franklin to compromise his position by drafting a money bill which he and the Penns could settle on in England, but Franklin, incensed at this "mean Chicanery," refused to undercut the privileges of the Assembly in this way. By De-

21. Penn to Richard Peters, September 5, 1757, Thomas Penn Letter Book, Penn Papers, HSP. Before Franklin began his political activity in 1755, Penn seems to have looked on him with some favor. But many times thereafter he expressed a low opinion of Franklin's activities. See Penn to Richard Peters, July 3, 1755, January 10 and August 13, 1756; and Penn to Robert Hunter Morris, September 19, 1756, all in ibid.

22. Franklin to [Isaac Norris?], January 14, 1758, *Franklin Papers,* 7 : 362. The letter was copied by a proprietary sympathizer for Thomas Penn's enlightenment.

23. Penn to Richard Peters, July 5, 1758, Thomas Penn Letter Book, Penn Papers, HSP.

cember 1758 all negotiations were over.[24] Instead of improving relations between the Assembly and the proprietors by personal confrontation, Franklin worsened them. He had hoped to convince, not to compromise. The Penns would hearken to neither, in any meaningful way. The agent's talents, which had won over Pennsylvania, were of little service against the headstrong proprietors secure in their wealth and influence.

Franklin was forced to fall back to the original plan of appealing to the government against the Penns' instructions. Two lines of approach seemed possible: to win allies in high places who might influence or compel the Penns to make reforms; or to defeat the Penns before the Privy Council in the course of an appeal concerning some Pennsylvania case or a review of a Pennsylvania law. Because the second approach would depend on events in Pennsylvania, Franklin began preparing the ground for the first approach, during the time that he was negotiating with the Penns. He claimed that he made important contacts. "The agreable Conversation I meet with among Men of Learning, and the Notice taken of me by Persons of Distinction, are the principal Things that sooth me for the present under this painful Absence from my Family and Friends," he informed his wife.[25] Thomas Penn was not impressed with Franklin's attainments and thought few others would be. The agent's scientific knowledge might charm the Royal Society, but "it is quite another sort of People, who are to determine the Dispute between us." [26] Nor were the chief British leaders impressed. Franklin's dream that he could immediately take his case to William Pitt was quickly punctured. He did make acquaintance with some

24. The Penns were willing to allow the governor to agree to bills on the model of those previously agreed to, which gave the Assembly control of disbursements, and the Penns also agreed to permit alterations in the method of tax assessment. On the negotiations, see Franklin to Norris, January 19, 1759, *Franklin Papers*, 8 : 233.

25. Franklin to Deborah Franklin, November 22, 1757, ibid., 7 : 279.

26. Penn to Richard Peters, May 14, 1757, Thomas Penn Letter Book, Penn Papers, HSP.

important British figures and properly cultivated the secretaries of administrative bureaus, yet he failed to make the impression he apparently had anticipated making.[27] Scientific doors opened to him; political doors did not.

The claims of the Pennsylvania Assembly, Franklin soon discovered, did not appear in the same light to Britain as they did to Pennsylvania. Richard Jackson, a lawyer and Franklin's closest British associate, advised him that the ministry would not now support his attack on the Penns. He recommended that Franklin and his Pennsylvania allies, rather than pressing for a settlement, "keep up the Ball of Contention, 'till a proper Opportunity offers" and the government became more favorable.[28] Franklin got a sobering taste of ministerial hostility to colonial ambitions when Lord Granville, president of the Privy Council, mistakenly asserted to him that the king's instructions had the force of law in royal colonies—and proprietary instructions had a like character.[29] Franklin consequently discovered that the Penns were not only immune to his attempts at conciliation but also were supported by official attitudes.

The Board of Trade and the Privy Council would, however, listen to Franklin if he were to represent the Assembly in a case involving an appeal or a law sent to England for review. Thus, raising a case and providing evidence became the responsibility of his friends in Pennsylvania, especially Galloway. In 1758–60 Franklin undertook, with Galloway's cooperation, to present the cause of the Assembly before the Privy Council three times.

The first instance in which Franklin had an opportunity to plead for the Assembly was in the appeal of William Smith

27. Michael G. Kammen, *A Rope of Sand: The Colonial Agents, British Politics, and the American Revolution* (Ithaca, N.Y., 1968), pp. 69–70, critically discusses Franklin's methods of lobbying.

28. Richard Jackson to Franklin, [April 24, 1758], *Franklin Papers,* 8 : 26–27.

29. Franklin, *Autobiography,* pp. 261–62. Franklin knew that Granville's view was incorrect, but he realized he would have difficulty convincing the ministry of this. Granville was related to the Penns by marriage, so his opinion was all the more damning to Franklin's cause.

from his libel conviction. In February 1758 Smith petitioned the Privy Council to have the verdict of the Assembly reversed. His claim to being an innocent Anglican cleric hounded by a bigoted Quaker Assembly was all too believable and all too embarrassing for Franklin. Reportedly, the agent was "very uneasy at the Assemblys taking this most extravagant step [jailing Moore and Smith], as it is a matter that makes a great deal of noise here." [30] Franklin, however, never reproached Galloway or his other colleagues for the prosecution of the proprietary sympathizers; he had been informed that it had aided his party in Pennsylvania. Moreover, Smith's appeal could be turned to the Assembly's advantage. Franklin viewed Smith's case "as one Battery against the Privileges of the Assembly, and Rights of the People." [31] By defending the Assembly before the Privy Council, he might succeed in getting formal recognition of the power of the Assembly to act as a House of Commons. A favorable decision in this case would help to keep up the "Ball of Contention," as Jackson had advised him to do.

The Privy Council's committee on plantation affairs referred Smith's appeal to the attorney and solicitor generals, who held hearings beginning on April 20, 1758. After Smith's counsel opened with an attack on the Assembly and the Quakers, Franklin fought back with the arguments that Smith was an "old offender," that he had received due process, that he was jailed only during sessions of the present Assembly, and that he had no right of appeal in this case. In sum, his defense was the contention central to the Assembly's cause, that "the Assembly of Pennsylva. had as full powers, as the House of Commons had." [32] After these hearings, proceedings

30. Ferdinand J. Paris to William Allen, May 13, 1758, Penn Papers, HSP. Paris was attorney for the Penns.

31. Franklin, Notes on the Petition of William Smith, *Franklin Papers,* 8 : 46.

32. Ibid., 8 : 31–51; Franklin to Thomas Leech and the Assembly Committee of Correspondence, May 13, 1758, ibid., 8 : 61; Paris to Allen, May 13, 1758, Penn Papers, HSP; *Acts of the Privy Council, Colonial Series,* vol. 4, *1745–1766* (London, 1911), pp. 375–83.

stopped for over a year, perhaps because Franklin's arguments
convinced the attorney and solicitor generals that the Assembly was on solid constitutional ground. On June 26, 1759, the
Privy Council ruled for Smith on the technicality that the
Assembly of 1758 could not punish a libel on the Assembly
of 1757. The implication of the announcement of the "king's
high displeasure" at such proceedings was that the Assembly
did not, in the view of the ministry, possess the powers of a
little House of Commons.[33] That the Privy Council rendered
a decision on Smith's appeal when ordinarily no right of
appeal existed in such cases showed that the British government believed American legislatures quite inferior and subordinate to Parliament. The claim of parliamentary privilege
for the Assembly made by Franklin was not, however, totally
rejected. In basing the decision on technical points while admitting that an assembly could punish a libel against it, the
Council probably encouraged Franklin to push future cases
against the Penns in the hope that the Council might rule
for the Assembly. Nor did the decision prevent Galloway
from keeping the proprietary faction in Pennsylvania quiet.

While the Smith case remained undecided, another opportunity for the antiproprietary campaign presented itself,
and Franklin and Galloway attempted to take advantage of
it. In the summer of 1759, Franklin brought before the Board
of Trade and the Privy Council the issue of the Penns' Indian
policy, a bitterly controversial matter in Pennsylvania. Assembly leader Galloway, who helped to provide the evidence,
and Franklin, who presented the case in London, cooperated
closely to make the most serious challenge yet to the proprietors' ability to govern.

Although Franklin and Galloway opposed Quaker pacifism,

33. MS At the Council Chamber, Whitehall, June 26, 1759, Smith
Family MSS, Dr. William Smith and the Pennsylvania Assembly, HSP;
Acts of the Privy Council, Colonial Series, 4 : 383–84. The report of the
attorney and solicitor generals may have been delayed because Smith
had been freed from jail by Chief Justice Allen and was not molested
by the House after December 1758.

they were sympathetic toward Quaker efforts to keep peace with the Indians. Quakers in and out of the Assembly, and their non-Quaker supporters, reasoned that war had come because William Penn's traditional ideal of keeping friendship with the Indians had been subverted by the current proprietors. Franklin and Galloway were probably more interested in embarrassing the proprietors with the blame for the conflict with the Indians than in vindicating Quaker ideals or obtaining justice for the Indians. They worked toward a confrontation and a judgment against the Penns because they thought they had a good case that the British government would recognize as significant.

Evidence of proprietary mismanagement of Indian affairs, or of even more heinous crimes, was uncovered at a conference with the Delaware Indians at Easton in November 1756. Teedyuscung, who styled himself king of the Delawares but who really was only a spokesman, asserted that the French and Indian attacks on Pennsylvania were more fierce because the Penns had cheated the Delawares out of land that was rightfully theirs. The Penns had allegedly forged a deed of sale of Indian lands dated 1686, in which the Indians agreed to sell the "Walking Purchase"; and the Penns had bought a large tract extending from the Delaware to the Susquehanna rivers from the Six Nations, who, Teedyuscung averred, had no right to sell the land.[34]

The Penns, Governor Denny, and the proprietary supporters tried to blunt the threat of these serious accusations. They told each other that the Quakers, especially Israel Pemberton

34. Anthony F. C. Wallace, *King of the Delawares: Teedyuscung* (Philadelphia, 1949), discusses the career of this extraordinary Indian and deals in detail with the charges of fraud against the proprietors. The Easton conference of November 1756, is discussed on pp. 130–36. The "Walking Purchase" included as much of a large portion of northeastern Pennsylvania along the Delaware River between Easton and Trenton as one could walk around in a day and a half. When this purchase was made in 1737, the Penns' agent, James Logan, hired runners to circumscribe the boundaries of the sale, rather than walk around leisurely, as the Indians anticipated. See ibid., pp. 21–28.

and his Friendly Association for Regaining and Preserving
Peace with the Indians by Pacific Measures, had induced the
Indian "chief" to make these charges.[35] Thomas Penn reported the affair to the Board of Trade, which in February
1757, very likely as Penn desired, ordered Sir William Johnson, Crown superintendent of Indian affairs, to investigate the
Delawares' grievances.[36] Franklin, Galloway, and their colleagues had a different plan for settling the dispute. Johnson,
intent on keeping the Six Nations peaceful, would not likely
sustain Teedyuscung's charges. Thus, the antiproprietary
group wished to pursue these accusations through further
conferences and perhaps eventually go right to England.
After Franklin left for England, he maintained great interest
in the Indian claims and was kept informed by Norris and
Galloway concerning his friends' activities in this matter.

The Assembly took up the cause of the Indians at the Easton
Conference in July 1757. Galloway, several of his colleagues in
the Assembly, and Pemberton attended the conference to
help Teedyuscung stand up for his rights and to collect more
evidence against the proprietors.[37] The instruments of persuasion were well employed; throughout the conference Galloway and Pemberton continually conferred with Teedyuscung
to seal the alliance. According to witnesses, the chief appeared
"drunk and unfit for Business," and Galloway, trying valiantly
to coach the befuddled Indian, lost his temper at Teedyuscung's inability to remember his lines.[38] It must have been

35. *Minutes of the Provincial Council of Pennsylvania* (*Colonial
Records*), 7 (Harrisburg, 1851) : 325–26; Nicholas B. Wainwright, "William
Denny in Pennsylvania," *PMHB* 81 (1957) : 176–78; Richard Peters to
Penn, November 22, 1756, Penn Papers, HSP.

36. *Journal of the Commissioners of Trade and Plantations from
January 1754 to December 1758*, 10 (London, 1933) : 298.

37. Galloway and William Masters notified Denny that the House
wanted justice done to the Indians and that its representatives would
attend the Easton conference. Denny warned them that neither the
Assembly's representatives nor meddling Quakers would be welcome.
This did not stop Galloway, Hughes, Fox, and Masters from coming.
Pa. Arch., 1st ser. 3 : 160–61.

38. Ibid., 3 : 263–65.

frustrating for the politician and comical for the observers, but persistënce triumphed; Galloway and Pemberton finally drilled into the "king" that he must frame his charges in detail; he must ask for a clerk, a partisan of the Assembly, to set them down in writing; he must demand that proprietary officials produce the deeds recording Indian land sales; and, most important, he must demand that the king in England, not Johnson, judge his claims against the Penns.

Teedyuscung played his part well. He was so insistent in demanding a clerk that Denny had to accede. Charles Thomson, a close associate of Franklin and Galloway, filled the post, took careful note of what was said, and perhaps advised Teedyuscung on what to say. The charges of November 1756 were repeated with conviction. And, as Galloway and Pemberton had coached him to do, Teedyuscung insisted that before the Delawares made peace the king would have to judge his claims. This last threat was not made good, for the tribe agreed at this conference to make peace. But Teedyuscung, by demanding that his claims be ruled on in England, provided the Assembly with a strong case to use there against the Penns. In September 1757 the House forwarded all details of the proceedings at Easton to Franklin. Thomson prepared a detailed *Enquiry into the Causes of the Alienation of the Delaware and Shawanese Indians from the British Interest,* which was intended to indict the Penns before the British public for their alleged frauds.[39]

The proofs furnished Franklin from Pennsylvania seemed strong ones. The claims of the Indians were bound to have more significance in Britain than the Assembly's general grievances against proprietary government because the Indians had taken the warpath. Franklin evidently believed that he could prove to the Privy Council that the Penns "seem to have no Regard to the Publick Welfare," that those who would

39. *Votes,* 6 : 4649; Wallace, *Teedyuscung,* pp. 155–59. Thomson's work represented the orthodox Quaker view that the proprietary land policy was mainly to blame for the war, that the proprietary agents tried to cover up their delinquencies, but that the Assembly had done its duty in insisting that Teedyuscung get every opportunity to have justice done.

cheat Indians out of their land would also cheat Englishmen out of their rights.[40] After waiting until February 1759, by which time further information on recent Indian conferences was in his possession and Thomson's *Enquiry* was ready to appear, Franklin presented to the Privy Council a petition supporting Teedyuscung's claims.[41] It was referred to the Board of Trade the next month, and a hearing was scheduled for May 15. Meanwhile, Thomson's book was "more read than I expected," Franklin reported. The agent also prepared his case personally by lobbying with Lords Granville and Halifax to counter the proprietors' allegations that the Indians had no real claim against them. He convinced the ministers that, although Teedyuscung had retracted his charges against the Six Nations in October 1758, he still wanted the king to judge the charges against the proprietors.[42] At the hearing Franklin at least held his own. The Penns alleged that the Delawares' accusations were part of a plot of Franklin, the Assembly, and the Quakers. The proprietors hoped that the Board would recommend rejection of Franklin's contentions rather than report to the Privy Council that Sir William Johnson should investigate further. Franklin likewise desired that the Board make an immediate determination on the charges. He feared that a full inquiry in America would take

40. Franklin to Galloway, April 11, 1757, *Franklin Papers*, 7 : 178–79. William Peters reported to Thomas Penn, October 19, 1757, Penn Papers, HSP, that the original of the deed of 1686 could not be found, so the charge of forgery could not easily be disproved. Peters feared Franklin and the Assembly might cause the proprietors much embarrassment.

41. Franklin made some false starts on petitioning on behalf of the Indians. Thomson's manuscript arrived in plenty of time; he noted this fact to Israel Pemberton, June 10, 1758, *Franklin Papers*, 8 : 99–100. To Galloway, September 16, 1758, ibid., 8 : 150, Franklin wrote that "Sundry Circumstances" had prevented his petitioning. Perhaps he delayed because of his negotiations with the Penns on the instructions. Perhaps Thomson's book was delayed in publication until a time when it might be most influential on the 1759 session of Parliament. Franklin noted to Leech and the Committee of Correspondence, June 10, 1758, ibid., 8 : 89, that the *Historical Review* was to be published when it would be the most influential.

42. Franklin to Galloway, April 7, 1759, ibid., 8 : 313, 315.

too long and believed that the Assembly had a much better chance of making their claims stand up before the Board of Trade and Privy Council than before Johnson. Franklin presented his copies of the minutes of the Indian conferences which Galloway and Norris had sent over, averred that this evidence was sufficient to allow the Privy Council to make a final determination, and pressed for an award to Teedyuscung.[43]

Neither the Penns' influence nor Franklin's arguments completely prevailed. The Board of Trade retreated to its original position that the controversy be decided in America. It recommended, and on August 29, 1759, the King in Council ordered, that Johnson inquire into the matter to determine if and to what extent the Delawares had been defrauded.[44] In its report the Board, in a negative and compromising manner, found against both Assembly and proprietors. It noted that the proprietary land policies had raised suspicion among the Indians, but it also condemned the Assembly for interfering with Indian relations, which were the responsibility of the home government.[45] The report in this instance was much like that rendered in the Smith appeal—no complete condemnation for either side but slightly more favorable to the proprietary interest. Sir William Johnson's investigation, completed in 1762, vindicated the Penns. Teedyuscung retracted his charges which, Thomas Penn exulted, "established our right to the Land . . . to the satisfaction of even the great Champion of the Party [Galloway]." Galloway was obliged to work out a retraction of his accusations.[46] This episode must have been painful for him; he hated ever to admit that

43. Franklin, Petition to the King in Council, February 2, 1759, ibid., 8 : 273–76; Franklin to Isaac Norris, June 9, 1759, ibid., 8 : 397–98; *Journal of the Commissioners for Trade and Plantations from January 1759 to December 1763*, 11 (London, 1935) : 32, 36, 41.

44. MS Order in Council, August 29, 1759, Penn Papers, HSP; *Acts of the Privy Council, Colonial Series*, 4 : 402–03.

45. MS Report of the Board of Trade, June 1, 1759, Penn Papers, HSP.

46. Thomas Penn to Benjamin Chew, September 10, 1762, Thomas Penn Letter Book, Penn Papers, HSP.

his opponents were in the right. Yet his admission of error did him no harm politically; he lost some support in the election of 1762 but retained his prominence in the Assembly. The main impact of the attempt by the Assembly to support the Indian claims was the strengthening of the alliance between Franklin and Galloway. Galloway had worked with the Indian "king" and helped supply Franklin with evidence; the agent had used this support as best he could. Although Franklin and Galloway had not yet found a way to attack the proprietors successfully, they were discovering the formula for a transatlantic partnership which would, in time, prove its effectiveness.

A specific, effective approach was not readily discovered; Franklin and Galloway made some false starts before taking the right road. With Galloway in the lead, the Assembly attempted in 1757 and 1758 to tax the located unimproved proprietary estates when it appropriated large sums of money to support the war effort. Each time such a bill was sent up, Governor Denny refused it and the Assembly, in the interest of keeping up the defense posture of the province and the British offensives against the French, exempted the Penns in levying taxes. The Assembly considered complaints to England, but these came to naught.[47]

Franklin and Galloway also undertook a propaganda campaign; this tactic had worked well in Pennsylvania and might also prove effective in Britain. Franklin and William Franklin assisted Richard Jackson in writing *An Historical Review of the Constitution and Government of Pennsylvania,* which they had planned since late 1757 and which finally appeared in May 1759. Soon afterward, Galloway's *True and Impartial*

47. When Denny refused the Assembly's 1758 tax bill, the House on April 8 resolved to send the bill and the governor's objections to it to Franklin to be presented to the king and Parliament, if Parliament was still in session when it arrived in London. Apparently, it was not presented. *Votes,* 6 : 4791–92; Norris to Franklin, April 29, 1758, *Franklin Papers,* 8 : 55. In late 1758 the Assembly considered another petition against the proprietors, but this did not pass the House. Norris to Franklin, January 15, 1759, ibid., 8 : 228.

State of the Province of Pennsylvania, published in Philadelphia, arrived in England.[48] The *Historical Review,* as Franklin bluntly put it, was intended to arouse public opinion and to make the proprietors "rot and stink in the Nostrils of Posterity." [49] Galloway's book, hardly impartial, was a direct refutation of Smith's *Brief State.*[50] Neither were of much effect in aiding the Assembly's cause. Political arguments and literary talents impressed the electorate of Pennsylvania, but in Britain they could not arouse an apathetic public, a disinterested Parliament, and a preoccupied ministry to a general inquiry into the Penns' government. Franklin's only consolation for this failure was an ungenerous gloating over the reaction of Thomas Penn to the attacks on him. "The Pro-

48. Franklin and Galloway knew that Smith's *Brief State* and *Brief View* had been all too effective in arousing Britain against Quaker rule in Pennsylvania; the partners apparently hoped that their propaganda would get a more favorable reception. Richard Jackson was undoubtedly the author of *An Historical Review of the Constitution and Government of Pennsylvania, From its Origin; so far as regards the several Points of Controversy, which have, from Time to Time, arisen Between the several Governors of that Province, and Their several Assemblies,* although Franklin was long credited with it. Pamphleteering by agents was uncommon; Franklin's collaboration on the *Historical Review* was an important advance in the technique of making colonial appeals in Britain. He mentioned the preparation of the book in a letter to Galloway, February 17, 1758, *Franklin Papers,* 7 : 374. It was reviewed in the *Monthly Review* 21 (July 1759) : 46–57. Galloway's book was reviewed in the same periodical in October 1759, p. 367, indicating that the book was published in May or June.

49. The *Historical Review* was actually rather dull and heavy. It contained a detailed analysis of the controversies between governors and assemblies from William Penn's time to September 1756, made up largely of excerpts from messages that passed between them. Franklin to Galloway, February 17, 1758, *Franklin Papers,* 7 : 374.

50. Galloway argued that the mixed nature of the Pennsylvania constitution had to be preserved from proprietary encroachments, that the Pennsylvania Assembly should have all the privileges that the House of Commons had, and that the proprietors had no right to issue strict instructions. He concluded that the governing power of the province ought to be lodged in the Crown. It was a more able performance than were the Smith books. Galloway, *True State,* pp. 30, 36, 172.

prietor is enrag'd. When I meet him any where there appears in his wretched Countenance a strange Mixture of Hatred, Anger, Fear, and Vexation." [51] Lack of solid achievement, however, had made Franklin "almost weary of Business, and languish after Repose and my America." [52]

At about the same time Franklin wrote these words, the turn of events needed to get the Assembly's case against the instructions moving again occurred. The impasse between Governor Denny and the Assembly was broken. In March 1759 Denny, as he had done in 1756, 1757, and 1758, again vetoed a bill for raising £100,000 by taxing all estates, including the located unimproved lands of the proprietors. General Jeffrey Amherst, commander-in-chief in America, visited Governor Denny after his refusal of the bill and informed him that the army needed the Pennsylvania contribution as soon as possible to continue to defend the country. He urged the governor to agree to the bill taxing the proprietors rather than risk a long, drawn out battle with the Assembly before any money would be appropriated.[53] Added inducement was supplied by Norris and Galloway, who privately made it clear to Denny that his acceptance of the tax bill would be to his financial advantage. They also explained that he would not really be violating his trust, for the King in Council would make the final determination on the act. If it were approved in England, Denny would be vindicated and applauded for his contribution to the war effort. The governor weighed the alternatives and agreed to the bill on April 12, 1759. After a long struggle, the Assembly had finally won a victory over the instructions.[54]

51. Franklin to Norris, June 9, 1759, *Franklin Papers*, 8 : 402.

52. Franklin to Galloway, April 7, 1759, ibid., 8 : 310.

53. William Denny to Thomas Penn, April 17, 1759, Penn Papers, HSP; General Amherst to Denny, April 11, 1759, copy, ibid.; Wainwright, "Denny," pp. 190–91.

54. Norris to Franklin, April 12, 1759, *Franklin Papers*, 8 : 326–27; Richard Hockley to Penn, April 21, 1759, Penn Papers, HSP.

While the Penns raged at Denny's defection and prepared to dismiss him, Galloway and the Assembly gleefully rewarded the governor with £1,000 for his acceptance of the bill. Denny saw that it would profit him to maintain good relations with the Assembly; before the Penns could replace him more damage was done. Through the next four months Galloway drafted, and the Assembly passed, four important acts designed to give the House powers more like those of the House of Commons, curtail the prerogative of the proprietors, and hamper the activities of the proprietary faction in Pennsylvania. These were an act for appointing judges on good behavior, an act for recording warrants and surveys, an act for the suppression of lotteries and stage plays, and an act permitting the Pennsylvania loan office to reemit £80,000 in bills of credit.

The act for the appointment of judges on good behavior was the most important of these. It was Galloway's own pet which he had advocated since 1757. Galloway modeled it on the provisions of the Act of Settlement of 1701; the bill provided that judges could be removed only by the Assembly's address to the governor, which was the same privilege that Parliament enjoyed in Britain. It was probably Galloway who argued, in a pamphlet appearing at this time, that Pennsylvanians should enjoy the same valuable right belonging to Englishmen—protection from a subservient judiciary.[55] The other three acts had less noble purpose. Notable was the warrants and surveys act, which took the recording of land sales

55. *The Statutes at Large of Pennsylvania*, 5 : 462–65; [Galloway], *A Letter to the People of Pennsylvania Occasioned by the Assembly's passing that important Act for Constituting the Judges of the Supream Courts and Common-Pleas During Good Behavior* (Philadelphia, 1760 [Evans no. 8636]). This was hardly a "petty, unprincipled, and tyrannical" action, nor was it an attempt "to gain control over the judiciary," as Hanna, *Franklin*, p. 133, claims. Rather, it is the British policy of maintaining executive control over the colonial judiciary, and the consequent failure to extend to America the privilege guaranteed in the Act of Settlement, that should receive this harsh condemnation.

from the proprietary land office and made John Hughes the chief recording officer.[56] All of these acts, by design, violated the spirit and the letter of the proprietary instructions.

Under the spell of large stipends from the Assembly, Denny tore up the instructions and agreed to these acts. His formerly steadfast resolve evaporated when he assented to the bill taxing the proprietors; further indiscretions came almost automatically. Galloway coaxed him and promised him further rewards, and his assent to these bills was followed by an additional £2,000 from the grateful House. When, by September 1759, the proprietary instructions had been rendered meaningless, Denny retired to a newly purchased country house, his "Finances being at present in good Order." [57] The Assembly regarded the payments to the governor as salary arrears, not bribery. In any case, the legislature had no control over the executive other than financial. In order to make mixed government operate, the House had to employ its power over appropriations. Because its leadership, especially

56. The stated purpose of the warrants and surveys act was to rectify injustices perpetrated by the proprietary land office, which, Norris commented to Franklin, August 22, 1759, *Franklin Papers*, 8 : 428–29, had "Tyranized over this poor Colony so many Years without Controul." Lawrence H. Gipson, *The British Empire before the American Revolution*, 7 (New York, 1959) : 305, claims that the land office was "generally regarded as most correctly and efficiently managed." The lotteries and stage plays act was ostensibly to curb immorality in the Quaker commonwealth; yet, the College of Philadelphia was supported by a lottery, so in banning this form of gambling the Assembly may have been striking back at Provost William Smith. Placing more money in circulation, as provided by the reemitting act, was contrary to the proprietary policy of limiting the amount of paper money to prevent depreciation of their receipts from quitrents and land sales.

57. Norris to Franklin, August 22, 1759, *Franklin Papers*, 8 : 429. For Thomas Penn's reaction, see his letters to Richard Peters, June 28, August 1, 1759, Thomas Penn Letter Book, Penn Papers, HSP. Denny was dismissed, stayed in Pennsylvania for a while, and then went to London. James Hamilton replaced him. Wainwright, "Denny," pp. 194–95. Hanna, *Franklin*, p. 133; and James H. Hutson, "The Campaign to Make Pennsylvania a Royal Province, 1764–1770, Part I," *PMHB* 94 (1970) : 427, refer to the House's payments to Denny as bribery.

Galloway, was so resourceful and determined, the Assembly was able to employ many arguments, the pecuniary one included, to break Denny's resolve.

The magnificent victory over the instructions belonged chiefly to Galloway. He drafted the bills, he wrote a pamphlet supporting one of them, and he played a key role in winning over Denny. Galloway eclipsed all other assemblymen, including Speaker Norris. Norris resented his loss of influence to this young upstart but could do little about Galloway's direction of the Assembly except become "sick" while Galloway pushed these bills through.[58] Galloway's "capture" of Governor Denny completely justified the faith Franklin had placed in his abilities. In command of a strong party, influential in the Assembly and outside, and able to dominate the executive, Galloway had made himself the most powerful person in the province. He had more success in dealing with Denny than even Franklin had in 1756–57, proving that he was, as a politician, becoming more nearly Franklin's equal.

Galloway had raised in Pennsylvania a direct challenge to the Penns' instructions, a challenge the proprietors would have to meet before the Privy Council. Franklin, very pleased

58. According to a letter from William Franklin to Galloway, December 28, 1759, Yale University Library, Norris was piqued at Galloway. "It is not," wrote Franklin, "to be wonder'd at, if, as the Speaker grows more & more in Years he should be more & more capricious. . . . The Speaker having been long a member, & accustom'd to have considerable Weight & Influence in the House, it is not unnatural to suppose he would readily take Umbrage at any one whom he thought likely to interfere with his Power. I have myself seen several Instances where he has given such an Opposition to some measures propos'd by my Father, as could not be accounted for but from Motives of Jealousy. This, however, never created any personal Difference between them. Whenever the Speaker propos'd any Measure which appear'd to my Father not detrimental to the Public Welfare, he ever gave it all the Assistance in his Power, and whenever the Speaker oppos'd any Measure propos'd by my Father he never show'd any Resentment to him on that Account. This, I dare say, has likewise been my Friends Conduct; for no one can be more sensible than him, that public Business can never be well carried on where private Animosities are suffer'd to interfere."

with "the Firmness of the Assembly on this Occasion," now had to match Galloway's achievement. He had to defend the Assembly's legislation in its review by the Privy Council, where the Penns would attempt to have it voided.[59] This final stage of the battle opened in England on March 13, 1760, when the proprietors presented the recent acts of the Pennsylvania Assembly to the Council, entering objections to the five for which Galloway was primarily responsible and to several others. The Penns called upon all the official and prestigious aid they could muster to defend their privileges; they employed the most prominent attorneys in the realm, Attorney General Sir Charles Pratt (later Lord Camden) and Solicitor General Charles Yorke, as their counsel. Apparently Franklin's only countermeasure to this heavy battery was to argue that the £100,000 had already been issued and the laws were reasonable exercises of the Assembly's authority.

At hearings on the acts before the Board of Trade, which began May 21, 1760, the ministerial counsellors of the Penns charged that the Assembly had deliberately intended to destroy all proprietary prerogatives and had bribed Denny into collaborating with it. They claimed the Assembly's aim was "to establish a Democracy, if not an Oligarchy," under a charter which "betrayed the rights of the Crown." [60] Under such a system, they said, the Penns would be forced to pay most of the expenses of the colony, because of the unfair taxation of their lands, while the inhabitants would enjoy the benefits free of charge. The proprietors would not get a fair assessment of their lands from officers appointed by the As-

59. Franklin to Norris, June 9, 1759, *Franklin Papers*, 8 : 396. William Franklin wrote to Galloway, December 28, 1759, Yale University Library: "I wonder, when there was so good an Understanding between the Assembly and Governor they did not make an Attack on the Licences for Taverns, Marriages, &c. It would have been worth while for the Province to have given him a considerable Sum of Money to have the Matter put on a different Footing."

60. Thomas Penn to James Hamilton, May 24, 1760, Thomas Penn Letter Book, Penn Papers, HSP. *Journal of the Commissioners for Trade and Plantations,* 11 : 108–12.

sembly. Their quitrents would be depreciated by the Assembly's inflationary monetary policy. The two acts concerning judges and warrants and surveys would deprive them of their rights. All of Galloway's five bills, as well as several others of less importance, they deemed democratical and dangerous.

Franklin, through his counsel, based his defense of the acts on the charter rights of the Pennsylvania Assembly and on the impracticality of repeal. The proprietors enjoyed executive authority, but as landholders they were under the law and had to meet the obligations of landholders. The tax rates would be equal and, considering the vastness of the Penn estates, not burdensome. As Norris pointed out to Franklin, "Nine Tenths of the Whole," the unlocated unimproved lands, went untaxed.[61] Moreover, Franklin claimed, since Pennsylvania had already put the act for printing £100,000 into effect, and the money was in circulation, repeal would ruin the colony and hinder the war effort. It was the people's right to express their will through the passage of these acts by the legislature.[62]

Franklin's arguments, which he and his Assembly colleagues had used for five years, were outweighed by those of the ministerial lawyers of the Penns and by a general prejudice against a colonial legislature's claim to great privileges. On June 24, 1760, the Board of Trade reported to the Privy Council against these five acts and two others. It declared the taxation of the proprietors an injustice. It reported against the act for appointing judges on good behavior because, it argued, Pennsylvania possessed few qualified judges, and the Penns should be at liberty to make changes in the judiciary as more capable judges became available. This reasoning

61. Norris to Franklin, June 4, 1759, Copybook, HSP, in *Franklin Papers*, 8 : 392.

62. The summary of the arguments presented on both sides is reconstructed from letters from Thomas Penn to James Hamilton, May 24, June 6, June 27, 1760, Thomas Penn Letter Book, HSP; and from the Report of the Board of Trade, June 24, 1760, in *Franklin Papers*, 9 : 131–73.

sounds spurious now; judging from the attitude of the British
government toward Pennsylvania and other colonies in regard to this matter, it appears that the home government
feared the establishment of a colonial judiciary not totally dependent on executive authority. Showing that it had a far
different conception of the Assembly's privileges than did
Franklin and Galloway, the Board censured the Penns for
not safeguarding the king's prerogative against the encroachments of the House.[63]

Franklin did not accept the Board's report as final. Too
much was at stake for Pennsylvania for him to give up the
battle at that point. He carried his fight to the Privy Council,
trying at the same time to outweigh the influence that the
Penns had brought to bear. He wrote to William Pitt "im-
ploring his Protection for the Province," and he tried to get
London merchants to endorse the £100,000 act.[64] While these
attempts came to naught, Franklin did obtain some relief.
The Privy Council, in its orders on colonial affairs, usually
followed the recommendations of the Board of Trade, but
Franklin, at a hearing on August 27, 1760, succeeded in soft-
ening the blow dealt to the colony. His point that the economy of Pennsylvania would be gravely damaged if the act
for printing £100,000 were disallowed had more weight here.
Lord Mansfield, the chief justice, saw merit in Franklin's argument; at the hearing he and Franklin agreed on a compro-

63. Report of the Board of Trade, June 24, 1760, in *Franklin Papers,*
9 : 131–73. The warrants and surveys act was recommended for disal-
lowance because it made warrants clear titles to land before the land was
fully purchased. The Board argued that the College of Philadelphia
would be injured by the suppression of lotteries and that the prohibition
of plays was unnecessary. The reemitting act, it found, would inflate the
currency too greatly and reduce the sterling value of quitrents. An act for
the relief of heirs of unnaturalized decedents and a supplement to the
reemitting act also were reported against. Several unimportant acts and
the one appointing Franklin to collect the parliamentary grant to
Pennsylvania were recommended for approval because they did not
touch the proprietary prerogative.

64. William Franklin to Galloway, August 26, 1760, *Franklin Papers,*
9 : 189–91.

mise. Taxation of the proprietors would be permitted if their located unimproved lands and town lots were assessed at the lowest rate at which other lands in Pennsylvania were assessed, if waste lands were not taxed, if the Penns had a right to appeal their assessments within the province, if the governor was granted some voice in disbursements, and if quitrents were not depreciated. Franklin agreed to these stipulations because they were minor reservations compared to the establishment of the principle that the Penns were not above the law and had the same responsibilities as ordinary landholders of the colony. The Penns, reversing their stubborn stand, also agreed. They now believed that their financial burden was guaranteed to be minimal, and they could not afford to appear obstructionist to the Council. Only the act for printing £100,000 was allowed to stand, however; the others that the Board of Trade had reported against were voided.[65]

It was a shallow victory for Franklin and Galloway, but meaningful nevertheless. Although the chief Pennsylvania politicians had by no means brought the Penns to book, their efforts had gotten British authorities to inquire into the proprietary handling of Indian affairs and had established the power of the Assembly to tax the proprietors. The amount the Penns had to pay was small, but, as Norris correctly pointed out, "we have been contending for a Matter of Right rather than Mony." [66] The continued uncompromising stand of the Penns did them no credit. Thomas Penn later admitted that the Assembly's taxation of the proprietary estate was equitable with its taxation of land in general, showing that the proprietors' earlier fears were groundless.[67] In order

65. Franklin, *Autobiography*, pp. 265–66; *Acts of the Privy Council, Colonial Series*, 4 : 440–42; Thomas Penn to James Hamilton, August 30, 1760, Thomas Penn Letter Book, HSP. In April 1760 Hamilton had agreed to a money bill taxing the proprietors' located unimproved lands as had the bill of 1759.

66. Norris to Franklin, July 28, 1760, *Franklin Papers,* 9 : 181.

67. Thomas Penn to John Penn, October 13, 1764, Thomas Penn Letter Book, HSP, comments on a tax bill which the proprietor thought equitable but excessive.

to have effective government in Pennsylvania, it was necessary
to make the Penns realize that they had to deal forthrightly
with their subjects and their subjects' representatives. Yet, the
proprietors were correct in assuming that they could not give
way to the Assembly with impunity. Franklin and Galloway,
having cracked open the door, would not be satisfied until
proprietary power was completely reduced.

The limited gains against the Penns were secondary to a
more important development, the maturation of the partnership of the agent and the Assembly leader. Before 1757 Galloway played a political role much subordinate to Franklin's.
By 1759 the two men were virtual partners, pulling in tandem, Galloway right behind Franklin, as they labored toward
a final confrontation with the proprietors. With Franklin's
blessing and support, Galloway rose in prominence in Pennsylvania. He challenged Governor Denny and won—Denny
lined his pockets and the proprietary instructions were broken.
He challenged the popular Norris and won again—Norris
quit the Assembly temporarily while Galloway led it in bold
attack. Franklin did not publicly single out Galloway above
Norris, Hughes, and his other colleagues, for he was much
too shrewd a politician to risk alienating his other followers.
Nevertheless, he recognized that Galloway had most ably supported his cause while he was absent from Philadelphia and
had amply repaid Franklin for giving him his start and his
first promotions in politics. The aims of the two men, their
methods, and their political ideas were identical. They cooperated as closely as possible over a 3,000 mile separation.
They were acknowledged as the chief leaders of their party
in the Assembly. In short, they were partners in their political
ventures, just as if they had made a formal written agreement
to do business together.

The Philadelphia electorate also recognized Galloway's
ability and his attachment to Franklin. In 1756 and 1757
Galloway, young and relatively unknown, placed seventh in
the race for eight seats. The Moore-Smith trials brought him
to the forefront in the Assembly and helped to advance him

to third place on the ticket in 1758. His leadership in persuading Governor Denny to break the proprietary instructions boosted Galloway to second place on the ticket in 1759, right behind Speaker Norris. In 1760 and 1761 Galloway had no good issue with which to build his popularity, so his support fell off slightly. Teedyuscung's admission that the Penns had not defrauded the Indians hurt Galloway in 1762; he slipped back to seventh place.[68] Galloway's slow decline in popularity after 1759 meant little, however, for his previous achievements firmly established his partnership with Franklin. Thomas Penn paid him the crowning backhanded compliment when he accorded him the title, well-deserved, of "great Champion of the Party."

Franklin, in contrast, had gained little from his London mission. Although flattered by his reception by the learned, he did not receive in political circles the attention and respect to which he was accustomed in Pennsylvania. His opponents were too strong; after the partially favorable decision on the Pennsylvania legislation, he hoped to escape quickly from the tangle of British affairs. "I grow weary of so long a Banishment, and anxiously desire once more the happy Society of my Friends and Family in Philadelphia," he wrote to Galloway in 1760.[69] Obliged to remain in Britain to manage the parliamentary reimbursement of Pennsylvania's military expenses, he was unable to leave until August 1762. Probably he was especially anxious to join forces with Galloway and his party to continue to press the Assembly's cause in more congenial Pennsylvania. By 1763 Franklin and Galloway were seasoned veterans who had built a strong party organization, worked together in a transatlantic cooperation, and won important constitutional battles in Pennsylvania and in London. Their success against the Penns, however limited, made them

68. *Votes*, 6 : 4886, 5068, 5157, 5280, 5367. Assemblymen were listed in order according to vote totals. Election returns which would show the number of votes for each candidate have not been found for these years.

69. Franklin to Galloway, January 9, 1760, *Franklin Papers*, 9 : 17. Also see Franklin to Deborah Franklin, [March 28, 1760], ibid., 9 : 37–39.

all the more determined to continue the fight. United on the same soil, pitting their combined abilities and their party against the proprietors, they thought they could soon deliver the final blow.

3 The Change of Government

Honored by English scientists and savants, doctor per St. Andrew's and Oxford, father of the new royal governor of New Jersey, but only partial victor over the proprietors, Franklin returned to Pennsylvania in November 1762 in triumph.[1] Galloway and his many other friends in Philadelphia flocked to his house to congratulate him and, presumably, to consult on the next political actions to be taken against the Penns. The philosophical prestige Franklin had gained in Britain probably made him more determined to gain political success as well. So much had been won in Pennsylvania; Galloway's first grasp on the political machinery of the Assembly provided a strong base from which to attack the proprietors. So little had been won in England; despite the vindication of the Assembly's claim to tax the Penns, the executive prerogatives of the proprietors remained generally intact.

Franklin was absent from Philadelphia throughout much of 1763 on post office business, but many times during the year he and his closest colleague, Galloway, must have discussed their next move against the Penns. Very likely as they lingered at dinner over their favorite delicacy, sea turtle, they considered how they could win full privileges for the Assembly. There seemed little point in further attacks on the instructions; by the end of 1763 Franklin and Galloway had probably concluded that their partnership should com-

1. William Franklin was appointed through the influence of Lord Bute, probably to guarantee that his father would be obligated to the ministry. Thomas Penn to James Hamilton, March 11, 1763, Thomas Penn Letter Book, Penn Papers, HSP.

mit itself to a change of Pennsylvania's government from proprietary to royal.[2]

Before the partners finally decided that they would undertake to dissolve the Penns' government and persuade the
king to assume direct control over the colony, they had
dropped many hints that royal government might be the cure
for the ills infecting the province. In the disputes between
the governors and the Assembly in the early 1750s, messages
of the Assembly, which Franklin helped write, suggested that
Pennsylvania should be under direct royal control. "We cannot but esteem those Colonies that are under the immediate
Care of the Crown, in a much more eligable Situation," a
1753 report of the House declared.[3] One Penn supporter believed Franklin was planning, on the eve of his trip to England, to put Pennsylvania in such an "eligable" situation.[4]
When Franklin went off to London in 1757, he apparently
considered the substitution of the king's government for the
Penns' as a last resort to be sought only if all efforts to get
the proprietary instructions revoked failed. He recognized
that Pennsylvanians had no great inclination for a change
of government while the possibility existed that the Penns
could be cured of their intransigence by less drastic surgery.
In June 1758 Franklin reported that he had sought opinions
on the effect that a change of government would have on the
privileges of the colony, but he followed this line no further.
On September 16, 1758, he wrote to Galloway that, "as to a
Change of Government, that perhaps is at some Distance, unless the Province, heartily tir'd of Proprietary Rule, should
petition the Crown to take the Government into its own
Hands." [5] A letter to Norris of the same date speculated,

2. Apparently, Franklin and Galloway planned an arrangement dupli-
cating that in New Jersey, where the Crown controlled the government
but the proprietors retained the unsold lands and collected quitrents.

3. *Votes,* 5 : 3826–27; also in *Franklin Papers,* 5 : 57.

4. Extract of a letter from Robert Hunter Morris [to Thomas Penn?],
October 8, 1756, Penn Papers, HSP.

5. Franklin to Galloway, September 16, 1758, *Franklin Papers,* 8 : 150.
Also see Franklin to Thomas Leech and the Assembly Committee of
Correspondence, June 10, 1758, ibid., 8 : 88–89.

"Tumults and Insurrections, that might prove the Proprietary Government insufficient to preserve Order, or show the People to be ungovernable, would do the Business immediately; but such I hope will never happen." [6] Yet if reform of Pennsylvania's government required internal disorder, such disorder was not necessarily a distant prospect with Franklin and Galloway controlling the political situation.

The agent's relations with the proprietors had so deteriorated by September 1758 that Franklin was becoming more firmly committed to the total overthrow of Penn government than he had indicated to Galloway and Norris. In that month he raised the issue of the change of government publicly in a newspaper article. "[The question is] Whether the frequent clashings of interest between the Proprietors and people of our colonies, which of late have been so prejudicial to His Majesty's service, and the defence of his dominions, do not at length make it necessary for this nation to enquire into the nature and conduct of these Proprietary Governments, and put them on a better footing?" [7] Throughout the succeeding months, repeated failures to persuade the Penns to resign some of their privileges made Franklin more convinced. "I am tired of Proprietary Government," he confided to Galloway in April 1759, "and heartily wish for that of the Crown." [8] Galloway echoed the same sentiment in the conclusion to his *True State*. In 1761 Franklin investigated the possibility that the rightful owner of the province was Springett Penn, descended from the elder branch of the family, who was much more amiable than surly Thomas and willing to sell his right of government to the Crown.[9] Before 1764, talk and inquiry came to nothing except to help Franklin and Galloway con-

6. Franklin to Isaac Norris, September 16, 1758, ibid., 8 : 157.

7. Franklin, "Queries Addressed to a Friend of Lord Baltimore," *London Chronicle*, September 19, 1758, reprinted in *Benjamin Franklin's Letters to the Press*, ed. Verner W. Crane (Chapel Hill, N.C., 1950), no. 1, p. 7.

8. Franklin to Galloway, April 9, 1759, *Franklin Papers*, 8 : 315. Also see Franklin to Norris, January 19, 1759, ibid., 8 : 236; and Franklin to Israel Pemberton, March 19, 1759, ibid., 8 : 299–300.

9. Franklin to Edward Penington, May 19, 1761, ibid., 9 : 315–17.

vince themselves that making Pennsylvania a royal province ought to be attempted when the time was ripe. Franklin, and probably Galloway also, knew that events would dictate their course of action. Both were men of reaction, having in past years utilized for their benefit political crises not entirely of their own making. For the time being, they adopted a conciliatory manner. In debating the issue of additional paper money in the Assembly in January 1764, both Franklin and Galloway argued against fruitless controversy with the governor.[10] However, they were intellectually committed to and prepared to work for royal government once something like the "Tumults and Insurrections" occurred.

The issue that started the push for royal government arose in backcountry Pennsylvania in late 1763. By December of that year Pontiac's conspiracy had stirred up fires which would lock Assembly and governor in combat again. The Scotch-Irish and Germans of the frontier, wearied to desperation by repeated attacks on their homes and families, could not and did not want to discriminate between friendly Indians and Pontiac's allies. The Assembly tried to alleviate their condition by raising 1,000 men for defense; in addition, the legislature tried to prevent possible outrages by taking Indians from Bethlehem under its protection and quartering them at Philadelphia. But the Assembly was not thorough enough in its measures. Some intrepid Indian fighters from the Paxton district of Lancaster County, rather than seek out the warring redmen, took the noble course of revenging themselves on friendly and innocent Indians. At the Indians' homes on Conestoga Manor and at the Lancaster workhouse, these "Paxton Boys" attacked and massacred twenty defenseless Indians.

10. Franklin wrote to Peter Collinson, December 19, 1763, ibid., 10 : 401, about John Penn, the new governor: "I think we shall have no personal Difference, at least I will give no Occasion." To John Fothergill, March 14, 1764, ibid., 11 : 101–05, Franklin related how Governor Penn had first had his confidence and then lost it. For the paper money debate, see Howard M. Jenkins, "Fragments of a Journal Kept by Samuel Foulke, of Bucks County, While a Member of the Colonial Assembly of Pennsylvania, 1762–4," *PMHB* 5 (1881) : 68–69.

The horrible atrocity aroused all Pennsylvania. Franklin spoke for human decency and justice in his pamphlet *Narrative of the Late Massacres in Lancaster County*. Castigating the cowardly murderers, he called on every honorable citizen to "join heartily and unanimously in Support of the Laws, and in strengthening the Hands of Government, that JUSTICE may be done, the Wicked punished, and the Innocent protected." [11] This clarion to suppress rioting and lawlessness went largely unheeded by Governor John Penn, nephew of Thomas and Richard. The Assembly resolved that it would provide for troops to suppress the rioters, but the governor merely issued a proclamation against the criminals.[12] Penn was convinced that a conspiracy of silence and collusion with the rioters existed among the Scotch-Irish settlers in the neighborhood of the massacre. Against this, he believed that he could do nothing and so did not act with vigor.

Supineness encouraged the Paxton Boys to march on Philadelphia to deal with the Indians there as they had dealt with those in Lancaster County and to convince the Assembly that they should have a greater voice in formulating governing policies. When the approach of the marchers was discovered on February 3, 1764, the governor gave over the command of the defense of the city to Franklin. Franklin exulted over John Penn's predicament and his dependence on Franklin's natural leadership ability; the governor "did me the Honour . . . to run to my House at Midnight, with his Counselors at his Heels, for Advice, and made it his Head Quarters for some time." [13] Franklin took charge, and in two days the reception for the Paxton Boys was prepared. The city bristled with artillery. Companies of infantry, composed even of Quakers resolved to stave off what looked like revolution, were or-

11. Franklin, *Narrative of the Late Massacres in Lancaster County*, in *Franklin Papers*, 11 : 68.

12. *Votes*, 6 : 5501; *Minutes of the Provincial Council of Pennsylvania*, 9 (Harrisburg, 1852) : 95–96, 107–08; *Pa. Arch.*, 1st ser. 4 : 153–54.

13. Franklin to John Fothergill, March 14, 1764, *Franklin Papers*, 11 : 103.

ganized. The Paxton Boys, on reaching the outskirts of Philadelphia, learned of the defenses and consequently were quite
ready to treat. A committee composed of Franklin, Galloway,
Daniel Roberdeau, and representatives of the governor met
with the Paxton leaders at Germantown, northwest of the
city. For the westerners, discretion proved to be the better
part of valor. They rather meekly presented the committee
with a list of grievances, chief among which was that the backcountry counties did not have as many representatives in the
Assembly as the counties in the eastern part of the province.
The marchers dared do no more than present their protests,
and on February 8 they returned to their homes. The committee promised to permit the Paxton Boys' spokesmen to lay
their grievances before the Assembly. Franklin and Galloway,
however, had no sympathy for the western demands for equal
representation; they later argued that the backcountry counties did not pay taxes sufficient to entitle them to as many
representatives as the eastern counties.[14]

Franklin and Galloway believed that they gained two ad-

14. Brooke Hindle, "The March of the Paxton Boys," *WMQ*, 3d ser.
3 (1946) : 461–86, covers this episode very well. For the grievances of the
backcountry see *Votes*, 7 : 5542–47. John R. Dunbar, ed., *The Paxton
Papers* (The Hague, 1957), is a useful collection of contemporary accounts
of the events. More comprehensive study of such accounts can be made
by consulting the titles referring to Pennsylvania listed in Evans, for
1764. Hindle, "Paxton Boys," p. 463, provides a table showing the in-
equitable apportionment of representatives. Using Philadelphia County
as the base, he shows that Bucks County was 100 percent overrepresented,
while Philadelphia City, Lancaster, York, Berks, and Northampton were
more than 50 percent underrepresented. The backcountry settlers, as well
as Franklin's and Galloway's party, had no real conception of democratic proportional representation. The Paxton Boys' request that "we
may be no longer deprived of an equal number with [the eastern coun-
ties]" was answered by an Assembly party broadside, *To the Freeholders
and other Electors for the City and County of Philadelphia, and Counties
of Chester and Bucks* (Philadelphia, 1764 [Evans no. 9854]), which argued
that the backcountry wanted more representatives regardless of "Numbers,
or the Proportion of the public Tax they pay."

vantages from their handling of the Paxton Boys' march. Franklin's political reputation was immensely strengthened by his prominence and leadership through these hectic days when both Quakers and proprietary leaders quaked in fear of mob violence in Philadelphia. This prominence was now coupled with the issue the partners needed, the "tumults" that Franklin had speculated to Norris "would do the Business immediately." Murders, riots, a march on the capital— what more proof was needed to demonstrate to the citizens of Pennsylvania and to the home government that the proprietary government could not keep order? Judging from their retreat, the Paxton Boys appear to have been no real threat to the control of the Assembly by Franklin and his Philadelphia allies; they constituted only an annoyance. The partners apparently believed that they could use the actions of the rioters to indicate to the citizens that the collapse of law and order was near at hand unless strong measures were taken. The authority and power of the king seemed to the politicians to be required to replace the apparent weakness and stubbornness of the proprietors and to save Pennsylvania. The campaign for royal government could now begin.

The advocates of royal government had a ready-made pattern for proceeding, for the Indian menace and the riots had raised the issues of 1755–56 all over again. Following the blueprint of 1755, the Assembly in February 1764 passed bills to create a democratically officered militia and to print £50,000 in bills of credit for military purposes, to be redeemed by taxing all estates. This tax bill, and a substitute providing for the raising of £55,000, interpreted the Franklin-Mansfield agreement rather loosely, for it stated that all lands would be assessed on the same basis and that proprietary lands would not necessarily be taxed at the lowest rates.[15] Franklin explained that he interpreted the agreement of 1760 with the Penns to mean that all lands ought to be taxed at a fair rate. To tax rich meadowland owned by the proprietors at the

15. *Votes*, 7 : 5576–79.

same rate as valueless swamp would be "inconsistent with all Notions of Common Honesty." [16] Franklin's interpretation was probably just; later in 1764 the Penns would agree to it. However, Governor John Penn would not agree in February or March; determined not to admit that the Assembly had any right to reinterpret the agreement, he sent down these money bills. Moreover, he refused the militia bill. Very likely, Franklin and Galloway expected him to do so; they were giving the proprietary government the chance to be accommodating, but the governor remained steadfast. In return, the Assembly declared that the backcountry grievances were "founded on false or mistaken Facts" and blamed the proprietors for Indian unrest and for allowing the Paxton Boys to run wild.[17] The Assembly had attempted to act; the governor had rebuffed it and had sided with its opponents. Now the Assembly would have to strike directly at the root of the obstruction.

Under Franklin's and Galloway's leadership, the House now began an attack, not on the instructions but on proprietary government itself. Galloway, John Hughes, and George

16. The Franklin-Mansfield agreement lends itself to the interpretation held by the proprietors: their lands would be taxed at the lowest rate of any land in the province. But Franklin and the Assembly, in *Votes*, 7 : 5586–91, insisted that the agreement meant that the Penn lands would be assessed at the rate of other lands of the same kind, situation, and quality. It is unclear what Franklin, the Penns, or the Privy Council thought the agreement meant when it was drawn up, but certainly the Assembly's interpretation was the most equitable.

17. The House requested the governor to hold a public hearing at which it expected the Paxton Boys would be convinced of their errors. Penn refused; then in May 1764 the House appointed a committee, composed of Franklin, Galloway, and several of their adherents, to report on the backcountry grievances. The committee reported favorably to the backcountry position on one grievance, that the lack of circuit courts was a hindrance to justice. Later the House, under Galloway, would deal with this problem. The other grievances were virtually ignored. *Votes*, 7 : 5553–56, 5636–37, 5608. Franklin wrote to Richard Jackson, March 14, 1764, *Franklin Papers*, 11 : 107, that it was rumored that the "Governor's Party" encouraged the rioters.

Ashbridge of Chester County lined up Franklin's supporters. On March 24, 1764, five days after the governor's second refusal of a tax on proprietary lands, Franklin and Galloway presented twenty-six resolves, which the Assembly passed *nemine contradicente*. The resolves declared that all mischiefs in the province were chargeable to the proprietors, who constituted an unwarranted interposition between the sovereign and his subjects. The major particular grievances were much the same as those that Galloway and his allies had drawn up for Franklin to take to England in 1757. They stated that the proprietary instructions restricted the lawful powers of the Assembly and that the proprietors infringed on the rights of Pennsylvanians as Englishmen by appointing judges to serve at their pleasure. The House then adjourned until May, delaying further action until it determined whether its constituents were equally resentful of proprietary rule and wished their representatives to petition the king to take over the government.[18]

Contemporary opponents of Franklin and Galloway, as well as later observers, have viewed the quest for a change of government as the product of either the foolishness or the knavery of the two men and their allies. The partners appear, in the light of historical hindsight, to have been collaborating, unwittingly or by design, with those in Britain who wanted to extend and tighten imperial control. Franklin had firsthand evidence that the British ministry cared little about the privileges of legislative assemblies in the colonies and considered Americans to possess fewer political rights than Britons. Bringing royal government to Pennsylvania would seem to defeat the avowed intentions of Franklin and Galloway

18. *Votes*, 7 : 5591–95. Some other grievances were that the proprietors held all the good land for exorbitant prices while not paying fair taxes on it, that they took advantage of their subjects while the "Knife of Savages [was] at their [subjects'] Throat," and that they increased the number of tippling houses. Charles Thomson wrote Franklin, December 18, 1764, *Franklin Papers*, 11 : 522, that the proprietors attempted to "render them more abject Slaves by erecting Bagnios and public Inns," as the ancient Persians did.

to maintain and increase the rights of the citizens and their representative body. Could it be that they had sold out their principles and their constituents for material gain? Opponents of Franklin and Galloway believed that this was true. It was widely charged that the partners would acquire high office when the change of government was consummated. Franklin would become governor and Galloway, chief justice.[19] Franklin's enemies charged that "the only joyous thing in the world to him is great pay." Even Galloway's friends believed him overly ambitious; Thomas Livezey, a fellow assemblyman, chided Galloway good-naturedly for being a fee-seeking lawyer and an honor-craving politician.[20] These charges were coupled by the partners' political opponents with allegations concerning certain deceitful and unscrupulous political operations in the past. At that time and in later studies, the partners' integrity was, and has been, called into serious question.

Two general considerations tell heavily against the charge that Franklin and Galloway pushed the change of government to advance their own interests. First, both men had declined past opportunities to take the road to great wealth in Pennsylvania politics: the proprietary side. Franklin could have cooperated with his erstwhile friends, Allen and Smith, or joined Thomas Penn when on his London mission. Galloway's father-in-law could have found him a proprietary place.

19. *Pennsylvania Journal*, September 27, 1764.

20. For Franklin's love of Mammon, see Edward Shippen to William Logan, February 24, 1758, Shippen Letter Books, APS. Thomas Livezey to Galloway, December 14, 1765, printed in *PMHB* 12 (1888): 367, comments obliquely on Galloway. Neither Franklin nor Galloway was really very wealthy; their circumstances were, in 1764, merely quite comfortable. Franklin profited some £600–£700 yearly from his printing partnership with David Hall; he received £300 a year as deputy postmaster general; and he had been paid £3,000 plus expenses for his mission to London. Galloway had wealthy relatives, a profitable law practice, and a wife who was heiress to a large fortune. Although in 1778, in his *Examination*, p. 71, Galloway claimed he had an estate worth £40,000, he probably acquired much of this after 1764—and especially after the death of his father-in-law in 1770.

Thomas Penn probably would have "bought" both men with land grants if he could have, although he certainly considered the attempt not worth the effort.[21] Franklin and Galloway demonstrated by their actions that they considered the Assembly more congruent to their political ideals and a surer base for their advancement that the proprietors in far off British estates.

Second, Franklin and Galloway felt themselves propelled by events, not tugging against the tide. Truly, they were ambitious, but the ineffectiveness and stubbornness of the current government, more than their own aspirations, impelled them to seek the change. In 1764 they were concerned only with the immediate problem of obtaining royal government; they made little reference to the future problem of who would occupy the royal posts after the change. In 1765 Franklin indicated that "when I am quit of these [duties of his agency], I will engage in no other," and would lead a life of "Ease and Leisure." Galloway never made his plans clear.[22] One should not confuse the political maneuvers which Franklin and Galloway employed to deceive their opponents, silence their detractors, and break the resolve of the proprietary governors with their primary attitudes toward and expectations from political activity. These political methods cannot be applauded, but they were not used merely to advance the partners' own interests. In all their actions, especially in promoting the change of government, Franklin and Galloway were, first, concerned with furthering the privileges of the representative assembly.

Nor were Franklin and Galloway fools. Royal government conducted by able officials on the spot, distant from home authorities in England, would, they thought, be far more flexible and more responsive to the popular mood than was government by a deputy who was under heavy obligation to

21. Warden, "Proprietary Group," pp. 383–84, notes how Penn rewarded favorites with land warrants. Also see chapter 5, n. 4, for the case of Joseph Fox.

22. Franklin to Lord Kames, June 2, 1765, *Franklin Papers*, 12 : 161–62.

proprietors always concerned about their revenues. Proprietary government had given the colony the advantages of William Penn's Charter of Privileges of 1701, but the partners were confident that the liberties of conscience and politics guaranteed therein would be continued under royal government. They rejected the notion that proprietary government was an interposition between Crown and colony that safeguarded Pennsylvanians' liberties. Good officials were the best safeguard. The future royal officials might be the present leaders and members of the Assembly party, but they, having spent their careers in the cause of strengthening the representative part of the government, could hardly conceive that they might become embroiled in conflicts with the Assembly in a royal colony. Franklin and Galloway had already shown that they were not rubber stamps for the Board of Trade. They may have been unrealistic about the ability of a royal government to maintain the liberties of the colony in the face of new imperial measures, but thus far in their careers the Assembly party leaders had shown themselves much less subservient to the British ministry than were the Penns. The partners were not trading the birthright of free Pennsylvanians for a bowl of the king's pottage. They wanted both birthright and pottage.[23]

It remained for the political leaders to persuade the voters of Pennsylvania, who had supported them through former controversies, to permit them to push a bit further. Franklin and Galloway apparently anticipated minimum difficulty, for the electorate was already familiar with their political services to date and had little about which to complain. Turning the responsibility for the decision over to their constituents was

23. Franklin favored the corporate form of government enjoyed by Connecticut and Rhode Island. In his plans for two colonies to be founded on the Ohio River, drawn up in 1754, he proposed that these colonies have an elected executive and council, "for extraordinary privileges and liberties, with land on easy terms, are strong inducements to people to hazard their persons and fortunes in settling new countries." Franklin, *A Plan for Settling Two Western Colonies, in Franklin Papers,* 5 : 460.

an adroit maneuver, for the issue of proprietary mismanagement and intransigence would attract popular interest and make the demand for a change of government seem more of a spontaneous grass-roots movement than it actually was. Soon after the Assembly adjourned in March, Franklin and Galloway put their persuasive abilities to work. They held a meeting outside the Statehouse, attended by many Philadelphians, to acquaint the inhabitants with the Assembly's reasons for proposing the change and to solicit their support. The younger partner was called upon to put his vaunted oratorical powers to the test. "Mr. Galloway made a long and . . . very silly Speech to the Mob, he was prompted by Mr. Franklin," John Penn reported to Uncle Thomas. Galloway told the "Mob" that "the way from Proprietary Slavery to Royal Liberty is easy &c." [24] All the voters had to do was to sign petitions, then being circulated by the Assembly party, and reelect the Franklin-Galloway group in October; the change would then be as good as accomplished.

Galloway's specialty was oratory; Franklin also contributed his specialty: well-reasoned and well-argued pamphlets. On April 12 Franklin presented his case for a change of government in *Cool Thoughts on the Present Situation of Public Affairs*. The title suggests the theme—reasoned argument rather than impassioned emotional pleas. Franklin pointed out that the governor had failed to keep order and that the proprietary instructions thwarted the Assembly's efforts in all directions. As he often did in his writings, Franklin adapted scientific principles to political situations. The proprietors, he charged, were an unnecessary interposition between the British government and Pennsylvania's citizens, and, "like unnecessary Springs and Movements in a Machine, are so apt to produce Disorder." [25] Direct royal control was the only

24. John Penn to Thomas Penn, May 5, 1764, Penn Papers, HSP.
25. Franklin, *Cool Thoughts on the Present Situation of Public Affairs*, in *Franklin Papers*, 11 : 162. Franklin wrote Israel Pemberton, March 19, 1758, ibid., 8 : 299, that proprietary government was "too much Weight in one Scale."

solution. Anticipating possible objections, Franklin claimed that the charter liberties granted by the founder would remain unaltered and that the rights of all citizens would be protected. If the ministry was determined to impose taxes, bishops, or a standing army on Pennsylvania, these scourges would come no less quickly under a proprietary government than under a royal one. The charter rights of Pennsylvanians, Franklin asserted, could be altered only by act of Parliament. To prevent this, he argued that "we may rely on the united justice of King, Lords, and Commons, that no such Act will ever pass, while we continue loyal and dutiful Subjects." [26] Such reliance may have been naive, but Franklin could envision no conflicts between British authority and the colony as serious as those between proprietors and Assembly.

The controversial scheme of the partners could not long go unchallenged; opposition quickly sprang up from five groups. Of course, the proprietary officeholders, small in number but large in wealth and influence, decried the plan. Religious opposition came from the Presbyterians and some Quakers. Franklin and Galloway, by disregarding religious differences in shaping their party to their own principles, and by attempting to consign the term "Quaker party" to oblivion after 1756, had sought to place politics on a more secular basis. The Presbyterians were not entirely prepared to unite with Quakers and Anglicans. George Bryan, once a member of the Scourge triumvirate with Galloway and William Franklin, was a Presbyterian who backed away from Franklin perhaps at the time of the Moore-Smith trials. Of the change-of-government proposal, Bryan wrote, "all dissenting from the Church of England, would do well to consider how far their privileges would be likely to be impaired." [27] To this group, royal government meant royal church and an end to the traditional religious liberty. On March 24, 1764, when the Assembly had drawn up its grievances, Presbyterian ministers

26. Ibid., 8 : 171.

27. See Burton A. Konkle, *George Bryan and the Constitution of Pennsylvania* (Philadelphia, 1922), p. 51, quoting Bryan's diary.

and elders of Philadelphia sent out a circular letter to the
other Presbyterian churches in the colony asking them to
subscribe to a plan for more joint action by Presbyterians
to prevent "evil-minded persons" from encroaching on "our
essential and *charter* privileges." [28] The Quakers, also by
British standards dissenters who would be forced to pay
tithes to an established church, divided on the scheme of the
politicians. Most supported Franklin because they believed in
him, shared his principles, and hankered for profits from royal
offices when the change came. A few influential ones feared
the coming of the king's church and the departure of cherished
liberties. Fourth, the Pennsylvania Germans, numerous but
not very active politically unless they perceived a direct challenge to their ethnic group, were concerned about the preservation of their religious freedom and about their safety from
oppression by a strong royal government that might have no
sympathy or toleration for their traditional ways. A fifth
group opposing the scheme was the backcountry settlers. Because Franklin and Galloway advocated royal government to
suppress riots and lawlessness, backcountry men feared that
royal troops might soon be chasing after the murderers of the
Indians in Lancaster County. The government might be
changed, but the easterners would remain in control, the
backcountry representation in the Assembly would not be
increased, and Quaker Indian policies, which held that there
were other good Indians besides dead ones, would be continued. Moreover, nearly all backcountry settlers were Germans or Scotch-Irish Presbyterians. Among these five groups,
political and religious grievances forged an alliance against
the powerful Assembly leaders.

Samuel Purviance, Jr., a Philadelphia merchant and a
Presbyterian, led in uniting the five groups into a party

28. This letter was termed a "jesuitical bull" by Franklin's supporters.
It is printed in Galloway, *Historical and Political Reflections on the Rise
and Progress of the American Rebellion* (London, 1780), pp. 49–53. Franklin and Galloway, hardly avid Churchmen, had no intention of establishing Anglicanism or permitting the violation of liberty of conscience.

rivaling that of Franklin and Galloway. Purviance worked with proprietary officeholders and other Presbyterians to set up an efficient political machine to draw supporters from the Assembly party and to arouse previously uncommitted voters. Soon hard-hitting propaganda appeared from the pens of writers whom Purviance encouraged to attack Franklin and Galloway.[29] The stated aim of this Proprietary party, or New Ticket, as it was called in contrast to the Franklin-Galloway Old Ticket, was to oust the partners and their colleagues from their seats in the House and thus kill their political scheme. If the Assembly leaders were not reelected in the October election, "the rest wou'd be like a Body without a Head." [30] Now Franklin and Galloway were confronted with an organization nearly as formidable as their own; they would need all their political skill to save their seats and their plans for the change.

As the petitions for a change of government circulated in Philadelphia—among children and inebriates, the Proprietary party charged—a host of pamphlets appeared to praise or damn the plans of Franklin and Galloway. Franklin's *Cool Thoughts* opened the printed debate; in reply, Hugh Williamson published his *Plain Dealer* series. Williamson charged that the change-of-government issue was a red herring designed to obscure the real problem, which was the need of the backcountry for equal representation. Proprietary partisans supported the backcountry's demand because greater representation from that section would break the monopoly of the Franklin-Galloway party.[31] Williamson also shrewdly

29. Technically, the Assembly's power to punish libels on it had been upheld by the Privy Council in Smith's appeal, as long as it was the libelled Assembly that tried the accused. But the new party organization apparently believed that the Assembly was hesitant to employ this parliamentary privilege; indeed, the House never considered it.

30. [Isaac Hunt], *A Looking-Glass for Presbyterians, Number II* (Philadelphia, 1764 [Evans no. 9703]), p. 30.

31. [Hugh Williamson], *The Plain Dealer: or, a few Remarks upon Quaker-Politicks, and their Attempts to Change the Government of Pennsylvania, Number I* (Philadelphia, 1764 [Evans no. 9876]), p. 19.

noted that the British imperial system was beginning to manifest its new character. He charged that if the Assembly petitioned the Crown to take over the government, Parliament would alter the charter. "It is very probable that we shall soon have stamp offices, customs, excises and duties enough to pay, we don't want to pay tythes into the bargain." [32] Galloway replied to Williamson in defense of the proposed change in *An Address to the Freeholders and Inhabitants of the Province of Pennsylvania,* which Franklin helped him prepare.[33] Williamson then concentrated his fire on the more vulnerable younger partner, charging him with bribing Governor Denny and sponsoring the warrants and surveys act of 1759, which was "calculated for making estates for some Quakers." [34] The attacks of Williamson and other proprietary writers were not easily answered; the opposition's propaganda had enabled it to seize the initiative and put the Assembly party on the defensive. Franklin and Galloway were attempting to make revolutionary changes, but they made the mistake of letting the proprietary side issue all the revolutionary, inflammatory propaganda.

The circulation of the petitions was not a successful tactic; the attempt to demonstrate that the change-of-government plan was a popular move did not work. A petition with 1,500 signatures and another signed by many Quakers were brought into the House when it resumed sessions. The petitions were clearly not a mandate, although it cannot be determined whether the low number of signatures resulted from apathy or opposition. At any rate, Franklin and Galloway determined to proceed and let the voters ratify the Assembly's action in

32. Ibid., pp. 17–18.

33. "The Philosopher is also said to have corrected this piece [*An Address*] before it was presented, but the Philosopher is excusable, for he did not observe the falsehoods contain'd in it, as he seldom understands words in the plain natural meaning in which his Majesty and the English nation commonly use them"—a reference to Franklin's reinterpretation of his agreement with Lord Mansfield. [Williamson], *The Plain Dealer, Number III* (Philadelphia, 1764 [Evans no. 9878]), pp. 15–16.

34. Ibid., pp. 7, 11.

the coming election.[35] Before taking the final step, the Assembly tested Governor Penn with another money bill taxing the proprietary estate, just as it had tested Denny at the last moment before Franklin went to England in 1757. Penn failed the test and probably helped convince waverers that the government had to be changed. Franklin and Galloway mustered their supporters; and on May 23 the Assembly resolved to petition the king to take the province under his immediate care. The partners were appointed to draw up the petition, a task they had already performed. They brought it into the House that afternoon; debate on it began the next day.

Chief spokesman for the proprietary side was John Dickinson, then a rather obscure lawyer who had heretofore not given his allegiance to either group. Dickinson cared little for the Penns' government, but he preferred its certainties to the ambitious and perhaps impractical aims of Franklin and Galloway. His main argument was that Franklin's and Galloway's scheme contained no guarantee that Pennsylvania would retain any of her charter rights. All dissenters might lose their liberties. A standing army might be sent to Pennsylvania to enforce royal authority. In suggesting that Franklin and Galloway were playing right into the hands of those British ministers who sought more imperial control over the colonies, Dickinson summed up: "Have we not *sufficiently felt* the effects of royal resentment? Is not the authority of the Crown fully enough exerted over us?" [36]

---

35. *Votes*, 7 : 5604–06, 5608. A total of 3,500 eventually signed petitions favoring the change. Hutson, "Campaign, Part I," p. 442, terms the Assembly party's petition effort a failure. The opponents of the change of government later circulated petitions, and received about 8,600 signatures. Thomas Penn to Benjamin Chew, December 7, 1764, Thomas Penn Letter Book, HSP. Apparently both sides got many forged and invalid signatures. It is not certain which side had the most support; but it is clear that the change of government did not have overwhelming support.

36. John Dickinson, *A Speech, Delivered in the House of Assembly of the Province of Pennsylvania, May 24, 1764* (Philadelphia, 1764 [Evans no. 9641]), p. 28. David L. Jacobson, "John Dickinson's Fight against Royal Government 1764," *WMQ*, 3d ser. 19 (1962) : 71–77, summarizes the speech thoroughly.

It was seldom that members of the Assembly dared to oppose Franklin and Galloway on important issues; Galloway quickly rose to deflate this upstart. In rebuttal he argued that charter provisions protecting religious groups would be retained; that if a standing army was necessary to keep order against the Indians and Paxton Boys, the Crown should establish one; and that no rights would be surrendered but the government would be given more authority to protect the citizens. In answer to Dickinson's contention that Pennsylvania might be casting herself into the arms of a tyrannical ministry, Galloway rejoined:

> The Royal Government shews its Limits; they are known and confined; and rare it is, that any Attempts are made to extend them. But where Proprietary Power will terminate, where its Limits will be fixt, and its Encroachments end, is uncertain.[37]

The two speeches sparked a hot rivalry between Dickinson and the younger of the Assembly party leaders. Each man prided himself on his oratorical ability; some accounted Galloway the best speaker, while others thought the honor belonged to Dickinson. In their speeches, each had challenged the integrity of the other; consequently, each took offense and both lost their tempers. As they were leaving the Assembly that day harsh words passed between them. They quickly squared off and exchanged blows.[38] Perhaps Galloway got

37. Galloway, *Speech, in Answer to the Speech of John Dickinson, Esq.* (Philadelphia, 1764 [Evans no. 9671]), p. 41. Galloway's speech was not presented in published form until August 1764. A draft sheet of this speech in Galloway's handwriting is among Franklin's papers in the APS. Dickinson, in *A Reply to a Piece called the Speech of Joseph Galloway, Esq.* (Philadelphia, 1764 [Evans no. 9640]), p. 2, charged that the speech was a pretended one, never spoken in answer to him in the Assembly. Galloway then submitted a testimonial, *To the Public, September 29, 1764* (Philadelphia, 1764 [Evans no. 9674]), signed by his colleagues in the Assembly, which claimed that he did speak "the substance" of this printed version.

38. David Hall to William Strahan, June 12, 1767, David Hall Letter Books, APS.

the better of the fisticuffs, for Dickinson challenged him to a duel. Physical violence went no further; the Quaker background of both men had hardly prepared either to don swords or take up pistols.[39]

The boiling issue engendered other adverse reactions in the Assembly; the Old Ticket flew apart. Isaac Norris and Joseph Richardson, perhaps the most influential Quakers, sided with Dickinson and the few other proprietary partisans in the Assembly in registering a protest against the petition. Norris was convinced that Pennsylvania would lose the charter privileges that he had so long defended in the House. His defection was a heavy blow to the partners; yet Franklin and Galloway would not permit the opposition of the Quaker stalwarts to stand in their way, and they persuaded the Assembly to adopt the petition. Norris then resigned as Speaker, as he had done before when he did not agree with the turn of events. The partners interpreted this development to mean that they were in complete control of the party, although the defection of Norris could mean the loss of many votes at election time.

Franklin was immediately elevated to the post that Norris vacated, making himself supreme in name as well as in fact in the House.[40] The petition approved, he signed it on May 28, 1764, and sent it off to Richard Jackson, the agent in London, with instructions to present it to the King in Council. The Assembly's instructions also specified that the agent was to suspend action on the petition if he believed Pennsylvania would lose any civil or religious liberties in a change of government. Franklin and Galloway had presented strong constitutional arguments asserting that the change could be obtained without any infringement on charter rights, but some of their supporters desired this further reassurance.[41] The

39. [Isaac Hunt], *The Birth, Parentage, and Education of Praise-God Barebone, to which is added An Election Ballad, or the Lamentation of Miss ——* (Philadelphia, 1766 [Evans no. 10339]), p. 16.

40. *Votes*, 7 : 5611.

41. Ibid., 7 : 5615. Hanna, *Franklin*, p. 167, referring to identical instructions repeated in October 1764, argues that this instruction "ex-

deed done, the Assembly showed its good faith by passing a
money bill agreeable to the governor's terms. Franklin then
adjourned the House, certainly confident that the electorate
would approve its actions.

The two political leaders had found it easy to force an
Assembly that was almost completely in their power to approve the petition. But the Proprietary party was determined
to make it difficult for the partners to obtain the approval of
the voters. Before the Assembly debated and approved the
petition, this new party had an organization of proprietary
sympathizers and Presbyterians, but it had no candidates. The
speech of Dickinson and the defections of Norris and Richardson from the Assembly party made the New Ticket a real
ticket. Dickinson became the hero of the new party because he
stood up against Galloway, verbally and physically fighting it
out with him. He, Norris, Richardson, Henry Pawling, and
two Germans agreed to stand for election from Philadelphia
County. Presbyterians Thomas Willing and George Bryan
stood in the city. Purviance also set up New Ticket slates in
the counties outside Philadelphia.[42]

Franklin and Galloway already had their ticket and their
party organization prepared. With a few exceptions, Assembly
party incumbents stood behind their plans. The popular

---

pressed the growing doubt in the Assembly that royal government was
either necessary or desirable." But since the privileges of Pennsylvania
had long ago been confirmed in laws allowed by the Privy Council, as the
instruction noted, there appeared to be no reason why Pennsylvania could
not obtain royal government and keep its privileges intact. As Franklin
had pointed out in *Cool Thoughts,* nothing short of parliamentary inter-
vention could deprive Pennsylvania of its charter privileges. Franklin and
Galloway had no intention of letting this occur. The wording of this
instruction suggests that it was a safeguard that Franklin probably
regarded as superfluous—as well as reassuring to any Assembly party
waverers.

42. The other Proprietary party candidates for the eight Philadelphia
County seats were Amos Strettle and Henry Harrison. Norris, Richardson,
and Dickinson were incumbents; Strettle and Pawling were Anglican
merchants; the Germans were Henry Keppele and Frederick Antis; and
Harrison remains unidentified. Election return, Philadelphia County, 1764,
Franklin Papers, 69 : 97, APS; also in *Franklin Papers,* 11 : 394.

Norris and Richardson, although now in opposition to the partners, were retained on the Philadelphia County slate to attract more votes.[43] The Assembly party depended heavily on the support of the different groups in Philadelphia that Franklin, Galloway, and their friends had kept united since 1756; and on the traditional domination of the counties outside Philadelphia by other Old Ticket assemblymen. Rich merchants and professional men, anticipating lucrative offices and more favors from the executive when royal government came to Pennsylvania, were ready to risk their fortunes to elect Franklin and his Philadelphia associates.[44] Franklin and Galloway also had the support of lesser merchants and mechanics, who admired the former printer as the mechanic who had made good. Many of this latter group were members of a club called the White Oaks. This organization's earliest political activity is unclear. It participated in the defense of the city against the Paxton Boys and by the later months of 1764 apparently operated as an arm of the Assembly party. Its assignment was to bring in the voters on election day. The more apathetic and pliable Germans would be made to vote for the Assembly party by this club. George Ashbridge from Chester County and the other assemblymen from outside Philadelphia County were supposed to muster strong support for the party in their bailiwicks. The Franklin-Galloway party had a clear advantage in organization, leadership, and the incumbency of its candidates. The opposition made up in spirited propaganda what it lacked in other respects.[45]

43. The Old Ticket for Philadelphia County was Franklin, Galloway, Fox, Hughes, Norris, Richardson, Rowland Evans, and Plunkett Fleeson—all incumbents. As well as standing for the first time from the county, Franklin also stood from the city. Election return, ibid.

44. Thomas and Samuel Wharton, and Nicholas Waln, all fervent supporters of Franklin, anticipated royal offices. *Pennsylvania Journal,* September 27, 1764; Samuel Wharton to Franklin, November 23, 1764, *Franklin Papers,* 11 : 476–77; Nicholas Waln to Franklin, October 11, 1765, ibid., 12 : 311.

45. James H. Hutson, "An Investigation of the Inarticulate: Philadelphia's White Oaks," *WMQ,* 3d ser. 28 (1971) : 3–25, identifies the core of this group as ship carpenters. They took their name from their material.

The pamphlets and broadsides issued by the parties before the October election were unprecedented in number and in vituperation—not even in 1755–56 had there been such a quantity of publications and such a quality of scurrility. The question of the change of government had great emotional appeal; the broadside writers consequently attempted to appeal to the baser emotions. The partners' skirts were not clean; Franklin's illegitimate son, Galloway's haughty demeanor, and both men's reputations for political trickery were weaknesses to be exploited by clever writers. Franklin was blasted, according to his own count, by "five scurrilous Pamphlets and three Copperplate Prints." One of the former, called *An Answer to the Plot,* resorted to something like poetry:

> F——n, tho' plagu'd with fumbling Age,
> Needs nothing to excite him.
> But is too ready to engage
> When younger Arms invite him.[46]

Another Williamson effort, *What is Sauce for a Goose is also Sauce for a Gander,* was more of a shotgun. Franklin allegedly stole others' scientific discoveries, begged and bought honorary degrees, and mistreated the maidservant who was reputed to be the mother of his son William.[47]

Galloway also received some vulgar knocks. He was attacked as a mere puppet of the scheming Franklin; his speech against Dickinson was

> Midwif'd by Philosophic Paw,
> Tho' Mother'd by a Man of Law.[48]

The younger partner's alleged ambition to replace William Allen as chief justice was also exposed in a ribald manner.

46. *An Answer to the Plot* (Philadelphia, 1764 [Evans no. 9581]).

47. [Williamson], *What is Sauce for a Goose is also Sauce for a Gander* (Philadelphia, 1764 [Evans no. 9879]), pp. 2–7. The maternity of the younger Franklin has never been fully explained; it is not at all certain that his mother was this maidservant.

48. *Advertisement, and not a Joke* (Philadelphia, 1764 [Evans no. 9562]).

They vow to get eternal Fame,
All things they'll *change,* yet keep the *same;*
Thro' Rocks and Shelves our Bark they'll paddle,
And fasten G—— in Will's old Saddle;
Just as they please they'll make him fit it,
Unscrub'd, tho' Will, they say, be-sh-t it.[49]

Mudslinging would make the electorate laugh, but it would not necessarily insure the defeat of the Old Ticket. The Proprietary party soon found more damaging evidence against Franklin than bawdy revelations about his personal life. In 1751 Franklin, then just beginning his career in the Assembly and unaware that a politician can easily incriminate himself by opening his mouth, wrote, "Why should the Palatine Boors be suffered to swarm into our Settlements, and by herding together establish their Language and Manners to the Exclusion of ours?" [50] Some industrious proprietary partisan found this extract in the *Gentleman's Magazine* for 1755. It was translated into German in a broadside with appropriate commentary and circulated among the German voters. In this broadside "Boors" was rendered as "Bauerntolpel," or blockhead. The broadside naturally inquired whether the "Deut-

49. Ibid. Thomas Penn thought it might be easier to attack Galloway than to go after the highly respected Franklin. Penn requested his nephew, the governor, to forward "any injurious expressions to us made use of by Galloway, that it may be considered whether we cannot prosecute him for scandal, and get some considerable damages from him." Thomas Penn to John Penn, July 13, 1764, Thomas Penn Letter Book, Penn Papers, HSP. John Penn replied to his uncle, September 22, 1764, ibid.: "I send you enclosed among other Pamphlets a speech of Mr. Galloway (that was never spoke) in answer to one of Mr. Dickinson in the house of Assembly. I think you will find injurious expressions enough to answer your purpose, in this most scurrilous and impudent Piece." Yet Galloway's *Speech,* and the prefatory remarks by Franklin, were mild in comparison to the broadsides that blasted the partners. Certainly, the Penns would have been guilty of a breach of civil liberties had they attempted to prosecute; likewise the Assembly leaders took no legal action against their detractors.

50. Franklin, *Observations concerning the Increase of Mankind, Peopling of Countries, &c.,* in *Franklin Papers,* 4 : 234.

scher Nation" could accept Franklin as its representative, since he had such a low opinion of the Germans.[51]

Franklin's rather loosely translated insult, coupled with the fear of many Germans that a royal government would deprive them of their rights, turned the German community leaders against the Assembly party. Christopher Sauer, Jr., a Dunkard who had formerly supported the Franklin-Galloway party because of its favors to Germans and its general adherence to Quaker policies, and whose newspaper carried great weight among the Germans, reversed his allegiance and opposed royal government for Pennsylvania. A broadside that he printed quite aptly inquired whether "unser Herr König und sein hohen Rathe geneight sein mochten, neuen Most in alte Schlauche zu fassen, oder alles neu zu machen." [52] Sauer feared losing the "alte Freiheit und alte Berechtigheit" which the German colonists treasured, and he recommended that Franklin and Galloway be turned out of the Assembly. These arguments, borrowed from Dickinson's speech, were more logical than personal attack, but Sauer was not above repeating the charges concerning Franklin's "boorish" opinion of the Germans.

Franklin and Galloway, half-buried under the avalanche of innuendo and slander, did not themselves counterattack in the same vein. Conceiving of their campaign as a noble crusade, they declined to descend to the same level as Williamson and other refuse spreaders. However, some rebuttal was offered to the proprietary defamations by Isaac Hunt, a Quaker lawyer who supported the Old Ticket and who had a talent for vulgarity. Hunt was able to taunt the proprietary

51. *An die Freyhalter und Einwohner der Stadt und County Philadelphia, Deutscher Nation* (Philadelphia, 1764 [Evans no. 9575]).

52. (Our King and his Privy Council would be inclined to put new wine in old bottles, or to make everything new.) [Christopher Sauer, Jr.?], *Anmerckungen über Ein noch nie erhört und gesehen Wunder Thier in Pennsylvanien, gennant Streit-und Strauss-Vogel, Heraus gegeben von einer Deutschen Gesellschaft freyer Burger und getreuer Unterthanen seiner Gross Brittanischen Majestät* (Philadelphia, 1764 [Evans no. 9578]), p. 2.

leaders in the same coarse manner their propagandists used. What if William Franklin was illegitimate? He was a worthy son, "while the illegitimate Progeny of [Franklin's] Adversaries are so *numerous* so *scandalous* and so *neglected,* that the *only* concern of the Parents is least their *unhappy* By-Blows should commit Incest." [53] Hunt also referred to the Proprietary party as "Piss-Brute-tarians." [54]

It was more necessary to answer the damaging charges concerning what royal government would mean for the Germans and to show the Assembly party's affection for them. *Ein Anrede an die Deutscher Freyhalter der Stadt und County Philadelphia* answered Sauer's charges and pointed out Franklin's virtues. In this piece, "Boors" was translated as "Pfalzer Bauern," giving the word the more innocuous meaning of Palatine peasant. This *Anrede* falsely asserted that "das Englishe Wort Boors hat keine weitere Bedeutung, dann Bauern." Franklin was here depicted as the friend of Germans, who got them good contracts with Braddock. The Germans were reminded that *Kurzen Zustand von Pennsylvanien* (Smith's *Brief State*) had called them wicked, stubborn, and stupid enemies of the king.[55] All was in vain. The original insult had done the damage, and the Assembly party

53. [Isaac Hunt], *The Scribbler, Being a Letter from a Gentleman in Town to his Friend in the Country, concerning the present State of Public Affairs, with a Lapidary Character* (Philadelphia, 1764 [Evans no. 9831]), p. 10.

54. [Hunt], *A Letter from a Gentleman in Transylvania to his Friend in America giving some Account of the late disturbances that have happen'd in that Government, with some remarks upon the political revolutions in the Magistracy, and the Debates that happened about the change* (Philadelphia, 1764 [Evans no. 9702]), pp. 4–5. Franklin attacked the Penns personally in an "epitaph" he wrote for Thomas Penn as part of his preface to Galloway's *Speech,* but only, he claimed, after the strongest provocation. See Franklin, *Preface to Joseph Galloway's Speech,* in *Franklin Papers,* 11 : 298–99. Otherwise, he and Galloway left the dirty work to Hunt.

55. (The English word Boors means nothing more than peasants.) *Ein Anrede an die Deutscher Freyhalter der Stadt und County Philadelphia* (Philadelphia, 1764 [Evans no. 9576]), pp. 2, 5, 6.

could not convince the Germans of the purity of either its motives or its leader.

The vast amount of recrimination and libel hurled back and forth showed that the parties depended on the voters to make a choice based on the issues, be they bastardy or better government. A sizable proportion of the electorate was indeed literate and knowledgeable; this group would weigh what the propagandists told them. Yet the outcome of the election depended much more on how many voters, both sensible and ignorant, the party managers could entice to the polls to vote for their candidates. The method of getting out the vote, which seems to have been traditional with the Assembly party, was personal appeal and personal influence, backed up by promises of treats and rewards. The vitality of the issues and the electioneering tactics insured the biggest turnout in the history of Pennsylvania. Over 3,800 voted in Philadelphia County, where the leaders of both parties were candidates. By mutual consent, the polls remained open a day and a half to accommodate all the voters that the party workers could round up. Galloway, Franklin, and their aides canvassed the city and county, as did Purviance and his friends. William Franklin came over from Burlington, New Jersey, to lend his father and his father's partner a hand. He "left his own Government to keep open house at Germantown in favor of his father, & Mr. Galloway. He was several days there Canvassing among the Germans & endeavoring to get votes by propagating the most infamous lies he could invent; he is as bad as his father," John Penn reported. It was a great loss to colonial American history that no Hogarth was available to paint the royal governor of New Jersey, in ruffles and wig, passing out punch and beer to thirsty "Boors." John Penn inquired quite pointedly, "Is this a Conduct becoming a King's Governor?" [56] But Franklin, Galloway, and their allies had to conduct a personal campaign, had to circulate among the lower ranks to garner support. Right up to election day, they were confident that their personal appeal,

56. John Penn to Thomas Penn, October 19, 1764, Penn Papers, HSP.

their former valued service, and their plans for Pennsylvania would give them victory.[57]

The partners' electioneering was not good enough. The Proprietary party achieved a stunning reversal, unseating the titans of Pennsylvania politics and weakening their party in Philadelphia. In a very close election in both city and county, only Fox and Hughes among Franklin's supporters retained their seats. The other six county seats and the two city seats were captured by the Proprietary party. The Assembly party machine kept control of most of the seats they had formerly held in counties outside Philadelphia, although the New Ticket did gain in Lancaster County, scene of the Paxton Boys' atrocities. About twenty seats remained to the Old Ticket, which proved to be a substantial working majority. Yet the two leaders were discredited, and the plan for a change of government appeared to be in jeopardy. The Proprietary party was jubilant.[58]

Conflicting reasons were given for the startling defeat of Franklin and Galloway. The losers charged fraud and the winners took credit for the effectiveness of their propaganda. Franklin, exuding his characteristic optimism, made light of the defeat to his friends, terming it "quite a laughing Matter" that his reference to the Germans of years before had en-

57. Franklin to Richard Jackson, September 25, 1764, *Franklin Papers,* 11 : 358.

58. The following table, drawn from the Election return, Philadelphia County, 1764, Franklin Papers, 69 : 97, APS, illustrates the closeness of the election. The figures show the number of votes.

Winners—eight highest		*Losers*	
Norris	3,874	Harrison	1,921
Richardson	3,848	Galloway	1,918
Dickinson	2,040	Antis	1,914
Fox	1,963	Evans	1,911
Pawling	1,955	Franklin	1,906
Keppele	1,932	Fleeson	1,884
Strettle	1,930		
Hughes	1,925		

The editors of the *Franklin Papers,* 11 : 394, read 2,030 votes for Dickinson—the figure is written over.

couraged 1,000 German voters to turn against him.[59] In truth, his laughter was forced and counterfeit, for both he and Galloway were bitter in defeat. Franklin sourly charged that the election was stolen.[60] Galloway blamed an insidious conspiracy of Presbyterians who by vile slanders seduced the lower classes. Neither man was accustomed to losing, so they both looked to the unfair activities of their opponents for an excuse.

In truth they had only themselves to blame. They had proposed a plan that possessed real merit, for proprietary government was clearly defective, but that was so drastic that it was bound to create a storm of protest. The evidence of the election campaign and the petitions circulated does not show conclusively whether Pennsylvanians were opposed to or in favor of the change of government.[61] Regardless, the plan was a very difficult one to get the voters of Philadelphia to accept, for many wanted to preserve the *alte Freiheit;* royal government was for them an unknown quantity; and the Assembly, even with its difficulties with the Penns, had been successful under the old system in maintaining liberties and in providing effective, unburdensome government. Franklin and Galloway left themselves open to propaganda attacks. It did no good for them to offer *Cool Thoughts,* which in effect asserted that the leaders knew best and all should blindly follow them. It was too easy for the Proprietary party to reply with "Answers to the Plot," which were devastating in effect.

More helpful to Franklin and Galloway than rational and deliberate presentation of the issues was their political machine. In the face of enormous antagonism to their scheme,

59. Franklin to Jackson, October 16, 1764, *Franklin Papers,* 11 : 397.

60. Franklin, *Remarks on a Late Protest against the Appointment of Mr. Franklin as Agent for the Province of Pennsylvania,* ibid., 11 : 434.

61. The petitions show a lack of support for Franklin and Galloway but not the proportion of this. The election results throughout the colony are about as indefinite an index as the petitions. William Allen, not always a reliable source, reported to Thomas Penn, October 21, 1764, Penn Papers, HSP, that in the counties outside Philadelphia the Quakers told the Germans that it was the Proprietary party that was attempting to change the government. Most likely, tradition was more important than issues in the back counties.

the party organization they had built up was strong enough to turn out almost enough voters to win. Its strength was a tribute to Galloway's activities during Franklin's London mission and to Franklin's leadership during the early months of 1764. The vigorous campaigning immediately before election day was, unfortunately for the partners, too brief and too restricted to lure to the polls the few extra supporters required to convert defeat into victory. Probably the campaign taught the partners three lessons: a dramatic issue cannot be pushed solely on its merits; being on the defensive in a hot propaganda campaign is a great disadvantage; and a political organization must expend maximum effort to bring the voters to the polls—numbers more than issues produce victories. As events proved, Franklin and Galloway came to appreciate the need for both a more thorough broadcasting of their case and a stronger political organization.

Because it was not clear to Franklin and Galloway that they were defeated solely on the change-of-government issue, they did not resign themselves to defeat. They pressed ahead with their grand design, confident that at the next election their plans would be vindicated. Since Ashbridge and the other party leaders from the counties outside Philadelphia had saved the Old Ticket's majority in the Assembly, the partners thought it quite legitimate to attempt the change of government and convince the voters at the election next year.

The Assembly party majority was, in the main, quite malleable under the hammering influence of the absent leaders. Hughes was now the nominal leader of the Franklin-Galloway group in the House, but the party leaders would not trust Hughes to lead their fight alone. To prevent the Assembly from slipping out of their grasp, they retained close contact, "the measure & plan of each Day's proceeding being settled by them every Evening at private meetings & cabals held with their Friends in the house." [62] To their chagrin, Franklin and Galloway found that they could not completely control affairs, for some of their adherents wavered in support of the

62. Benjamin Chew to Thomas Penn, November 5, 1764, Penn Papers, HSP.

party. Their friends had to compromise on the choice of a speaker to replace Norris, who had had enough of that arduous post. Hughes nominated George Ashbridge, whom the proprietary members, led by Dickinson, opposed as being too close to Franklin and Galloway. After an uproarious session, both sides agreed on Joseph Fox, a more moderate Assembly party member.[63] Moreover, the appointment of committees in the Assembly and the selection of members to draw up various bills were made without much regard for party lines. Governor Penn began to use more industriously the proprietary patronage to reward those who had aided in the defeat of Franklin and Galloway.[64] Much of the work of Galloway and Franklin's other friends of the previous seven years was undone; much more would have been ruined if the partners had not had considerable influence among the majority of assemblymen.

In the most important respect this influence held firm. The Assembly, acting under the orders of its ousted leaders, refused to rescind the petition to the king and resolved, on October 26, 1764, to send Franklin back to London to guide the petition through the Privy Council. At least the change-of-government plan was not yet frustrated. No one in the Assembly party saw any incongruity in supporting Franklin or in continuing the petition even after Franklin and Galloway had been defeated—in part because of the petition. None thought that the Assembly party would suffer politically for defying the decision of the Philadelphia electorate. The strength of the partners' hold on their party is shown in the fact that their determination to press the change of government despite all obstacles was shared by their colleagues.[65]

63. There was a near riot in the Assembly chamber as Dickinson's backers and Franklin stalwarts faced each other over the issue of the Speakership. John Dickinson to Isaac Norris, October 24, 1764, Copybook, HSP. *Votes,* 7 : 5687–91.

64. Galloway to Franklin, November 23, 1764, *Franklin Papers,* 11 : 468. Charles Thomson to Franklin, December 18, 1764, ibid., 11 : 522–23.

65. Hutson, "Campaign, Part I," p. 456, argues that after the 1764 defeat the rural Quakers in the Assembly, not really desirous of royal government, sent Franklin to England to intimidate Thomas Penn to give

Franklin probably regarded a return to London with mixed feelings. On leaving there in 1762 he indicated that he wanted to return, but by 1764 he had built a new house and was settled more firmly in Philadelphia. Nevertheless, going back to England enabled him to stage a graceful retreat from an arena in which he had failed. He was probably tired of the dirty political infighting that was alien to his moderate nature, and he was distressed by his loss of popularity. By undertaking this mission he could escape the local political battles and re-establish his prestige. He had every confidence that his mission would be short, high hopes that his petition would be accepted, and he looked forward to returning to Pennsylvania in triumph.[66] The conviction that he and Galloway were correct in their plans for Pennsylvania, the desire to serve his friends and his province in the best way he knew, and the need to vindicate himself after his first political failure were most likely his chief reasons for going.

By leaving Pennsylvania at this critical time, Franklin showed the great confidence he had in his partner. A difficulty which neither man had faced before now confronted them; a vigorous Proprietary party threatened to wrest control of the Assembly from its antiproprietary leaders. Yet Franklin could return to London with little fear of the consequences in Pennsylvania. Galloway would take charge, preserve the party, and recover all losses.

----

in on the issues that the twenty-six resolves raised. Perhaps some in the House wanted a compromise rather than royal government. For Franklin, and very likely for most of his colleagues, there would be, constitutionally, very little difference between royal government and the kind of settlement with the Penns that the Assembly party would accept. Either the recognition of the Assembly's privileges by the proposed royal government or great concessions by the Penns—too great for anyone to expect them to make—would make the Assembly supreme. This was why Franklin, writing to John Ross, February 14, 1765, *Franklin Papers*, 12 : 67, thought that trying to deal with the Penns at this point was a waste of time. Indeed, it proved to be so.

66. Franklin to Deborah Franklin, February 9, 1765, *Franklin Papers*, 12 : 42.

Left to face defeat without Franklin at his side, Galloway could hardly be so confident. The younger partner's prospects were black indeed; he had no formal power and only a shadowy informal hold on his followers in the Assembly. He had no Franklin to prompt his speeches and help him plan strategy. Franklin was fifty-eight, Franklin was secure, Franklin had many successful activities to his credit; Galloway was thirty-four, and he was burning with unfulfilled ambition and unrealized plans. He was basically a politician who had just suffered defeat in his most cherished vocation. With Franklin setting off for England, he must have felt lost and alone. However, his hope that the change of government would be accomplished and his awareness that Franklin depended on him probably buoyed him up. All seemed to depend on Franklin's efforts with the petition. Consequently, when the White Oaks rowed Franklin to his ship on his departure for England, Galloway had reason to sing the loudest the anthem "suitable to the occasion." [67]

> O LORD our GOD arise,
> Scatter our Enemies,
> And make them fall.
> Confound their Politicks,
> Frustrate such Hypocrites,
> *Franklin,* on Thee we fix,
> GOD Save us all.
>
> Thy Knowledge rich in Store,
> On *Pennsylvania* pour,
> Thou great Blessing:
> Long to defend our Laws,
> Still give us greater Cause,
> To sing with Heart and Voice,
> GEORGE and FRANKLIN.

67. *North Carolina Magazine and Universal Intelligencer,* December 14–21, 1764, p. 227. Also see *The Election, a Medly* (Philadelphia, 1764 [Evans no. 9650]).

God save great George, our King,
Prosper Agent Franklin;
Grant him Success:
Hark how the Vallies ring;
God Save our Gracious King,
From whom all Blessings spring,
Our Wrongs redress.

4 The Stamp Act

The determination and tenacity of the partners were, after the defeat of 1764, their principal assets. These provided reassurance for Franklin and Galloway that loss of office, difficulties with the petition in London, and a resurrected opposition in Pennsylvania could all be overcome. Franklin acted much as if he were living out the sayings of Poor Richard. Would not virtue be rewarded? Would not those who persevered without surrender win in the end? Galloway's faith in the abilities and achievements of his partner prevented him from giving up. Reason, justice, and right seemed to them to be on their side. And since the petition had been approved by the Assembly despite their electoral defeat, they foresaw little difficulty. But their calculations had not included drastic shifts in British policy toward the colonies.

Franklin apparently was so certain that his cause was just that he never entertained the thought that Britain might reject the petition for the change of government. He believed that when the Privy Council heard about the Paxton riots, the murder of the Indians, the refusal of the governor to cooperate with the Assembly, and the continued arbitrary nature of the proprietary instructions, it would surely take the provincial government from the hands of the Penns.[1] The discouraging report of Richard Jackson, who had written Franklin that the expense of making Pennsylvania a royal province would be great and the results perhaps not worthwhile, and the experience with British hostility toward colo-

1. Franklin expressed his confidence to Deborah Franklin, February 9, 1765, *Franklin Papers*, 12 : 42; and to John Ross, February 14, 1765, ibid., 12 : 67–68.

nial aspirations that Franklin had encountered on his previous
mission did not deter him in the slightest. His first mission,
he thought, had won him some influence and respect in British
official circles. Far from the emotional issues raised by his
Pennsylvania opponents, "cool thoughts" would persuade the
ministry to change the government. It was a pardonable delu-
sion. Franklin misjudged the British government's position,
not because he was naive but because he fervently believed in
the power of reason to alter men's convictions. The philosopher, the honest agent, could act on no other principle.[2]

Galloway, meanwhile, had to sway the Philadelphia electorate. His task was more crucial to the future of the Assembly
party. As Samuel Wharton, a Quaker supporter of the partners, concisely put it, "For if Galloway does not get in [the
Assembly], We shall have no Leader in the House & advantages will therefore be taken, of *Our Members.*"[3] Galloway had to regain his seat to maintain party unity and to
support Franklin in his quest for royal government. Spurred
on by the responsibility thrust upon him in Franklin's absence, he set to work to win the election of 1765. The ap-
petites of the wealthy merchants who provided funds for
the party's campaigns—Thomas and Samuel Wharton, Abel
James, Cadwalader Evans, and others—and who could almost taste the royal offices Franklin was supposed to bring
back for them from Britain, drove them to greater efforts in
Galloway's behalf. The White Oaks, stung by defeat, were
fully determined to bring the Germans back into the fold. A

2. Richard Jackson to Franklin, August 11, 1764, ibid., 11 : 312–13.
Hutson, "Campaign, Part I," pp. 442–50, argues that Franklin relied for
support in Britain on both the advice of Jackson and his self-imagined
influence with the Earl of Bute. Franklin seems to have placed more
confidence in his own powers and in the facts of Penn misgovernment
than in his influence in Britain.

3. Samuel Wharton to William Franklin, September 29, 1765, Franklin
Papers, 1 : 159, APS. Much of the material concerning events in Pennsylvania in this chapter has been drawn from Benjamin H. Newcomb, "Effects of the Stamp Act on Colonial Pennsylvania Politics," *WMQ*, 3d ser.
23 (1966) : 257–72, and used by permission of the editor.

few months after the disastrous election, Galloway completed the rebuilding of the Assembly party so that it was probably better prepared to wage a campaign than it had ever been before. Barring an unforeseen calamity, Franklin's mission was expected to be short and successful, and Galloway would easily be able to reverse the electoral result of the previous year.[4]

Then calamity struck. Franklin arrived in London in December 1764 to face a ministry which planned to extend parliamentary authority over America by imposing a Stamp Act. All the new developments in imperial policy since 1763 were familiar to Franklin and Galloway, but they had previously paid them only scant attention. Through most of 1764 they had found it expedient to refrain from public comment on the Proclamation of 1763, the prohibition on legal tender paper money, the Sugar Act, and the proposal for a Stamp Act. The first, which would limit settlement in backcountry Pennsylvania, did not alarm politicians whose power was based on eastern predominance. The second, Franklin believed, could be evaded simply by printing paper money that was not declared to be legal tender and paying an interest on it, which would maintain its value. Nor was Franklin "much alarm'd about your Schemes of raising Money on us." Not clearly understanding that the Sugar Act was designed to raise revenue in America from a heretofore illegal trade, he asserted to Richard Jackson that the high duties on foreign sugar would raise the price of British West Indies sugar and thus be objectionable to the British consumer. Blinded by their enthusiasm for their own schemes, Franklin and Galloway at first failed to perceive that these British policies were in direct conflict with their basic principles.[5]

4. Galloway to Franklin, January 23, 1765, *Franklin Papers*, 12 : 26. Cadwalader Evans to Franklin, March 15, 1765, ibid., 12 : 83, comments on the propaganda efforts made by Franklin's friends.

5. Franklin to Jackson, January 16, June 25, 1764, ibid., 11 : 19, 235–36. Franklin's attempt in January 1764 to be more conciliatory toward Governor John Penn involved a proposal to issue interest bearing notes in

The partners were inspired to give more recognition to the new British policies by John Dickinson's attempt to inject the issue of imperial taxation into his attack on the proposed change of government. Although Franklin and Galloway continually argued that the real enemy of Pennsylvania was proprietary government, Franklin in June 1764 turned some of his attention to putting forward a way to obviate the problems that imperial taxation would raise. In that month he wrote to Jackson that as an alternative to taxation for revenue, he "could propose a better Mode by far, both for us and for you." [6]

The unspecified "better Mode" presumably became a "Plan" by the end of the summer of 1764. Franklin perhaps decided that he needed to have a plan to refute the Proprietary party's charges that he and Galloway were selling the province into slavery. On September 22, 1764, the Franklin-Galloway–led Assembly passed, and Speaker Franklin signed, instructions to agent Jackson to oppose the Sugar Act and the Stamp Act. These instructions mentioned a "Plan" under consideration by the House, which would grant aids to the Crown and contribute to the general defense without violating colonial rights. [7] Despite what the instructions said, however, the Assembly apparently had seen no plan; only Franklin had one. He kept the particulars secret from Galloway and his other colleagues, perhaps because it was not completely formulated in his own mind or perhaps because he feared the plan might add fuel to the torches with which the incendiary Proprietary party was trying to burn up his career. [8] In the heated election campaign,

---

providing for supplies. Galloway, in a rare instance of differing with his partner, voted with the majority of the House to reject this new mode. Jenkins, "Fragments of a Journal Kept by Samuel Foulke," pp. 68–69.

6. Franklin to Jackson, June 25, 1764, *Franklin Papers*, 11 : 237.

7. *Votes*, 7 : 5643–45. It is unlikely that Franklin would have written to Jackson in the singular if more than one plan were under consideration. Nor would he have permitted the Assembly, which he controlled, to suggest one plan while he proposed another.

8. Edward Shippen, who usually believed the worst of Franklin, thought that he planned a tax of some sort less odious than the Stamp Act. Edward Shippen to William Shippen, December 24, 1764, Shippen Letter

there was no advantage to letting anyone, even Galloway, know about what was probably a tentative scheme. The Pennsylvania Assembly consequently took about the same sort of measures against the acts that most other colonies did: they protested through the colonial agency. New York and Virginia sent strong petitions to Parliament, but Pennsylvania was satisfied that Jackson, collaborating with Franklin in London, could protect its rights.

Franklin carried the petition for the change of government and the undisclosed plan to raise revenue constitutionally with him to Britain in an overfilled pocket. The first order of business was the petition, but the agent would ignore neither his instructions nor the convictions of his conscience that the new policies also were unjust. Very shortly after his arrival, he realized that British policy was a more immediate and pressing danger to Pennsylvania's rights than was proprietary policy. Accordingly, he "let what related particularly to our Province sleep a little for the present" in order to work against the proposed Stamp Act.[9] Joining the other American agents, he attended a meeting with Prime Minister George Grenville on February 2, 1765. The agents insisted that the constitutional rights of the colonies be preserved; the minister insisted on an American revenue; and never the twain did meet. However, Franklin took Grenville's invitation to the agents, to propose a method of raising revenue which would be as satisfactory as the contemplated Stamp Act, in good faith.[10] He saw it was time to bring forward his "better Mode." He thought that if he could persuade Grenville to

Books, APS. William Allen wrote Thomas Penn, December 13, 1764, Penn Papers, HSP, that Franklin's friends were claiming that he had a tax plan.

9. Franklin to John Ross, February 14, 1765, *Franklin Papers*, 12 : 67.

10. The agents at the meeting included Charles Garth, South Carolina; Jared Ingersoll, Connecticut; Richard Jackson, Massachusetts and Pennsylvania; and Franklin. They offered the weak proposal that Americans supply the Crown by taxing themselves. Grenville rejected this as uncertain and impractical. Edmund S. and Helen M. Morgan, *The Stamp Act Crisis*, 2d ed., rev. (New York, 1964), pp. 89–92, discuss this episode and describe Grenville's overture to the agents as "an opportunity to refuse to tax themselves."

recommend it to the colonies and to Parliament, British revenue needs would be filled with no objections from America. Remaining secretive, Franklin did not take the other agents into his confidence concerning his plan. Neither he nor they had any official authority to recommend an alternative, nor could they be confident that colonial assemblies would approve. Quietly, Franklin and Thomas Pownall, former Governor of Massachusetts, member of Parliament, and friend of Franklin since the Albany Conference of 1754, proposed to Grenville what became known as the paper money scheme.[11]

The paper money scheme, as Franklin recounted it later, was a plan to allow the home government, by colonial consent, to superintend an imperial currency. Paper currency, printed in Britain, would be placed on loan to individuals in America through loan offices established by the British government and the colonies. To prevent depreciation, Franklin proposed that the Bank of England back this imperial currency at an exchange rate of 4 : 3, or £1 6s. 8d. in paper bills to one pound sterling. Franklin never explicitly stated how much currency would be issued according to this plan. He calculated roughly that a province of 40,000 families might require £80,000 to be emitted on loan.[12] Colonial America contained perhaps 400,000–500,000 families who would, according to Franklin's figures, borrow £800,000–£1,000,000. Each borrower would give security for the loan in the form of land worth double the value of the loan. The borrower

11. Crane, *Franklin and a Rising People*, p. 109. Franklin reported ambiguously to John Ross, February 14, 1765, *Franklin Papers*, 12 : 68, that "a Scheme is under Consideration to furnish us a Currency, without which we can neither pay Debts nor Duties." James A. Ernst, "The Currency Act Repeal Movement: A Study in Imperial Politics and Revolutionary Crisis, 1764–1767," *WMQ*, 3d ser. 25 (1968): 182, accepts the Crane version. Jack M. Sosin, *Agents and Merchants: British Colonial Policy and the Origins of the American Revolution, 1763–1775* (Lincoln, Neb., 1965), pp. 59–60, note, questions Franklin's statement that he presented the plan at this time because none of the other agents was informed of it.

12. Fragment of a pamphlet on paper money, in draft, Franklin Papers, 50, part ii : 34, APS.

would repay the principal within ten years and also remit an annual interest of 6 percent. If £800,000–£1,000,000 were borrowed, the interest would amount to about £48,000–£60,000 per year. This was less revenue than Grenville expected from the Sugar Act and the Stamp Act combined.[13] Franklin thought his plan would be an adequate substitute; he concluded that there would be "a great annual Sum continually increasing [which would] arise to the Crown for Interest, to be apply'd to American Purpose. It will operate as a general Tax on the Colonies, and yet not an unpleasing one." The paper money plan would be enacted by Parliament and in part implemented by the colonial legislatures, giving it a constitutional foundation.[14]

Franklin believed that his plan, if successful in providing considerable revenue through interest receipts, would solve three of the empire's most pressing difficulties. Britain would receive tribute from the colonies in a manner quite painless to sensitive Americans. And Americans would be glad to borrow from British loan offices as long as they were guaranteed that the currency they borrowed would hold its value and circulate easily. Secondly, the commerce of Britain and America would be more firmly tied together. British merchants would accept this paper money because the Bank of England guaranteed the exchange rate. Americans could thus get out of debt to British merchants by mortgaging their lands. Thirdly, under Franklin's plan the colonies would easily be able to increase the circulation of money and augment the money supply, as currency would be available on demand. The inconveniences of barter and disparate currencies would no longer hamper colonial commerce.

13. Ibid. Lawrence H. Gipson, *The Coming of the Revolution, 1763–1775* (New York, 1962), pp. 66, 71, claims Britain expected £45,000 from the Sugar Act and £60,000 from the Stamp Act.

14. Fragment of a pamphlet on paper money, in draft, Franklin Papers, 50, part ii: 18, APS. Thomas Pownall, *The Administration of the Colonies*, 4th ed. (London, 1768), pp. 230–53, contains a published version of this plan, with textual variations from Franklin's draft. The draft and Pownall's version are in *Franklin Papers*, 12 : 47–60.

The paper money scheme was not the complete substitute for the Stamp Act that Franklin believed it to be. In times of prosperity, it probably would have provided the Americans with currency and the British with revenue; in depressed times American borrowers would probably have defaulted on loans and interest payments. One can imagine the reaction of the colonists to the seizure of the security—their land—by the British government or the Bank of England. By contrast, Grenville's plan for direct taxation would raise revenue more dependably. It was characteristic of Franklin that he saw America's future only with great optimism; he was certain that his paper money scheme would work because American prosperity would make it work. Grenville was not interested. Certainly to him the scheme must have looked exactly like a South Sea Bubble. And, as Franklin later reported to Galloway, the minister was so "besotted with his Stamp Scheme" that he would not seriously consider any alternatives.[15]

Grenville's intransigence placed Franklin in an unhappy dilemma. Employing the press to continue opposition to the Stamp Act, which was the type of strategy Franklin had used so often in Pennsylvania and on his first British mission, would win him no friends in the ministry. Yet he needed friends to aid him in getting approval for his cherished petition. Franklin's conscience would not permit him to glide over to the side of the ministry, support the Stamp Act, and then hold out his hand for favors; the act was too obviously oppressive and unjust in principle. After failing to sell his plan to Grenville, it was easy for Franklin to convince himself, probably correctly, that he had done all he could. He watched helplessly as the Stamp Act passed Parliament on March 22, 1765, and then he returned to work on the main business, that of getting his petition approved. In a political and a personal sense, obtaining a hearing on the plans for a change of gov-

15. Franklin to Galloway, October 11, 1766, *Franklin Papers*, 13 : 449. Crane, "Benjamin Franklin and the Stamp Act," *Colonial Society of Massachusetts, Publications* 32 (Boston, 1937) : 56–77, gives full details on Franklin's activities in this period.

ernment was much more important to him and to Galloway than was bewailing an accomplished fact.[16] Certainly it seemed more likely to Franklin that the Stamp Act would be repealed without his aid than that the petition would be approved without his lobbying. Ministries had changed rather frequently in recent years; perhaps the next ministry would see the folly of the act and repeal it. Franklin resigned himself to an oppression which he hoped would be temporary, and he wrote his friends in Pennsylvania to do likewise. To Charles Thomson he explained that in attempting to forestall the Stamp Act "we might as well have hinder'd the Suns setting. That we could not do. But since 'tis down, my Friend, and it may be long before it rises again, Let us make as good a Night of it as we can. We may still Light candles." [17] The agent had no anticipation that such resignation would be construed as acquiescence to injustice.

Nor did Franklin see any harm in bringing himself and his party into closer cooperation with the ministry. Probably to eradicate all hard feelings, Grenville offered several Americans in London, including Franklin, the opportunity to nominate stamp distributors in the colonies. Franklin accepted this task, hoping to ingratiate himself further with the ministry, to aid the defeated Old Ticket in Pennsylvania, and to make an embarrassing resistance to the act less likely. John Hughes, leader of the decimated ranks of Franklin's party in the Assembly, was in the best position to dispense the patronage attendant on the post of stamp distributor.[18] When nominated by Franklin, Hughes took the job with relish.

16. Besides the obvious political commitment to the petition, Franklin's position as deputy postmaster general, worth £300 per year, and his Pennsylvania agency, worth £500 per year, helped convince him that in this case silence was truly golden.

17. Franklin to Charles Thomson, July 11, 1765, *Franklin Papers,* 12 : 207–08. See also *Franklin's Letters to the Press,* ed. Crane, no. 18.

18. John C. Miller, *Origins of the American Revolution* (Boston, 1943), p. 114, notes that the stamp distributor for Virginia expected to employ twenty-five assistants. Hughes, in hiring assistants, would certainly distribute this patronage to benefit the Assembly party.

In a few weeks, however, on hearing that other colonies were expressing resentment against the act and the "ministerial agents" who were to carry it out, Hughes communicated to Franklin some second thoughts concerning his acceptance. Franklin advised his lieutenant to brace up. "If [the Stamp Act] continues, your undertaking to execute it may make you unpopular for a Time, but your acting with Coolness and Steadiness, and with every Circumstance in your Power of Favor with the People, will by degrees reconcile them." [19] Agitation in Pennsylvania was futile and could only harm Franklin's chances of getting the petition accepted. If mob violence and murders in the backcountry were chargeable to proprietary adherents, the Crown might be encouraged to take over the province leaving the Philadelphia-dominated Assembly party in command. If disturbances and riots against the Stamp Act occurred in Philadelphia, the Crown probably would not assume control of the government without altering the traditional liberties of the people and the House. Violence in Philadelphia might also enable the Proprietary party to increase its strength in the Assembly. A gain of about six members would give the New Ticket a majority; it could then rescind the petition and recall Franklin. Clearly, the political futures of Franklin, Galloway, and their allies seemed to depend on the ability of the Assembly party leaders to keep Pennsylvania loyal and dutiful.

Having failed in opposing the Stamp Act, but having, he apparently thought, gained some influence with the ministry, Franklin went back to work on his main consideration in the summer of 1765. He rather vaguely reported progress in getting his pleas for a change heard. When London Quakers, who during the spring and early summer of 1765 negotiated with the Penns about changing the instructions, failed to make any progress, Franklin probably pushed his petition more forcefully.[20] In July 1765, Rockingham replaced Gren-

19. Franklin to Hughes, August 9, 1765, *Franklin Papers*, 12 : 234-35.
20. Franklin to John Ross, June 8, 1765, ibid., 12 : 173; Franklin to Samuel Rhoads, July 8, 1765, ibid., 12 : 205; Franklin to Hughes, August

ville; Franklin did not reopen the question of the Stamp Act.
Throughout the summer came news of the adverse reactions of
several colonies to the act; Franklin wrote to Hughes that
these were rash and foolhardy and could do no good. Believing Galloway competent to meet any contingency, he expected his partner and Hughes to pursue a moderate course
in this regard, one that would not turn voters against them
and would not jeopardize the chances of obtaining royal government.

The Assembly party in Pennsylvania soon faced much the
same dilemma that its leader had, he thought, solved in
Britain. Wholly committed to the change of government to
protect the rights of the Assembly and the colonists, the party
now watched British authority being extended to the colony
in violation of those rights. Franklin had solved his dilemma
by giving up opposition to the Stamp Act when all seemed
hopeless. But Galloway's problem was compounded by the
activities of his political opponents. Gleefully, the New Ticket
pointed out that the Assembly party was trying to turn over
the provincial government to those who were seeking to deprive the citizens of their charter rights. The distinction between advocating for Pennsylvania the direct executive authority of the Crown and advocating legislative authority for
Parliament was easy to blur. The antiroyal arguments of
1764 became anti–Stamp Act arguments in 1765. Many believed that the Proprietary party's contention that the colony
would lose its rights and privileges if it were taken over by
the Crown was verified by the imposition of these new duties.
Perhaps, some charged, the seekers of the change of government planned it this way. Was not Franklin very likely
trading a change of government for a Stamp Act? Was not the
leader of the Assembly party in the House the stamp distributor? By June 1765 the Proprietary party was whipping

9, 1765, ibid., 12 : 235–36. Hutson, "Campaign, Part I," pp. 459–63, gives
an account of the Quakers' negotiations with Thomas Penn. Franklin
apparently played no part in these. He may have delayed pushing his
petition while they went on, however.

up sentiment against the Stamp Act, and its proponents, among the mechanics and others formerly loyal to the Assembly party in order to "alienate their Affections from the Mother Country" and the Old Ticket.[21] Unwittingly, Franklin had helped put Galloway and his party in a position all too vulnerable to attack and to further losses in the October election.

Despite the difficulty in communicating with his distant partner, Galloway knew what was expected of him. Franklin's acquiescence to the fait accompli would have to be duplicated in Pennsylvania. The best way to convince the restive populace to keep quiet, Galloway reasoned, was to use the Franklin approach. He would, as he reported to Franklin, "state the Conduct of the Mother Country with regard to her Colonies in a true Light, and endeavor, if possible to Check the growing Mischiefs—By Proving the reasonableness of our being Taxed—the Opportunity the Crown afforded the Cols. of Taxing themselves in the Manner which they contend they ought to be Assessed." [22] Cool reason would prevail against hot words; loyal and moderate sentiments would put disloyalty and violent action to shame.

Galloway put much cool reason into his newspaper appeal, which appeared over the pseudonym "Americanus" in both New York and Philadelphia in late August 1765. Adroitly he trod the thin line between advocating acceptance of the Stamp Act and denying parliamentary authority. Americans should peacefully remonstrate against the act. They should not make threats. "It is a proof of the greatest infatuation, to conceive, that we can bully the British nation, now at peace with the whole world, and possessed of strength which the united powers of France and Spain could not subdue." Since "the most plain and evident principle of justice, pronounce the

21. Galloway reported to Franklin, July 18, 1765, *Franklin Papers*, 12 : 217–18, that Lord Bute was cursed openly on the streets of Philadelphia and that it was dangerous to espouse the cause of Parliament in public.

22. Ibid., 12 : 218.

equity of [the colonies] being taxed, in order to defray the expence which their own safety requires," Americans should, instead of stirring up violent resistance, point out some alternative to the act, "some rational method, which will afford a confident dedendence [*sic*] to the crown, that this shall be done whenever necessary for the safety of our country." Galloway suggested the alternatives of a separate American legislature, with the power to tax for the common defense, or American representation in Parliament. His hints about American union with Britain were hardly concrete, but they were more farsighted and constructive than the protests and threats of most American assemblies and individual remonstrants.[23]

It was quite in character for Galloway, who had long championed the cause of the representative assembly, to place his faith in new or modified representative institutions. He failed to realize that the Stamp Act was a direct challenge to the very right of representative government. By advocating only peaceful protest and long-range solutions, Galloway avoided the question of how to stop immediately this imminent and flagrant invasion of colonial rights. He did not consider that Britain would also have to listen to the American position and make concessions if the crisis were to be solved. Certainly, once the home government could collect stamp duties, the question of what rights the colonists possessed would become academic.[24]

Objections notwithstanding, Americanus' arguments provided a rationale for the moderate position espoused by the leaders of the Assembly party. Despite the clamors of the Proprietary party, the merchants and the White Oaks rallied around the banner of moderation and compromise, resolving

23. *Pennsylvania Journal*, August 29, 1765. Goddard, *The Partnership*, p. 65.

24. An anonymous reply to Americanus, in the *Pennsylvania Journal*, September 19, 1765, pointed out that the author was really defending the Stamp Act because he did not consider the question of colonial rights and the protection of these rights at the time when American liberty was threatened.

to stand firm against violent resistance to the Stamp Act. However, the Proprietary party, spurred on by developments in other colonies, fully intended to commence violence. News of riots against Stamp Act sympathizers in Boston (August 14 and August 26) and Newport (August 29) encouraged Galloway's opponents to arouse a large number of Philadelphians against their homegrown Stamp Act supporters. If Bostonians could tear down the houses of those suspected of merely wanting to enforce the act, how would Philadelphians serve those suspected of imposing arbitrary government on Pennsylvania to gain their own selfish ends? Some Proprietary party leaders, acting much like the Boston Sons of Liberty, raised a mob and declared that the houses of Franklin, Galloway, Hughes, and Samuel Wharton, all allegedly involved in promoting the Stamp Act, "should be level'd with the Street." [25] Galloway sprang into action to repel this threat, just as Franklin had when the Paxton Boys were on the march. The White Oaks were now given the chance to prove that they were as sturdy as the wood for which they were named. From their numbers, and from other volunteers, Galloway organized an Association for the Preservation of the Peace of the City. Eight hundred stalwarts posted themselves in strategic locations, mostly near the threatened houses. When news reached the coffee house, the Proprietary headquarters, that their opponents had turned out to knock heads, the Proprietary party leaders began to fear for their own safety, and the mob "quietly retired." [26] In word and in deed, Galloway demonstrated that he and the Assembly party would brook no violence.

On October 5, another mob gathered to prevent the land-

25. Samuel Wharton to Franklin, October 13, 1765, *Franklin Papers*, 12 : 315–16. Wharton averred that the Proprietary party leaders had stirred up the mob. That this mob met at the coffee house is circumstantial proof of this. Certainly the more important and wealthier New Ticket leaders were not likely to counsel or consent to mob action, since their own property might be damaged in a riot.

26. Ibid., 12 : 315–16. Also Galloway to Franklin, September 20, 1765, ibid., 12 : 269–70.

ing of the stamped paper, which was reportedly being conveyed up river. This gathering induced Stamp Distributor
Hughes to swear that he would not put the act into operation
until other colonies did. Galloway could do nothing to save
his colleague from embarrassment, if indeed his stubborn refusal to resign his commission as distributor merited his salvation.[27] Threats and violence went no further, for the Association succeeded in preventing any hotheads from burning the
stamped paper or insulting Franklin. Galloway proved his
courage; he stood up against the rioters and put himself in
firm control of the situation in Philadelphia. His actions were
in striking contrast to those in Boston and Newport, where
local leaders like Thomas Hutchinson could arouse no pre-
servers of the peace and had to flee before the mob. Ener-
getic leadership and a moderate populace thwarted the house
wreckers. As Galloway bragged to William Franklin, if the
violent faction tried anything, "we can Muster ten to their
one." [28]

If Galloway could translate these heavy odds against violence into a victory over the Proprietary party at the polls,
Philadelphia would be secured for loyal behavior under the
renewed dominance of the royal party. Galloway, William
Franklin, and the Whartons selected a ticket for the October
election that reflected the moderate position and sentiments
of the party. Hughes's obstinate refusal to compromise his adherence to the Stamp Act forced his old friends to repudiate
him; for the first time in ten years, he was left off the ticket.
To replace Hughes and the absent Franklin, merchants who
supported Galloway and moderation were nominated. Otherwise the Old Ticket was much the same as in 1764.[29] The

27. Hughes to Franklin, September 8, 1765, ibid., 12 : 264–65, and
Hughes to the Commissioners of the Stamp Office, [October 1765?],
November 2, 1765, APS, castigated Presbyterians and argued for royal
government to keep the "disloyal" subdued. He demanded that his hands
be strengthened so he could put the act into effect.

28. Galloway to William Franklin, Novmber 14, 1765, *Franklin Papers*,
12 : 374.

29. On the Old Ticket for Philadelphia County were Norris, Fox,

party also put up full slates in the counties outside Philadelphia. Although victories there had helped continue the Assembly party majority in the House, the leaders were not primarily concerned about most of these seats. It was in Philadelphia, where violence against Stamp Act supporters was advocated, that the leaders of both parties sought votes using this highly charged issue; and it was in Philadelphia that the Proprietary party would make its most determined attempt to block Galloway and his allies from recovering their power.[30]

The New Ticket leaders made the mistake of concentrating on issues and ignoring organization and strategy. The proprietors themselves weakened their case when, in January 1765, Governor Penn finally admitted to the Assembly that Franklin's interpretation of his 1760 agreement with Lord Mansfield, that all lands of the same sort should be equally assessed, was justified. Penn also bungled the management of patronage in appointing justices. The ineptitude of the New Ticket leaders caused the defection of Henry Pawling, who went straight over to the Assembly party and supported Franklin's agency, as well as Dickinson, who threatened never to serve in the Assembly again, for "He had been used very ill." [31] Samuel Purviance could not easily find replacements.

Richardson, Rowland Evans, Thomas Livezey, Michael Hillegas, Henry Pawling, and Galloway. Pawling, the proprietary apostate, Hillegas, and Livezey replaced the absent Franklin, the stubborn Hughes, and Plunkett Fleeson, low man in the 1764 election. All these candidates had important property or mercantile interests which they would not sacrifice to the mob. Election return, Philadelphia City and County, Bucks, Chester, and Lancaster Counties, 1765, Franklin Papers, 69 : 98, APS. James Pemberton ran for burgess from Philadelphia City for the first time since this strict Quaker had retired in 1755. He hoped to inject a more Friendly spirit into politics again, and to "keep out an Envious Pres——n [George Bryan]." Pemberton to John Fothergill, December 28, 1765, Pemberton Papers, vol. 34, HSP.

30. The Philadelphia delegation in the Assembly was still controlling the policies of the House, as they had for many years.

31. John Penn's concession to the Assembly is in *Votes*, 7 : 5730–31. Pawling was welcomed with open arms by the Assembly party, as shown in n. 29. Dickinson's complaint was directed against Norris and Pember-

He was unable to put fervent Stamp Act nullifiers on the
ticket because that would alienate the moderate voters. A
rather weak anti–Stamp Act ticket, headed by Dickinson, who
changed his mind about resigning, was nominated.[32] Purviance did not ignore the backcountry, but, like Galloway, he
concentrated on Philadelphia, where he hoped the New Ticket's unequivocal opposition to the Stamp Act would bring another victory.

Again the campaign was conducted on two levels—vicious
propaganda and thorough vote collecting. The broadside blasts
of the Proprietary party abounded with malicious jibes at
Galloway, such as this comment on one vulnerable point, his
proud and vain nature:

> Glad would he be (cou'd he but find the way)
> To make Mankind to him low Homage pay.[33]

The Proprietary party made much of the charge that the leaders of the Assembly party had played some sinister part in
promoting the Stamp Act. James Biddle read to an assemblage
at the Statehouse a paper charging that Benjamin Franklin
had helped write the act, that William Franklin had blocked
the New Jersey Assembly from petitioning against the act,
and that William and Galloway had also attempted to keep
the Pennsylvania Assembly from sending delegates to the

---

ton. Charles Thomson to Franklin, December 18, 1764, *Franklin Papers*,
11 : 522–23; Samuel Wharton to Franklin, December 19, 1764, ibid.,
11 : 525–29.

32. Henry Keppele, Frederick Antis, and Jacob Winez were the candi-
dates who were supposed to draw the votes of the Germans. Norris was
on both tickets again, because he was the traditional Quaker leader and
because he had opposed Franklin and Galloway in 1764. Strettle and
Dickinson had run on the New Ticket in 1764. Isaac Jones and Rodman
Cunningham were probably Philadelphia shopkeepers. Election return,
Philadelphia City and County, Bucks, Chester, and Lancaster Counties,
Franklin Papers, 69 : 98, APS.

33. This couplet was part of a longer, scurrilous poem in *The Counter
Medly, being a proper Answer to all the Dunces of the Medly and their
Abbetors* (Philadelphia, 1765 [Evans no. 9943]).

Stamp Act Congress in New York.[34] To these monstrous accusations Galloway and his party could reply only defensively, as they had in 1764, emphasizing that they wanted effective royal government to protect the province from riots and declaring that they had had nothing to do with the Stamp Act. The Assembly party rebuttals apparently had some salutary consequences: William Franklin declared that had he not replied to Biddle's defamations, he "should have had my House pull'd down about my Ears and all my Effects destroy'd." [35]

The specialty of the Proprietary party was libel; that of the Assembly party was machine politics. Using the money liberally supplied by the merchants and the strong arms and legs of the White Oaks, the machine rounded up Germans to be naturalized so they could cast ballots; held open houses for thirsty voters who promised to mark for the Old Ticket; and delivered the voters to the polls. Galloway allegedly hired a minion to stand drinks in all the taverns for those who promised to vote for the Old Ticket.[36] The polls were kept open for three days to make certain that all possible supporters of the Assembly party cast their ballots. Galloway had learned his lesson the year before and was determined to profit from it.

In an astounding reversal of the results of 1764, the Assembly party captured all eight seats in Philadelphia County,

34. James Biddle, *To the Freeholders and Electors of the Province of Pennsylvania* (Philadelphia, 1765 [Evans no. 9915]).

35. [Galloway?], *To the Freeholders and other Electors of Assemblymen, for Pennsylvania* (Philadelphia, 1765 [Evans no. 10184]). William Franklin answered Biddle in *The Answer of his Excellency William Franklin, Esq; Governor of His Majesty's Province of New Jersey, to the invidious Charges of the Proprietary Party, contained in a Libel, read by Mr. James Biddle, Clerk of the Common Pleas for the County of Philadelphia, on Saturday last, and afterwards published and injuriously dispersed through the Province* (Philadelphia, 1765 [Evans, no. 9973]). William Franklin commented to his father on the effect of his answer, April 30, 1766, *Franklin Papers*, 13 : 256.

36. *Pennsylvania Chronicle*, September 23–30, 1771. Thomas Wharton declared to Franklin, October 5, 1765, *Franklin Papers*, 12 : 290–91, that he had never before worked so hard in an election.

the one contested seat in the city, and about twenty seats in the counties outside Philadelphia. By a strenuous election campaign, Galloway and his friends had saved themselves. The fiery leaders and the audacious tactics of the Proprietary party had failed to convince the electorate that resistance to the Stamp Act should necessarily be radical and riotous or that Franklin and Galloway were traitors. On the contrary, Franklin and Galloway had won a vote of confidence. The election was, as Galloway put it, "a strong proof of the people's Disapprobation of their [opponents'] Conduct." [37]

A comparison of the election results of 1765 with the totals of 1764 shows how Galloway and his party managed to win and how the Stamp Act issue injured the Proprietary party. In the Assembly party strongholds outside Philadelphia, the New Ticket was beaten very badly; the elections in Bucks, Chester, and Lancaster counties were landslides. In the key contests in Philadelphia City and County, the Proprietary party showed strength, but the Assembly party did about 25 percent better than in the previous election. All the Assembly party candidates who ran in both 1764 and 1765 got about 500 more votes in 1765 than they had in the previous year. This includes Isaac Norris, candidate of both parties. Because Norris was on both tickets, we may assume that nearly every voter chose him. If Norris, on both slates, garnered about 500 more votes than in the previous year, and the other Assembly party candidates received approximately the same increase, the conclusion must be that the Assembly party turned out about 500 more voters in 1765 than it had in 1764—and that nearly every one of them voted the straight Old Ticket. The returns for the New Ticket in 1765 were almost exactly the same as in 1764. John Dickinson even lost some support while his chief rival gained a huge bloc of votes. The Assembly party demonstrated the efficiency of its machine by drawing out a large number of people who had not voted before, while the opposition could achieve no real increase. The election of 1765 proved that the Franklin-Galloway party, principally under

37. Galloway to Franklin, [October 1765], *Franklin Papers*, 12 : 305.

Galloway's direction, had become a real party with effective techniques for getting out votes and with the ability to survive a serious crisis.[38]

Political skill won the election, but the Assembly party's espousal of moderation and Galloway's countermeasures against violence were also important. Dickinson's loss of about 3 percent of his 1764 support in 1765 indicates that the New Ticket's anti–Stamp Act stand gained it very little. Incendiary appeals to pull down houses and bully supposed Stamp Act advocates could not be converted into votes. Politically, Stamp Act radicalism was dead; moderation had killed it.[39]

Consequently, Galloway was well prepared for the fatal first of November, when the Stamp Act went into effect. As leader of the Assembly, he insisted on protests that were "Decent and Moderate and not negative of the Parliamentary Jurisdiction." [40] Since no stamps were landed in Pennsylvania, no further violence was attempted, but the colony was in many

38. The following table compares the election results of 1764 with those of 1765. The figures show the number of votes.

	1764	1765
Isaac Norris	3,874	4,332
Joseph Richardson	3,848	2,451 (on Assembly party ticket only)
Joseph Fox	1,963	2,466
Joseph Galloway	1,918 (lost)	2,400
Rowland Evans	1,911 (lost)	2,427
John Dickinson	2,040	1,980 (lost)
Henry Keppele	1,932	1,927 (lost)
Amos Strettle	1,930	1,955 (lost)
Frederick Antis	1,914 (lost)	1,917 (lost)

Henry Pawling, who after the 1764 election switched from the New to the Old Ticket, got 1,955 votes in 1764 and 2,432 votes in 1765. Election returns, Philadelphia County, 1764, 1765, Franklin Papers, 69 : 97, 98, APS.

39. The argument of Morgan, *Stamp Act Crisis*, pp. 255–62, that the colonists were ready to revolt if the Stamp Act were enforced, seems not to apply to Pennsylvania. See Benjamin H. Newcomb, "Effects of the Stamp Act on Colonial Pennsylvania Politics," *WMQ*, 3d ser. 23 (1966): 257–72.

40. Galloway to Franklin, [November 1765], *Franklin Papers*, 12 : 378.

respects in chaos. Ports and newspapers were temporarily closed, but they soon reopened for business as usual. Galloway objected to opening the courts of the province without stamps unless the judges agreed that the decisions rendered would be binding notwithstanding their technical illegality.[41] They would not agree, and the courts remained closed. The merchants of Philadelphia, following the example of those of New York, resolved not to import goods from Britain and petitioned the London merchants to press Parliament for repeal. Galloway believed that the merchants were too uncompromising in their petition, and he persuaded them not to send it. He drew up another which emphasized the feeble economic condition of America and the impossibility of paying the stamp duties. Much to Galloway's chagrin, the merchants added the harsh word "unconstitutional" to his draft in describing the Stamp Act.[42] On the whole, Galloway performed well what he thought Franklin expected of him. Compared to other colonies, Pennsylvania had a clean record; no riots and house wreckings would cause anyone to question its loyalty. Galloway urged his partner in London to make use of the evidence of Pennsylvania's loyal behavior to help procure the change of government. And he pleaded with Franklin to work for the speedy repeal of the Stamp Act.[43]

The connection between the Stamp Act and the Pennsylvania political situation was brought home forcefully to Galloway, but it dawned on Franklin rather slowly. While America was in turmoil over the coming of the duties, Franklin continued to press his petition. Apparently he met with real encouragement, for in early November 1765 he and Richard Jackson

41. Morgan, *Stamp Act Crisis*, pp. 206–08, 223–24. Galloway's political opponents accused him of being opposed to opening the courts no matter what the judges agreed. He denied this charge in an *Advertisement, December 20, 1765, To the Publick* (Philadelphia, 1765 [Evans no. 9977]).

42. *To the Merchants and Manufacturers of Great-Britain; The Memorial of the Merchants and Traders of the City of Philadelphia* (Philadelphia, 1765 [Evans no. 10185]), in draft, in Franklin Papers, 57 : 5, APS. Galloway to Franklin, [November 1765], *Franklin Papers*, 12 : 377–78.

43. Galloway to Franklin, [November 1765], *Franklin Papers*, 12 : 377.

presented the petition to the Privy Council. Franklin evidently was confident that they would get a fair hearing and perhaps a favorable decision.[44] Presumably, Franklin made use of Galloway's support, talking up the loyalty of his colony in contrast to the behavior of Virginia, Massachusetts, and Rhode Island in an effort to show that loyalty deserved the reward of good government. All in vain. He never got the chance to press the case of the Assembly before the Privy Council, for on November 22 all action on the petition was "postponed for the present" by the Council.[45]

Galloway's success in quelling disturbances in Pennsylvania had availed his partner in Britain very little. Nor did it do any good to argue that while the Assembly party preserved the peace in Philadelphia, the proprietors allowed the Paxton Boys to riot in the backcountry. The Privy Council would not act on this petition while America was in uproar over the Stamp Act. It saw no advantage to be gained in doing any favors for Americans while they refused to obey an act of Parliament. Franklin's and Galloway's scheme was in no way an aid in enforcing Pennsylvania's obedience to British authority. The cure for rioting and disloyal colonies would have to come from Parliament and would have to be much more thorough than the expropriation of the governing rights of an influential, respectable British family to oblige the questionable aims of its subjects.

The reports of resistance to the Stamp Act that Franklin received from Galloway awakened him to the full meaning of this attempt at establishing parliamentary authority over America. Before 1765 he had regarded the Penns as the chief enemies of the liberty of the colony and royal government as

44. Thomas Wharton to Franklin, December 30, 1765, *Franklin Papers*, 12 : 420. *Acts of the Privy Council, Colonial Series*, 6 (London, 1912) : 367–68. The date of entry in this source is May 23–28, 1764, when the petitions of the citizens of Pennsylvania were received by the Pennsylvania Assembly.

45. *Acts of the Privy Council, Colonial Series*, 4 : 471. Thomas Penn reported this postponement as *sine die* to John Penn, November 30, 1765, Thomas Penn Letter Book, Penn Papers, HSP.

the best means of salvation. Even when Grenville fell and
Rockingham came to power without moving to repeal the
Stamp Act, Franklin still clung to his hope that Britain
would see its mistake and disavow the taxation of the colonies
without any pressure from America.[46] By November he saw
that his hope was in vain. Postponement of action on his petition further demonstrated that the ministry cared little for
the rights or just aspirations of Americans. Charges of complicity in framing the Stamp Act, relayed from Pennsylvania,
stung him. He replied to the accusation of one Presbyterian
in a bitter vein: "I thank him he does not charge me (as they
do their God) with having plann'd Adam's Fall, and the
Damnation of Mankind. It might be affirm'd with equal
Truth and Modesty." [47] Galloway's pleading letters, full of
dismay at the disruption of trade, despair at possible violence,
and demands for repeal, showed him that he had greatly misjudged the impact of the act and the patience of his countrymen. They would not light candles to wait for the sunrise;
they would light bonfires to burn off the chill of oppression.

Never too proud to make amends, Franklin turned to firm
espousals of his long-held principles. No matter whether it
was the proprietors or Parliament that denied the Assembly
its primacy in Pennsylvania and its exclusive control over tax
revenues in that colony, Franklin would oppose them and uphold the rights of the representative body, as he had always
done. The blinders were off; he saw that the determined and
almost universal resistance by Americans deserved his support. Very quickly he blotted out of his memory his mistakes:
the appointment of Hughes and his advice to the stamp

46. Franklin may have been the author of two newspaper pieces appearing in *Lloyd's Evening Post, And British Chronicle,* August 30–
September 2, 1765 and September 9–11, 1765; see *Franklin Papers,* 12 : 244–
246, 253–55. These asserted firmly that Americans were loyal, not
ungrateful, and they very tentatively argued that Americans might be
correct in their constitutional claims against Parliament. If these were
Franklin's writings, they were not followed up for several months.

47. Franklin to Deborah Franklin, November 9, 1765, *Franklin Papers,*
12 : 360–61.

distributor to stand firm.[48] He would make others forget these actions, and redeem himself, by vigorous and unequivocal defenses of American rights.

Franklin began his public work of redemption in his time-tested and favorite manner: with newspaper contributions. British writers in London newspapers, in attacking American reactions to the Stamp Act, had contended that Americans were ungrateful, unpatriotic, and selfish in their refusal to contribute to the support of imperial defense. In a series of articles and letters beginning in November 1765 and extending into February 1766, Franklin refuted these mistaken and malicious views point by point. The Stamp Act, he argued, was not only wrong because it taxed without representation, but it was impractical to obey or enforce. Sarcastically, he claimed that Britain would need an army of 50,000 men, three or four years, and expenditures of ten to twelve million pounds to put the unjust measure into effect. If enough Americans were killed in such a war, the demand for manufactured goods in America would abate and, at any rate, the price of goods in Britain would decrease. Franklin was at his best in composing a stinging, backhanded reminder that the economies of both mother country and colonies were endangered by unjust and unwise legislation.[49]

48. Years later, in outlining his autobiography, Franklin at first made a note of his recommendation of Hughes and then crossed it out. His part here was a mistake which he wanted neither to remember nor to put into print. *Benjamin Franklin's Autobiographical Writings*, ed. Carl Van Doren (New York, 1945), p. 215.

49. In all, fourteen newspaper pieces containing these and similar arguments appeared over pseudonyms used by Franklin in the period November 1765–February 1766. The piece referring to war between Britain and America appeared in the London *Public Advertiser*, January 2, 1766, reprinted in the *Pennsylvania Chronicle*, February 16–23, 1767. Another very biting article, recommending that the British set Highlanders, French Canadians, and Indians on the colonists to make them obey, appeared in the *Public Advertiser*, January 26, 1766, reprinted in *Franklin's Letters to the Press*, ed. Crane, no. 30, pp. 54–57. The other pieces appeared in the London *Gazetteer*, December 19, 27, 28, 1765, and January 2, 11, 14, 15, 23, 29, 1766; and in the *London Chronicle*, November 11, 1765, and January 9, February 8, 1766. All are listed in *Franklin's*

Franklin's propaganda was limited in its effect. He was not now in microcosmic Philadelphia, where his pen had swayed voters and voters had swayed assemblymen. Yet it was more successful than his earlier efforts in Britain, for his activities brought him into close contact with British merchants who feared that their trade would be ruined by disorder and by nonimportation agreements in America. Franklin and other agents, such as Charles Garth of South Carolina and Dennys De Berdt of Massachusetts, worked closely with a committee of London merchants who sought repeal of the act. The Pennsylvania agent and Barlow Trecothick, leader of this committee, forwarded to the ministry letters from America detailing the impossibility of enforcing the act.[50]

With the Rockingham ministry, Franklin had another game to play: the paper money scheme again. In December 1765 he and Pownall presented the plan for an imperial loan office to the prime minister.[51] The plan was received enthusiastically, Franklin reported, because the ministry was desperately searching for a way to repeal the Stamp Act, collect revenue from the colonies, and retain the theoretical, but not the actual, power of Parliament over America. The ministers "had frequent Conferences with me upon it, and readily strengthened one another and their Friends in the Resolution of Repealing the Stamp Act, on a Supposition that by this Plan of a Loan Office they could raise a greater Sum with more satisfaction to the People." [52] Probably because of the opposition to such a plan among the Grenville faction and the king's friends, notably the Earl of Hillsborough of the Board of Trade, the paper money scheme never became a part of the Rockingham program. But the ministry took note of Franklin and allowed him to play a leading role in effecting repeal.

In the House of Commons, an examination of colonial rep-

Letters to the Press, ed. Crane, nos. 18–23, pp. 35–44, and nos. 25–32, pp. 45–63.

50. Sosin, *Agents and Merchants*, pp. 73, 76–77.
51. *Franklin's Letters to the Press*, ed. Crane, p. 27.
52. Franklin to Galloway, October 11, 1766, *Franklin Papers*, 13 : 449.

resentatives and experts who opposed the Stamp Act was staged. Franklin, among other agents and merchants, appeared to testify. He put on an outstanding performance, responding with pat answers to those questions the friendly ministry had told him would be asked, and also answering with tact and determination the attempts of the proponents of the Stamp Act to trap him. He readily presented views calculated to mollify parliamentary reluctance to backing down on the act, and he suppressed his own opinions, which might have made Americans seem more rebellious. He firmly and unequivocally opposed sweeping taxation for revenue, via such methods as the Stamp Act, as harmful to the empire economically and unjustified constitutionally.[53] Franklin was less definite about the legality of duties on commerce. Parliament, he stated, had the authority to regulate commerce and might be entitled to some revenue from such regulation to support the British navy; but, Americans might also be within their rights in resisting duties on commerce by refusing to buy any products excessively or unnecessarily taxed.[54] In short, Franklin implied that Britain should abandon all attempts to obtain revenue from America by taxation.

The efforts of Franklin and Galloway to smooth troubled waters, in the Americanus piece and in the examination before Commons, were strikingly parallel. Both partners developed moderate compromise positions which they hoped would refute the arguments of the extreme anti-British and pro-British positions. Yet, the compromise stands they took were quite different; these differences opened the first cracks

53. Franklin, *Examination*, in ibid., 13 : 131, 135, 137.

54. Ibid., 13 : 137, 139–40, 144–45. Morgan, *Stamp Act Crisis,* pp. 152–54, points out the American objections to both internal taxes and customs duties. Franklin had opposed the Sugar Act as well as the Stamp Act in 1764. Before Commons, however, he wanted to confine himself to the issue at hand—getting the Stamp Act repealed. He was willing to admit that Parliament could resolve that it had a right to govern the colonies —if it never put that right into practice. Cecil B. Currey, *Road to Revolution: Benjamin Franklin in England 1765–1775* (New York, 1968), pp. 184–90, discusses how Franklin stated the American case in London in a light calculated to bring about repeal.

in the long partnership of the two men. Franklin made concessions to parliamentary authority with which not all Americans would agree, but he strongly avowed that Americans were
correct in their resistance to the Stamp Act as a violation of
their rights as Englishmen. Galloway implied that the act was
impractical and unwise, but he ignored the question of colonial rights and advocated very restrained resistance. The
younger partner thought it expedient to ignore the question
of rights partly because he wanted to promote conciliation—
but also because he believed that Americans had a weak case
against parliamentary supremacy. Franklin consistently held
to the principle of the primacy of the representative assembly, but Galloway had not followed his mentor in adopting a
consistent set of political ideals. He stood with Franklin for
the supremacy of the Pennsylvania Assembly over the proprietors, but it was quite another matter for him to take a firm
stand against the authority of the mother country. Probably
Galloway failed to follow Franklin because another consideration loomed larger for him. Britain was, for Galloway, the
source of all law and justice. His eyes were so fixed on the goal
of bringing law and justice to Pennsylvania, in the form of
royal government, that he failed to think through the challenge to the primacy of the representative assembly.

Franklin, in his efforts to get the Stamp Act repealed, presented as a basic principle the exclusive competence of a
colony's little House of Commons to legislate on matters affecting that colony. Governors should not be restrained by instructions. Parliament should not attempt to legislate on
internal colonial affairs. By 1765, Galloway, while not repu-
diating his earlier views on the powers of the colonial assembly, began to consider the possibility that the lack of restraint
on the little houses of commons in some colonies would open
the door to rebellion and mob rule. As he saw it, radical New
Englanders, involved in a "Presbyterian conspiracy," had
treacherous designs.

Several of their Governments are nearly Democratical,
and Consequently very liable to discontent and Insurrec-

tions. Their Distance from their mother Country will Lessen her Awe, and the Idea of her Power, and when in a more Opulent State, and increased in Numbers, will probably prompt them to throw off their Subordination. I do not think this can possibly Happen in our Day, God Grant it never may—I am sure no good man woud wish to see it. But certainly these Considerations indicate the Prudence, if not the Necessity of Uniting the Colonies to their Mother Country by every Prudential Measure that can be devised.[55]

In advocating union to suppress these dangerous tendencies, Galloway placed the need for harmony and peace between mother country and colonies before political rights. The partners' views on which was more important, American rights or the preservation of the empire, opened a split between them.

Yet the breach could be easily healed. Franklin and Galloway, according to their correspondence, saw no real breach at all; they realized that they possessed honest differences of opinion but that to the practical function of their partnership these differences meant little. Not iron-bound ideologues, but practical men, they both decided to ignore the implications of their divergent views. "I thank you sincerely for the Notice you take of the Piece Signed Americanus," Galloway replied to Franklin on receipt of commendations for his conciliatory effort. "Be assured I shall ever esteem your Approbation of my Conduct among the highest Rewards." [56] The Americanus piece earned Franklin's praise because it helped to rally moderate opinion. Franklin probably took private exception to some of Galloway's points. The latter's opinion on the justice of raising a revenue in America and his criticism of New England "democratical" governments very likely irritated Franklin. The agent did not debate the

55. Galloway to Franklin, [November 1765], Franklin Papers, 58 : 36a and b, APS. The printed version, in *Franklin Papers*, 12 : 376, reads "meerly Democratical."

56. Galloway to Franklin, January 13, 1766 [misdated 1765 by Galloway], *Franklin Papers*, 13 : 35–36.

points with his young partner, however, because Galloway's strategy of supporting moderation had apparently worked so well.

Galloway sponsored the publication and circulation of Franklin's *Examination . . . in the British House of Commons, Relative to the Repeal of the American Stamp Act, in 1766* in Philadelphia. He wanted to insure that the leader of his party got full credit for his part in the repeal of the Stamp Act, regardless of the fact that British merchants were most responsible.[57] Probably Galloway did not completely approve of Franklin's views either. He never expressed any disagreement to his partner, for he could only applaud the results of the *Examination* in both England and America. Writing to William Franklin, he waxed poetic—a rarity for the solemn lawyer—on the effect the *Examination* had in proving that Franklin and his party were in favor of repeal of the act.

> True Merit and exalted Virtue [may be] like the Sun, overshadowed for a while. But the force and Brilliancy of their Rays will [before] long Dispell the Mists, and break forth notwithstanding opposing Clouds and Darkness.[58]

Both men were fundamentally politicians who knew full well the value of saying the right thing at the right time. They assumed each other's arguments to be not absolute statements of position but assertions made relative to time and place. For both, the chief considerations were to keep Pennsylvania loyal

57. Repeal came on March 18, 1766. Franklin deserved applause for his espousal of the colonial cause, but the merchants were more important than the agents. John Fothergill wrote to James Pemberton, February 25, 1766, Miscellaneous MSS collection, APS, printed in the *Pennsylvania Gazette,* May 8, 1766: Benjamin Franklin has served you ably and uprightly. He also was examined, and gave the House sufficient Proofs of his Abilities, your distress'd Condition, and the absolute Necessity of relieving the Americans, by repealing the Act."

58. Galloway to William Franklin, April 29, 1766, Franklin Papers, 48 : 123, APS. The original is torn; I have conjecturally supplied the missing words in brackets.

and to get the Stamp Act repealed. Thus, it was easy for them to gloss over the implicit and explicit conflicts between their views and to continue their collaboration. Their partnership, devoted in this instance to moderation and conciliation on both sides of the Atlantic, was a practical example of how Britain and America might, after this crisis, become reconciled.

The repeal of the Stamp Act added more cement to the partnership. Together the two men attempted to bury the animosities generated between Britain and her colonies. Franklin encouraged Galloway to draft and put through the Pennsylvania Assembly an humble and dutiful address of thanks to the king and a resolution promising that Pennsylvania would always be willing to provide aids to the Crown upon requisition.[59] Seldom did Franklin direct Galloway to take such specific action, for time and distance between the two partners made very close cooperation impractical. In this instance, though, Franklin wanted to gain beneficial recognition of Pennsylvania's loyalty in Britain in order to aid his chances of getting the petition accepted. Galloway consequently organized the White Oaks to guard against any "indecent Marks of Triumph and Exultation." [60] On May 20, 1766, when news of the repeal officially arrived in Philadelphia, rejoicing was enthusiastic but restrained. The king, the Rockingham ministry, and Franklin were liberally praised and toasted. Galloway and Franklin almost tasted mob rule and ruin, but they had cooperated, albeit belatedly, in Britain and in Pennsylvania to restore peace and order.

More confident than ever because of his personal victory over the rabble-rousing Proprietary party, Galloway anticipated a glorious future leading moderate Pennsylvania toward royal government. "I have now no doubt," he wrote to Franklin, "that all Discontent will Subside in America, for although I am every Day more and more Convinced that [torn—some?]

59. Galloway to Franklin, June 7, 1766, *Franklin Papers*, 13 : 292. *Votes*, 7 : 5884–85.
60. Galloway to Franklin, May 23, 1766, *Franklin Papers*, 13 : 285.

Peoples Views, went further than a Repeal, and even wishd
it might not take Place, in order to furnish them with a Pre-
text for other Designs, Yet their Number is so comparatively
Small, that they will, I beleive, generally withdraw their Intentions." [61] Franklin and Galloway could now proceed with
the fundamental business of the partnership. Having increased his political strength in Pennsylvania, Galloway was
better equipped to give Franklin the support he might need
to see the petition through. And Franklin would have to continue to supply the inspiration and leadership that had helped
keep the party together through the last ten trying years. If
he were to falter or be discredited, Galloway and the party
would likewise suffer.[62] Both Franklin and Galloway, by remaining true to the policies of moderation, accommodation,
and, when necessary, equivocation, had helped settle the
Stamp Act crisis and had survived it in good repair. Both
looked forward to the ouster of the proprietors and to the re-
sumption of good relations between mother country and
colonies. Yet basic philosophical differences concerning the
authority of Parliament had emerged between the partners
and would continue to plague their relationship.

61. Ibid.
62. Crane, *Franklin and a Rising People*, p. 116, divorces Franklin
from Galloway politically in 1766.

5 The Politicians and the Petition

With the Stamp Act—which to Franklin and Galloway was an unfortunate aberration in British imperial policy—repealed, the partners could now continue with the really important part of their business. No one would forget the yawning chasm between Britain and America that the question of parliamentary taxation of the colonies had opened; but now that it was at least temporarily closed, Franklin and Galloway did not believe that its effects would hamper their quest for the change of government. Politically, it was necessary for them to proceed as if the empire had never cracked open; at the same time, they had to endeavor to insure that it would never crack open again. Franklin's services to the British merchants and to the ministry appeared to give him increased influence. Galloway's electoral triumph gave him more confidence. Thus, the Stamp Act crisis dictated slight changes in strategy; it did not alter the basic aim of the partnership.

Franklin, undaunted by the postponement of the petition in November 1765, believed he could yet demonstrate that Pennsylvanians loved the Crown and that the proprietary government was subverting the British interest. After the American explosions of 1765, he also had to show that the home government would not be countenancing riot and rebellion by allowing the province to retain its charter privileges. Britain would not be inclined to do troublesome colonists any favors, nor to guarantee any rights which contradicted the authority of Parliament as stated in the 1766 Declaratory Act. Yet Franklin might be able to offset this effect of the Stamp Act. After his successful examination by the House of Commons, he was probably bolder and readier to lobby with officials. But he also probably saw that he would have to be more careful; that British policy was inimical to American rights was more evident. He would continue to press the petition for the change of government avidly, but he would be more cautious than before.

Galloway's moderation had strengthened the hold of the Old Ticket on Pennsylvania, but the Stamp Act crisis had for a time imperiled its hold and had cast doubt on the Assembly party's ability or willingness to perform its traditional function of defending the rights of the citizens. The experience changed Galloway for the worse. He became more suspicious of his opponents, who he thought were completely disloyal, and consequently he became more determined to crush them completely. He was more fearful of any political change in Pennsylvania—except of course that which he and Franklin planned—and he wanted to secure his hold on the colony. The crises of 1764–66 made Galloway tougher, more uncompromising, and more resolute. Like Franklin, he profited by his experience; he learned what he had to do to make his political career a success. Unlike Franklin, however, Galloway apparently learned little about the constitutional dispute between Britain and America.

The first problem which Galloway had to confront in 1766 was the discouraging news of the postponement of the petition. Thomas Penn, hoping to use the reversal of Franklin's plans against Franklin's party in Pennsylvania, wrote his supporters that the Privy Council's postponement should be interpreted as meaning "for ever & ever." "I am told Mr. Franklin was much shock'd when he was informed of it," Penn wrote to William Allen. "His Business is now over and I think I have nothing to fear from him." [1] In Pennsylvania the Proprietary party rejoiced in this interpretation; for the Assembly party the news, coming while Galloway and the other leaders were successfully calming Stamp Act radicalism, caused

1. Thomas Penn to John Penn, November 30, 1765, and Penn to William Allen, December 15, 1765, Thomas Penn Letter Book, Penn Papers, HSP.

near catastrophe. The New Ticket leaders attempted to persuade the merchants, the White Oaks, and the Germans to desert the partners because the petition had failed and the Stamp Act had arrived. Many Assembly party supporters were convinced that the petition was indeed dead and were ready to abandon the party. Through the early months of 1766, Galloway desperately cajoled and caressed the defectors back into line, reminding his adherents that Franklin was still in Britain and thus all was right with the world. "I have left nothing in my Power unessayed among our Friends to oppose the Torrent and to prevail on them to discredit this Account, and to believe that his Majesty will yet hear their Petitions and redress their Aggreivances," Galloway wrote his mentor, and he pleaded for some reassurance.[2] Franklin, characteristically optimistic in his belief that the postponement of the petition was not permanent, did not anticipate the effect of the Penn interpretation in Pennsylvania. He rectified this error by replying to the Pennsylvania Assembly's Committee of Correspondence in April 1766 that the postponement of the petition was only temporary and that, as soon as other American business was "out of hand," he could lobby with the ministry to get it revived. The agent was perhaps unduly confident, but his examination before Commons had been so successful that he and his party believed that his other efforts would likewise prove effective.[3] Aided by this news and by the repeal, Galloway countered the proprietary efforts to wreck his party.

To help Franklin revive his petition, Galloway would have to dominate a strong opposition to Governor Penn in the Assembly. When in command of the House in 1759, he had forced the issue of proprietary government to be sent before the British authorities and helped give Franklin what success he had on his first London mission. To repeat the earlier pattern was apparently the partners' best chance of fully van-

2. Galloway to Franklin, February 27, 1766, *Franklin Papers*, 13 : 181.

3. Franklin to the Pennsylvania Assembly Committee of Correspondence, April 12, 1766, ibid., 13 : 240. Galloway reported the reaction to this letter to Franklin, June 16, 1766, ibid., 13 : 317.

quishing the Penns. The opposition of the aged Isaac Norris, ready to retire, was little problem for Galloway. Joseph Fox, who now occupied the Speaker's chair, was a more formidable adversary. Fox not only blocked Galloway's ambition to dominate the House completely, but he failed to uphold the interests of the party. He took a much more conciliatory stance toward the proprietary opposition than Galloway could stomach.[4] The most galling example of the Speaker's ineptitude occurred when he allowed William Allen, in the House, to accuse Franklin of being the "greatest Enemy to the Repeal of the Stamp Act, of all the Men in England." Galloway, Ashbridge, and other Franklin supporters immediately rose to answer this false charge, but Fox would not let them speak and quickly adjourned to prevent an all-out battle on the floor.[5] A Speaker who would not support his party, a Speaker who permitted the leader of his party to be slandered, was intolerable. Fox would not resign voluntarily; Galloway would have to garner extensive popular support in the October election so that the Assembly would then elect him Speaker. The merchants, White Oaks, and, most important, Franklin, would support him over Fox.

It was, consequently, extremely important for Galloway to plan carefully for the October election. The first step was to improve the public image of the party by conclusively demonstrating that he, Franklin, and the Old Ticket were firm

4. According to *Votes*, 7 : 5851–57, Governor Penn and the House had almost no differences over legislation. James Pemberton, writing to John Fothergill, July 8, 1766, Pemberton Papers, vol. 34, HSP, was pleased that "the Spirit of Party in this province [was] very still," but this was exactly what Galloway did not want. Speaker Fox had apparently succumbed to the temptation of proprietary land, since he now believed that Franklin was not going to bring home any office for him. William Allen praised Fox's services to Thomas Penn, February 27, 1768, Penn Papers, HSP, stating that Fox "zealously Cooperated with me in our Assembly in opposing the extravagant conduct of a malignant party among us." Penn, writing to Allen, June 9, 1768, Thomas Penn Letter Book, HSP, authorized a reward for Fox—a land warrant.

5. Galloway to Franklin, June 7, 1766, *Franklin Papers*, 13 : 295.

defenders of American rights and never favored the Stamp
Act. Franklin's attacks on the act were convincing evidences
of his pro-American position. If the electorate was shown that
Franklin was unquestionably patriotic, it would impute the
same sentiments to his followers. Galloway, who had begun
politics at Franklin's side, especially had to appeal to the
voters as Franklin's partner and strongest supporter. If Franklin was praised in Philadelphia, his prestige would rub off on
Galloway. If Franklin was ruined by slander, Galloway too
would be ruined.

Galloway made certain that Pennsylvanians became familiar
with his substantial and prolific defenses of American liberties
as soon as they could be printed in the colony. In May 1766
"G. J.," obviously Galloway, caused to be printed in the
Pennsylvania Gazette a piece which Franklin had published
in London a few months earlier. This included letters from
Franklin to Governor William Shirley of Massachusetts written at the time of the Albany Conference of 1754. The letters
showed, according to "G. J.," that Franklin's "sentiments,
respecting a Parliamentary Taxation of the Colonies, have
been uniformly the same, for many Years past, and that he
had been one of the first and warmest Advocates against it." [6]
By the late summer of 1766 a Philadelphia edition of Franklin's *Examination* had been printed. A German edition was
also published, to appeal to that important bloc to vote for
the Old Ticket. Galloway encouraged the distribution of
Franklin's writings to enable the citizens to read for themselves how their agent had stood up to the mighty ministers of
Britain and told them what Americans thought of the Stamp
Act. If any Pennsylvanians disagreed with Franklin's state-

6. *Pennsylvania Gazette,* May 15, 1766, reprinted from the *London
Chronicle,* February 8, 1766; *Franklin's Letters to the Press,* ed. Crane,
no. 32, pp. 60–63. David Hall published private letters of Franklin "to
do Justice in some Degree to your traduced Character," as he wrote to
Franklin, July 12, 1766, *Franklin Papers,* 13 : 332. Franklin warned Hall
to be very cautious; the agent feared that these writings might be used
against him in England or Pennsylvania.

ments concerning parliamentary power over commerce and customs duties, they did not record their dissent. "You cannot conceive," William Franklin wrote his father, "the Satisfaction which the Accounts of your Examination at the Bar of the H. of Commons have afforded your Friends." [7]

For those who could not read or appreciate the significance of Franklin's condemnation of the Stamp Act, Galloway and his colleagues devised another means of persuasion. In celebration of the king's birthday, June 4, they staged a big party calculated to reunite the people behind the "loyal" ticket. By promising free treats for all, the Assembly party workers rounded up a large number of the "reputable" inhabitants, who assembled on the banks of the Schuylkill. The smack "Franklin" and the New White Oak barge were conveyed up the river to the point of the festivities, while the Old White Oak barge, on wheels, was pulled westward through the city streets by ships' carpenters and others of the faithful White Oak company. A sprightly band provided music for the parade and drew more people to the feast. When all had arrived at the river bank, the multitude heard speeches in praise of the king, Chatham, and Franklin. Guns saluted the royal family. Refreshments flowed freely, and the persons deemed responsible for the repeal of the Stamp Act were liberally toasted. Significantly, toasts drunk to Franklin preceded those drunk to the governor and the Assembly but, at least, followed the healths drunk to important British dignitaries. Fireworks capped the extravagant celebration. The crowds returned home full of punch and loyalty; Galloway probably went home congratulating himself that the Assembly party had shepherded all the wayward back into the fold. [8]

The activities of Franklin's partner had well prepared the Old Ticket for the perennial October contest. But his adversaries were far from resigning the game; the leaders and propagandists of the Proprietary party played some new cards,

7. William Franklin to Franklin, April 30, 1766, *Franklin Papers*, 13 : 254.

8. *Pennsylvania Gazette*, June 12, 1766.

hoping to trump both Franklin's *Examination* and the king's birthday celebration. The Proprietary party procured letters written by Hughes to the British stamp commissioners and by Galloway to Franklin, in which Hughes called for a strict enforcement of the act and in which Galloway identified himself as the author of the heretofore anonymous Americanus piece.[9] Quickly, denunciations of Hughes and Galloway appeared in the press.[10]

It was easy enough for the Assembly party to deal with the liability that was John Hughes. As in 1765, Galloway and his colleagues refused to put him back on the ticket. Any attempt to nominate him, Galloway declared to William Franklin, would "ruin our Party." [11]

The Proprietary party hoped that its propagandists would make Galloway a liability as well. Instead of continuing to portray Franklin and Galloway as united in a conspiracy against the rights of Pennsylvanians, a charge few could now believe, it shifted its propaganda attack in an attempt to drive a wedge between the partners. Forthwith, a comparison of Franklin's *Examination* and Galloway's Americanus piece appeared. The differences of opinion which the partners had ignored were now exposed for all to see. Galloway had charged that resistance to the Stamp Act was disloyalty, while Franklin

9. Hughes's letters were procured in Britain. Hugh Williamson, proprietary propagandist of 1764 now studying in Britain, got hold of the incriminating letter from Galloway to Franklin, according to Cadwalader Evans to William Franklin, December 7, 1766, Franklin Papers, 48 : 127, APS. Abel James predicted to William Franklin, September 1, 1766, ibid., 48 : 124, that "we shall have a good deal of Plagues about the Welsh Squire's Letters, for He was at that time very Angry."

10. *Pennsylvania Journal*, supplement, September 4, 1766; September 11, 1766. The Proprietary party published an "Essay toward Discovering the Authors and Promoters of the Memorable Stamp Act," ibid., supplement, September 18, 1766, which was based largely on charges resurrected from the 1765 campaign. But an accusation that Franklin was responsible for the Stamp Act was by this time certainly a dud.

11. Galloway to William Franklin, September 13, 1766, Franklin Papers, 42 : 4, APS. The Old Ticket was the same as in 1765, except that Norris died and was replaced by John Potts.

claimed that the responsible part of the American people were loyal, although they were clearly resisting. Americanus urged Americans to contribute to imperial defense, but the *Examination* argued that the colonists did not want or need British troops and would not pay for them. Franklin believed that the requisition system would supply Britain with sufficient revenue to meet emergencies, but Galloway denied this. Galloway argued that Parliament had the power to compel obedience, but Franklin assured Commons that the Stamp Act could not be enforced. Finally, Americanus claimed that Britain was entitled to some revenue to protect her in her present defenseless state, but the *Examination* viewed taxation for revenue as unconstitutional and unjust.[12]

Inspired to heavier attacks by the wedge they thought they had cleverly driven between Franklin and Galloway, the proprietary writers fired bigger broadsides than they had in 1765; these were designed to send Galloway's reputation to the bottom.

> Consider, O! Consider the irrevocable disgrace, the lasting infamy that must stain the reputation of Pennsylvania to the latest ages, should her generous free-born Sons call into her Assembly, the Author of AMERICANUS, the most daring, the most detestable ADVOCATE FOR AMERICAN SLAVERY . . . ever produced. . . . Must not all British America be convinced, THAT THE STAMP ACT WAS AGREEABLE To Us, when they see us advancing [Galloway] to a post of the most important trust, that very man who has most distinguished himself BY PLEADING FOR IT? [13]

The New Ticket based its attack on its own interpretation of Americanus and the *Examination*, not the interpretation that Franklin, Galloway, and the Assembly party held. The partners understood each other's position as relative to the time

12. *Pennsylvania Journal*, September 25, 1766.
13. *Friends, Brethren, and Countrymen* (Philadelphia, 1766 [Evans no. 10306]). Other campaign broadsides can be consulted from listings in Evans, for 1766.

and the situation into which each man was thrust, while their opponents tried to show the differences as absolute. The Assembly party did not permit the publication of the disparate views of the leaders or the scathing blasts at the leader in Pennsylvania to split the party. Galloway decided that the best strategy was to keep quiet, depend on the moderation and good sense of the thinking citizens, and let the White Oaks do the rest. He hoped that the more sophisticated voters would disregard the slanders and that the more ignorant would be swayed only by the treats and promises of his effective political machine.[14]

The election results were much as Galloway desired. The voting was considerably lighter in 1766 than it had been in 1765, indicating that the electorate was slipping back into its old apathetic habit. Vicious propaganda probably prevented Galloway from gaining votes at the expense of his intraparty rival, Fox; he was again eighth in the race for eight Philadelphia County seats. Dickinson and Keppele ran a very poor ninth and tenth. The contest in the city was close, but in the counties outside Philadelphia most of the Old Ticket candidates were returned handily, as usual.[15] Galloway personally vanquished all the force the Proprietary party had brought to bear. As the controversial standard bearer of his party, he drew on himself the full fury of the opposition's attack. Unlike the Quaker or German candidates, he could not count on a solid religious or ethnic bloc vote. However, his personal appeal,

14. Galloway reported to Franklin that he was confident of reelection, despite his opposition's slanderous efforts. Franklin offered his congratulations to Galloway, October 11, 1766, *Franklin Papers,* 13 : 447.

15. The Election return, Philadelphia City and County, 1766, Franklin Papers, 69 : 96, APS, shows that the Proprietary party was faltering badly. The figures in the following table give the number of votes.

Richardson	3,019	Galloway	1,848
Pawling	3,014	Dickinson	1,192 (lost)
Rowland Evans	3,000	Keppele	1,137 (lost)
Livezey	2,995	*Burgesses*	
John Potts	2,986	James Pemberton	1,419
Fox	2,875	John Ross	773
Michael Hillegas	1,927	Dickinson	739 (lost)

political ability, and attachment to Franklin enabled him to withstand the assault and, in turn, crush the opposition.

The Proprietary party, after viewing the disastrous results of this election, sounded its valedictory. Bitterly, Governor John Penn exclaimed, "The Quakers are a Macedonian Phalanx not to be broken by any force that can be brought against them in this Country." [16] The Germans who had supported the New Ticket in past elections were enticed to desert; Galloway reported to Franklin with much relief that they "are now generally come over to the Assembly Party, and have lost their former Prejudices." [17] The translation into German of Franklin's protests against the Stamp Act had frustrated attempts to keep many of that ethnic group on the proprietary side.

The election figures, when compared with the results of 1764 and 1765, show quite clearly that the Proprietary party lost German support. Only about 3,100 electors voted in Philadelphia County in 1766 as compared to about 3,800 in 1764 and about 4,300 in 1765. In 1764 Henry Keppele, prominent German Lutheran supported solidly by his ethnic group, won with 1,932 votes. In 1765 Keppele held on to 1,927 votes. In 1766, however, Keppele got only 1,137 votes, or about 800 less than in the previous elections. It seems likely that about 800 Germans who had voted for Keppele and his proprietary colleagues in 1764 and 1765 did not bother to appear at the polls in 1766. The Assembly party capitalized on the apathy of the Germans. It did not need the solid bloc of 500 votes turned out in 1765. Galloway lost with 1,918 votes in 1764 but won with 1,848 votes in 1766. The days of strenuous campaigning were over. The Assembly party had routed the New Ticket, permanently, as it turned out, and would hereafter rely on a smaller coterie of voters led to the polls by the White Oaks.[18]

16. John Penn to Thomas Penn, November 12, 1766, Penn Papers, HSP.
17. Galloway to Franklin, June 7, 1766, *Franklin Papers*, 13 : 296.
18. Election returns, 1764, 1765, 1766, Franklin Papers, 69 : 97, 98, 96, APS.

Galloway now turned his attention to attaining the Speaker's chair. His low position in the election returns gave him no good claim over the incumbent, Fox, but he was determined to displace Fox and use the post to increase his power and prestige. The Speaker could, if he were an able man, control the operations of the Assembly. He had much influence in the appointment of committees and in the dispensing of various jobs. The name of the Speaker was more often before the public eye than was the name of any ordinary assemblyman. Fox, and Norris before him, were partisan but moderate. Galloway, hotheaded, extreme in his attacks on the proprietors, and more interested in arousing controversy with them than in compromising matters, offered himself as quite a different sort of Speaker. Unseating the incumbent was against all tradition; Norris had been reelected since 1750, and Fox thought that his year in the chair entitled him to reelection. But Galloway was no traditionalist where his own ambition was concerned. He made it clear to his colleagues that he far overshadowed Fox in influence among the Old Ticket supporters, in political acumen, in ability to manage the Assembly, and in loyalty to Franklin.

Galloway rounded up support among the party members who had steadily followed his lead. Allen and Fox's other friends opposed the candidacy of their archenemy with a "spirit of party"; Galloway in the Speaker's chair would be a double blow to the proprietary group.[19] They could not prevail against Galloway's influence in the House, however, and Franklin's junior partner became the chief officer of the Assembly, although he was not accorded the customary honor of unanimous election.[20] He retained the post for eight years, exercising great influence over the House during that time.

Franklin was very pleased at Galloway's elevation. Congratulating him, he foresaw "great Good to our Country from your being in that Station, as I know you will fill it ably and

19. James Pemberton to John Fothergill, November 14, 1766, Pemberton Papers, vol. 34, HSP. Pemberton, a cautious Quaker, remained aloof.
20. *Votes*, 7 : 5938.

worthily." [21] Galloway interpreted Franklin to mean that he should bear down harder on their political opposition in Pennsylvania, make the agent and his party immune from scurrilous attack, and intensify the battle with Governor Penn until the proprietors gave up their privileges or until Franklin, armed with charges against the Penns supplied by Galloway, could procure the change of government. The strategy was much the same in 1757–59; but the partners were now in much stronger political positions.

Galloway undertook to deal first with the problem of the opposition's propaganda. The Old Ticket had for too long been on the defensive against the slanderous abuse of proprietary writers. The partners had been blasted by a torrent of calumny and half-truths: *The Plain Dealer, An Answer to the Plot,* Biddle's accusations of complicity in the Stamp Act, and the comparison of Americanus with Franklin's *Examination.* Galloway was, after the experience of the 1766 campaign, little mollified by Franklin's consoling sentiments that "Dirt thrown on a Mud-Wall may stick and incorporate; but it will not long adhere to polish'd Marble." [22] Franklin, far off in Britain, could stoically ignore attacks; Galloway was much more vulnerable and was not "polish'd" with a reputation comparable to Franklin's. His vanity made him greatly resent the continued scurrility issuing from nobodies and hireling writers. He had built for himself a high place in Pennsylvania, which he knew from experience was assailable if the Proprietary party took up some new issue. To beat back any attempt to unseat him, the new Speaker would have to mount a counteroffensive that would continue to blast at the New Ticket throughout the year and render its bothersome broadsides ineffectual.

The instrument required was a friendly newspaper. The *Journal,* printed by William Bradford, who had helped raise

21. Franklin to Galloway, December 13, 1766, *Franklin Papers,* 13 : 521.
22. Franklin to Galloway, November 8, 1766, *Franklin Papers* 13 : 488. This aphorism appeared in *Poor Richard Improved* (Philadelphia, 1757), in ibid., 7 : 85.

the mob against Galloway and Hughes in 1765, was, of course, of no use. Franklin's former partner, David Hall, retained a traditional nonpartisan stance in the *Gazette*. Therefore Galloway, William Franklin, and Thomas Wharton prepared to establish a newspaper that would be under their control and that could circulate Assembly party propaganda throughout the year.

William Franklin selected William Goddard, formerly a printer in Providence and New York, as the man to carry out the tasks assigned by the party chiefs. Galloway and Wharton became silent partners of Goddard; the politicians were each to receive 25 percent of the profits and the printer 50 percent. Neither Galloway nor Wharton put up any money, but Galloway undertook to persuade other members of the Assembly to sell advance subscriptions throughout Pennsylvania.[23] Galloway also promised Goddard the Assembly's printing concession, bragging to him that the government's printing business "was always at his command; whether he was a member of the House or not." William Franklin donated a press, not then in use, which belonged to his father. On January 26, 1767, the *Pennsylvania Chronicle* began publication and soon was firmly established.[24]

23. Goddard relates, in *The Partnership*, pp. 5–6, that he procured the job by happening to apply to Governor William Franklin at the time that the politicians were seeking a printer. Ward L. Miner, *William Goddard, Newspaperman* (Durham, N.C., 1962), pp. 62–66, deals with the arrangements of the partnership.

24. Goddard, *The Partnership*, p. 6. Because Hall held the government printing business, succeeding Franklin as official printer, he was not at all sympathetic to Galloway's enterprise. Galloway, aided by William Franklin, picked a quarrel with Hall, accusing the printer of refusing to publish material helpful to the Assembly party cause, to convince Galloway's friends in the House that Hall did not deserve the printing concession. Hall, who had endeavored to remain neutral during past political controversies, appealed to Franklin that he was being persecuted by Franklin's son and Franklin's friend on a trumped-up charge, which apparently was the case. Hall was furious at William Franklin, at "that mighty Man" Galloway, and even at Franklin for betraying him. He believed that Franklin was a party to the establishment of the newspaper,

The *Chronicle* became the best newspaper in Pennsylvania. It printed many interesting articles on a variety of subjects and was not reluctant to stir up controversy. Goddard sincerely believed that his press should be free and open to all contributors. The political views of his backers took up much of the space; the silent partners were not silent in the newspaper's columns. Galloway had most of Franklin's criticisms of the Stamp Act and defenses of America republished to show the patriotism of the Assembly party. Malicious pieces attacking the Proprietary party and its leaders, especially Dickinson, also appeared often. In presenting the Assembly party views and in damning the opposition, the *Chronicle* admirably repaid Galloway and his colleagues for their efforts. William Allen attested to the value of the newspaper in maintaining the party's hold on the White Oaks when he noted that it "stirs up the lower kind of people" with this "canal to disperse their poisonous productions among our people." [25]

While Galloway was busy with these fruitful political activities, Franklin was taking only halting steps toward getting the petition approved. After a well-earned vacation trip to the Continent in the summer of 1766, he returned to Britain to take up the problem of reviving the petition before the Privy Council. Franklin had many other irons in the fire: paper money for America and approval of the laws of Pennsylvania. But the change of government took up most of his time and was, from 1766 to 1768, the first-ranking matter. Franklin

---

which in Hall's view violated their old partnership agreement. He thought that Franklin should have forbidden Goddard to use Franklin's printing press. Hall's complaint against Franklin was neither valid nor fair, although he may well have been justified in his attitude toward William Franklin and Galloway. Franklin disclaimed any connection with the *Chronicle*, but he did not interfere in Hall's quarrel with the initiators, choosing the interests of his political partner over those of his former business partner. See Hall to Franklin, January 27, 1767, *Franklin Papers*, 14 : 17–18; Franklin to Hall, April 14, 1767, ibid., 14 : 126–28; Hall to William Strahan, April 30, 1767, May 26, 1767, June 12, 1767, July 4, 1767, and September 21, 1767, David Hall Letter Books, APS.

25. William Allen to Thomas Penn, May 25, 1767, Penn Papers, HSP.

realized Galloway's dependence on his success most fully when he was informed of the near collapse of the party after the petition was reported to have been rejected. Together with Richard Jackson, Franklin worked diligently throughout late 1766 and in the first months of 1767, "making all the Impressions possible wherever we can be heard, preparatory to reviving the Petition." [26] Apparently, British politicians were willing to humor Franklin; they seemed hopeful that he might, if induced by the prospect of sufficient rewards, support with his talented pen the British point of view in imperial affairs. The Earl of Shelburne, related to Penn's wife and unopposed to the proprietary interest, told Franklin, probably in order to gain his confidence, that he "was of Opinion Mr. Penn ought to part with the Government voluntarily and said he had often told him so." [27] Franklin also explored the possibility that the Crown might purchase the Penn's right to govern.[28] The proprietors, meanwhile, lost much of the confident air they had assumed when the petition was postponed. Thomas Penn was alarmed enough to keep close watch on Franklin's lobbying. He assured his Pennsylvania appointees that he would never surrender the government without twelve months' notice, so they could obtain commissions from the Crown before the transfer.[29] Penn betrayed his anxiety when he vowed he would never give up his province, even if compensated, "till I see Franklin removed far

26. Franklin to Galloway, December 13, 1766, *Franklin Papers*, 13 : 522.

27. Franklin to Galloway, October 11, 1766, ibid., 13 : 448.

28. John Penn to Thomas Penn, November 12, 1766, Penn Papers, HSP. William Penn had offered to surrender the government of Pennsylvania to the Crown in 1703 and in 1705. In 1712 the Board of Trade agreed with Penn on a price for the transfer of government and land rights, but Penn soon suffered a stroke and the resulting legal tangles precluded consummation of the sale. Franklin thought that this old agreement might still be binding on the proprietors; Thomas Penn was somewhat apprehensive that the British government might exercise whatever rights it had under this contract.

29. Galloway to Franklin, June 16, 1766, *Franklin Papers*, 13 : 318–19. Those Assembly party members who anticipated offices were not overjoyed at this report.

enough away from us"—a polite way of saying that the agent would have to go to hell in search of his change of government.[30]

Despite his efforts and the proprietors' fears, Franklin was not making much progress. Galloway and the Assembly party nevertheless remained convinced that final success was near, although they had little evidence of this.[31] The Assembly refused Franklin's offer to return home if it believed his mission was a waste of money; the party leaders predicted that this investment would eventually reward them handsomely. The agent sent William Franklin a copy of his journal for 1766–67, which William showed to Galloway as evidence that his father was indeed laboring diligently for his province. "[Galloway] is astonish'd how you are able to go through so much Business, and yet write so much," the younger Franklin reported to his father. Galloway went on to say, "If the People here did but know one-Half of what you are continually Saying, and doing for them, they would go near to deify you." [32] Reverence for Franklin and his works was not enough. Galloway saw that his partner would need material assistance from his Pennsylvania allies to speed the acceptance of the petition.

The partners had a good precedent on which to base a more vigorous transatlantic cooperation. As in 1759, Galloway as Speaker could initiate quarrels with Governor Penn and then send details of these disagreements to Franklin to be used as evidence of proprietary misgovernment. The issue of taxation of the Penns' estates had been settled by the proprietors' acceptance of the Assembly's interpretation of the Franklin-Mansfield agreement, and the quest for paper currency in-

30. Thomas Penn to William Allen, May 19, 1767, Thomas Penn Letter Book, Penn Papers, HSP.

31. William Allen reported to Penn, March 8, 1767, Penn Papers, HSP, that Franklin "still keeps feeding his associates in mischeif with the hope of wresting the powers of government out of your hands, when some accounts come of miscarriages in any of his attempts he writes some plausible story of his being like to renew them with great probability of success, and they either realy believe him, or pretend to do it."

32. William Franklin to Franklin, August 22, 1767, *Franklin Papers*, 14 : 235.

volved fighting against the parliamentary prohibition on legal tender of 1764, not against the Penns. But the appointment of judges at proprietary pleasure and the proprietary handling of Indian affairs were still sharp weapons with which the Assembly party could threaten its adversaries.

Failure to get judges appointed on good behavior in 1760 still rankled Galloway in 1767. He and Franklin corresponded concerning how the Assembly could best protect the province against a subservient judiciary. Franklin argued that the judges could be kept on their best behavior if the Assembly varied judges' salaries according to the performance of each judge. The proprietors influenced judges with their power of appointment and dismissal; the Assembly should influence them by financial controls. Drawing on a scientific analogy, Franklin pointed out that "for where the Beam *is moveable,* it is only by equal Weights in opposite Scales that it can possibly be kept even." [33] Galloway desired a more direct influence over the judiciary. By forcing the judges of the Supreme Court to ride circuit, he hoped that William Allen and William Coleman, devoted and aged proprietary supporters, would resign the bench rather than take to the saddle. In January 1767 the Assembly passed a circuit court bill, which attempted to supply a need recognized in the Assembly's response to the backcountry grievances of 1764, and which, by not providing for any additional judges, would make it very inconvenient for Allen and Coleman to serve.

Because it was quite clear what Galloway was trying to accomplish, Governor Penn refused the bill, arguing that the act should be of only three years duration and that more posts on the Supreme Court should be provided. The Speaker employed this refusal to "keep up the Ball of Contention," which he enjoyed doing very much. He threatened to send information about the dispute to Franklin for use against the Penns in England. It would appear in London that the governor was denying the people easily accessible justice. The intimidation

33. Franklin to Galloway, April 14, 1767, *Franklin Papers,* 14 : 122.

did not work at first; throughout February, and again when the Assembly met in May 1767, Governor Penn held out against Galloway, unmoved by his threat.[34] But by the middle of May he could hold out no longer, for he feared that Franklin was really making progress in London and that his refusal would aid the agent. On May 20 Penn approved the bill, finally deciding that it was better to surrender a point in Pennsylvania than to have to surrender the province in Britain. The Assembly backed down slightly by providing for one additional Supreme Court justice, but Penn's admission of the circuit court bill was a clear victory for Galloway.[35]

The long-range results were not very helpful to the Assembly party. Allen and Coleman continued on the bench rather than resign to complete the antiproprietary triumph. Franklin received no aid from the circuit court controversy; the home government probably would have had little interest in this dispute even if it had continued longer. And Galloway was no nearer to the establishment of appointments on good behavior or the ouster of his political opponents from the bench. All the same, a defeat for the governor and a weakening of the proprietary prerogative must have been gratifying to the Speaker.

The circuit court controversy having given him one modified success, Galloway was ready to challenge the Penns when the next opportunity presented itself. Proprietary management of Indian affairs was generally vulnerable to attack, and an incident in the backcountry soon gave Galloway his opportunity. In January 1768 one Frederick Stump and his servant

34. William Allen to Thomas Penn, March 8, 1767, Penn Papers, HSP. Penn agreed that court reform was necessary, but also noted to Allen, May 19, 1767, Thomas Penn Letter Book, HSP, that the law should be temporary and that fourteen to fifteen weeks was a long time to ride circuit. *Votes*, 7 : 5993–96, 6001–06, 6023.

35. The terms of the law are in *The Statutes at Large of Pennsylvania*, 7 (Harrisburg, 1900): 107–10. John Penn expressed his fears to Thomas Penn, April 29, 1767, Penn Papers, HSP. Thomas Penn advised his nephew, August 3, 1767, Thomas Penn Letter Book, HSP, that Franklin could do nothing.

murdered ten Indians because of real or imagined grievances. Stump was captured, but sympathetic backcountrymen who believed that killing Indians was no crime delivered him from jail at Carlisle. The episode contained many of the same elements of the Lancaster massacres of four years before: widespread backcountry sympathy for the criminals and suspicion of collusion between the murderers and proprietary officeholders. Consequently, the incident lent itself to use against the Penns. Under Galloway's direction, the Assembly accused Governor Penn and other proprietary appointees of conspiring with the jailbreakers to let Stump go unpunished. It further claimed that, because of repeated outrages against them, the backcountry Indians were ready to take to the warpath. The Assembly blamed the Penns for allowing settlers to move westward with little regard for Indian land claims or the consequent friction between Indians and settlers. The proprietors had failed to give the Indians protection from settlers like Stump. The Assembly recommended that the proprietors establish a boundary between the settlers and the Indians to prevent further conflict.[36]

Governor Penn met charges of failure to exercise strong executive authority in the backcountry with an attempt to clear the proprietors of responsibility. He replied to the Assembly by blaming the Quaker Indian traders for stirring up the Indians. Unwisely, he denied that the Lancaster outrage and the subsequent escape from punishment of the perpetrators was a cause of continued Indian discontent. Galloway in return produced a letter from Sir William Johnson, who averred that the 1764 massacres were indeed a partial cause of the Indian troubles.[37] In Pennsylvania the controversy blew over; the Indians remained at peace and Stump remained free. But the Assem-

36. *Votes*, 7 : 6081–82, 6129–34, 6135–40. Jack M. Sosin, *The Revolutionary Frontier, 1763–1783* (New York, 1967), p. 83.

37. *Votes*, 7 : 6141–47. Because Johnson backed up Galloway in this controversy with the governor, the Assembly resolved to pay the Indian superintendent a debt of £26 12s. 6d., which it had owed him for twelve years! Ibid., 7 : 6157.

bly had found an effective issue with which to embarrass the governor and make more charges against his uncles. Galloway gained some important points, for full reports were forwarded to Franklin who made good use of this evidence to show that the proprietors were incompetent governors.

In early 1768 Franklin, in pursuit of the revival of his petition, sought out the Earl of Hillsborough, newly appointed secretary of state for the colonies. Hillsborough was close to the king and a determined proponent of parliamentary authority over the colonies. He did not consider the Franklin-Galloway plan, under which the British government would assume control of the government of Pennsylvania while allowing the inhabitants to retain their claimed charter rights, to be consistent with British policy. Yet he encouraged Franklin's quest by promising to inquire into the status of the petition to see if it could be revived.[38] Soon, details arrived from Galloway about the Stump affair and the controversy with Governor Penn over Indian policy. In March 1768 Franklin presented to Hillsborough the Assembly's case. The secretary of state noted, with apparent suspicion, that "the governor had been tardy in bringing the former [Lancaster] murderers to justice." He seemed to Franklin to be partial to the Assembly's side in the dispute over Indian policy.[39] Hillsborough had long opposed backcountry settlements and favored the separation of Indians and settlers. To Franklin, he appeared to be no enemy to either the American cause or his own. After months of getting nowhere, the agent's hopes for final success were now bolstered.

Hillsborough apparently did make serious inquiries about the petition and investigated it in the light of British imperial policy. He presented the results of his study to Franklin in a lengthy meeting in August 1768. Here he exploded all the hopes of the partners. Franklin reported to Galloway that Hillsborough gave him "Advice . . . in order to obtain the

38. Franklin to Galloway, February 14, 1768, *The Writings of Benjamin Franklin*, ed. Albert H. Smyth, vol. 5 (New York, 1907), p. 99.
39. Franklin to Galloway, March 13, 1768, ibid., 5 : 111–12.

Change, being such as I assur'd him we could not take." As well, the minister manifested "a stronger partiality for Mr. Penn than any of his Predecessors." [40] Franklin's report seems somewhat contradictory, for Hillsborough did concede that the change was possible, and yet he favored the proprietors in their opposition to the change. Hillsborough pretty clearly was not anxious to support the change. His partiality for the Penns probably reflected Thomas Penn's influence with British officials. Since the 1750s, various ministries had supported the Penns against their subjects; there was no reason to reverse this stand in 1768.

What, then, was Hillsborough's "Advice" to Franklin? Almost certainly it involved seeking royal government on terms that would be far more suitable to British imperial practice than were the current charter and the standards of operation of the Penns' government. Only if the ministry believed it could make a better arrangement for governing Pennsylvania with Penn's opponents would it agree to the change. If Franklin were truly desperate in his quest for royal government, Hillsborough and the ministry hoped he would offer them some quid pro quo arrangement which would give the Assembly party their long-sought change, but which would also secure Pennsylvania's obedience to the Declaratory Act and insure that the Assembly and the colonial citizenry would lose many of their political liberties and privileges. Any such change would have made Pennsylvania a loyal and humble province and would have driven a deep wedge into American rights and American union. Complete surrender of these traditional charter rights by Pennsylvania would flagrantly violate the principles that Franklin had constantly espoused —and violate the instructions of the Assembly, continued since 1764, that he not permit the liberties of the province to be abridged.[41] The agent dismissed Hillsborough's advice at once;

40. Franklin to Galloway, August 20, 1768, *Autobiographical Writings*, ed. Van Doren, p. 180.

41. It is possible that Hillsborough advised Franklin to apply to Parliament for the change of government. Such a move was mentioned in Pennsylvania, although never seriously considered. British writers had claimed

he would just as soon have taken Thomas Penn's suggestion and gone to the devil for his change of government.

Galloway had won the battle, but Franklin had lost the war. The younger member of the partnership had, since the blow of the Stamp Act, rebuilt the party, completely confounded the opposition until it gave up in disgust, started an effective propaganda mill, become Speaker in defiance of tradition and political rivals, increased his own popularity at the polls, and capably challenged the proprietary governor. He had provided Franklin with solid support, but the stubborn adherence of British officials to the idea of parliamentary domination of the colonies was too much for the senior partner to overcome. Politically, Hillsborough's rejection of the petition had nothing like the effect that the postponement by the Privy Council in 1765 had had. By 1768 the Proprietary party was as dead as the petition it had opposed, and it could gain nothing from the Assembly party's defeat on this issue.

Galloway noted that it was discouraging to Pennsylvania to be so neglected by the ministry in the application for royal government, but he apparently did not let what was undoubtedly a great disappointment completely sink him.[42] By 1768 he found that the Speaker's post was sufficient gratification for his ambition. The Assembly was firmly in his control, and his popularity in Philadelphia had never been greater. In 1767 he was second in number of votes, and in 1768 he led the ticket for the first time.[43] Political success among the people

during the Stamp Act crisis that Parliament could set aside charters. However, an application to Parliament would have been unprecedented.

42. Galloway to Franklin, October 17, 1768, Franklin Papers, 2 : 143, APS. Hutson, "Campaign, Part II," *PMHB* 95 (1971) : 45–46, argues that after hearing of Hillsborough's decision from Franklin, Galloway became angry and indignant with the agent, and the two men split apart. Galloway did stop writing to Franklin for several months; but he was not a good correspondent anyway. According to William Franklin to Galloway, August 26, 1760, *Franklin Papers*, 9 : 192, Galloway had not written to him for a year.

43. Galloway was also sufficiently powerful to collect "extraordinary expenses" again. *Votes*, 7 : 6060, 6284, 6444, 6580; 8 : 6722, 6893, 7021, 7145. Galloway informed Franklin, October 17, 1768, Franklin Papers,

of Pennsylvania apparently satisfied Galloway's vanity. His whole world was political activity; now that he held the chief elective office in the colony, he did not feel so acutely the bitterness of defeat in the cause he had labored for. Galloway never accepted defeat as final, for through 1769 the Assembly instructed Franklin to continue to press for the change of government, and even after 1776 he continued to hope that Pennsylvania would become royal.[44]

The merchant and White Oak supporters of the Assembly party would get none of the royal offices they had asked Franklin for, but they felt no catastrophic loss. They could live with proprietary government as long as Franklin and Galloway were in command and as long as the patronage of the Assembly was in their hands. Moreover, imperial issues revived by the Townshend Acts were by late 1767 attracting so much attention from all groups that the change of government question paled in significance.

Franklin took the end of the quest for royal government in stride. Sixty-two years old in 1768, he was no longer so anxious for advancement. As he wrote to his son in July 1768, he no longer felt the same "spur of ambition." [45] Franklin's understanding of British colonial attitudes had fully matured by 1768. The imposition of the Townshend duties demonstrated to him that British officials agreed with none of his basic principles; Britain would not respect the rights of the colonists and insisted that Parliament was supreme over the colonial "little Houses of Commons." To work for a closer connection between colony and Crown seemed to him inconsistent with defending Pennsylvania against this latest challenge. After 1768 the agent saw few advantages and many dis-

---

2 : 143, APS, that only Allen had opposed the instructions to the agents for 1768, which included a direction to continue to work for the change of government.

44. The instructions in *Votes*, 7 : 5792, 5946, 6069, 6290, 6451–52, include the change, but reference to it was dropped in 1770.

45. Franklin to William Franklin, July 2, 1768, *Writings*, ed. Smyth, 5 : 148.

advantages in royal government. After observing how ineffectively the British government kept order against the raging Wilkesite mobs, he doubted that a British army would achieve better results in attempting to pacify riotous frontiersmen.[46] His 1764 prediction that the province could rely on the "united justice of King, Lords, and Commons" was exactly contrary to reality in 1768. Rather than showing that Franklin was incorrect earlier, however, it illustrates how readily he adjusted his views to changing circumstances. By the summer of 1768, when Hillsborough made his decision, Franklin was ready to give up his mission and return to Pennsylvania. Because of the continued anti-American sentiment in British official circles, and because of growing American resistance to the Townshend duties, Franklin finally resolved, in August 1768, to "stay however a little longer here, till I see what Turn American Affairs are like to take."[47] As the turns became sharper, the "little longer" extended to nearly seven more years.

The major objective of, and the motivation for, the partnership of Franklin and Galloway expired in August 1768. The partnership did not die with it, for such a long friendship and collaboration could not disappear at once. Galloway and his political party would need the symbol and the inspiration of Franklin, which did not appreciably weaken in Pennsylvania even though the source was 3,000 miles away. Since the main plank in the platform of the Assembly party had crumbled, Galloway, in the trying times ahead, would have to pin himself to Franklin's patriotic defenses of American rights. Franklin, in turn, needed Galloway and his colleagues to retain his position in Britain. He had to be free from worry about whether he would be recalled, free from worry about his reputation in Pennsylvania, so that he could continue his opposition to British imperial policy. For Franklin, imperial

46. Franklin to John Ross, May 14, 1768, ibid., 152–53.

47. Franklin to Galloway, August 20, 1768, *Autobiographical Writings*, ed. Van Doren, p. 180; Franklin to William Franklin, July 2, 1768, *Writings*, ed. Smyth, 5 : 146–47.

policy was becoming as serious a question as it had been during the Stamp Act crisis. The partners had subordinated the problem of relations between America and Britain to their drive for the acceptance of their petition, but this problem had never disappeared. After the repeal of the Stamp Act and during their pursuit of royal government, Franklin and Galloway had to face this problem again and turn their abilities toward attempting to smooth relations between the mother country and the colonies.

6 Papering the Empire Together

The Stamp Act crisis had temporarily disrupted Franklin's and Galloway's quest for a change of government, threatened to put an end to their political careers, and made each partner reconsider America's position in the empire. By the fall of 1766, the first two effects had been nullified. The petition for royal government, although never to be revived by the Privy Council, was being hotly pushed by the senior partner with the support of his second in command in Pennsylvania. The Assembly party had completely driven the New Ticket from the field and would soon launch its official organ. For Franklin and Galloway, the position of America in relation to Parliament was not clarified by the repeal of the Stamp Act. The Declaratory Act now affirmed the disputed right of Parliament to exercise authority over the colonies, probably to the point of taxation. Nor was any complete reconciliation of Britain and America in view. The Stamp Act left behind a lingering suspicion of ministerial motives in the minds of Americans. Moreover, there remained a residual resentment in Parliament because many members believed they had been forced to back down by the illegal activities of the inferior colonials.[1] Bad feeling on both sides of the Atlantic could only portend a repetition of the attempt to tax Americans, which next time might not be so easily repealed, and which also might lead to social and political unheavals overturning the current colonial leaders. Franklin and Galloway knew that their political positions and expectations depended in large measure on smooth Anglo-American relations—and that it was incumbent on them to keep relations amicable.

1. Charles R. Ritcheson, *British Politics and the American Revolution* (Norman, Okla., 1954), pp. 62–63, 67.

How could they do it? British policy was so uncertain and the ground of American rights so vaguely formulated that their chances of success were limited. The partners were prepared to concede that Britain should derive economic, diplomatic, and military benefits from the empire, but the mercantilistic regulation of the commerce, the manufacturing, and ultimately the wealth of America was burdensome and unfair. They believed that Britain deserved loyalty, perhaps she deserved even the right to sell her manufactures in America without competition, but American wealth could not keep flowing to Britain without sufficient return. They agreed that only if British policy were made rational, constitutional, and profitable for both mother country and colonies would further conflicts be prevented. As transatlantic partners, Franklin and Galloway had a great opportunity to aid in implementing any changes in British policy that might solve these perplexing imperial questions. Franklin could advise the ministry on policies that Americans would probably approve; Galloway could get Pennsylvania to agree to these policies and thus provide an example for other colonies.

The principal obstacle to solving the problem of the imperial relationship was that all parties concerned had different opinions as to what the empire actually was or should be. No complete agreement existed *within* Britain or *within* America. Franklin and Galloway epitomize the unclear middle ground; neither held anything like the opinions on the extremes, as represented by the Earl of Hillsborough and the more violent of the Sons of Liberty. Between themselves they differed, as the Americanus piece and the *Examination* showed. Moreover, neither man could firmly decide what position the colonies should occupy in the empire. Franklin often advocated something he called a "consolidating union." In May 1766 he suggested that America and Britain be united in Parliament as were England and Scotland, although he admitted that this was unlikely to happen.[2] Not long before this,

2. Franklin to Cadwalader Evans, May 9, 1766, *Franklin Papers*, 13 : 268–69. William Franklin to Franklin, August 22, 1767, ibid., 14 : 237–38,

he had argued in the opposite direction, claiming that Americans "are contented with their own little legislatures, if they be permitted to enjoy the privileges belonging to them." [3] Notes that he made in the margins of two British pamphlets, the two Lords' protests against the repeal of the Stamp Act, denied that Parliament was sovereign over America and that it had power to legislate for the colonists. Here Franklin also suggested that it was "now necessary to settle a Constitution for the Colonies." [4] Because Franklin was expressing these different ideas to himself, to close friends, and to the general public, it appears that in 1766–67 he was willing to accept a reorganization of the empire on any basis equitable to America—separation or a closer union.

Galloway was equally unsure how the demands for parliamentary authority and American rights should be reconciled. He never denied parliamentary authority, as did Franklin, but he aimed to make colonial assemblies equal to Parliament. As Americanus, he had suggested either an American legislature uniting the colonies and Britain or American representation in Parliament. By January 1766 he had prepared a manuscript, "Political Reflections on the dispute between Great Brittain and her Colonies respecting her Right of Imposing Taxes on them without their Assent," which likely con-

---

notes that in 1767 Franklin drew up a "Resolve" probably calling for American representation in Parliament; Thomas Pownall was to present this, but apparently he did not.

3. London *Gazetteer,* January 29, 1766, reprinted in *Franklin's Letters to the Press,* ed. Crane, no. 31, p. 59.

4. Franklin, "Marginalia in the Lords' Protests, 1766," *Franklin Papers,* 13 : 220–21, 224. Verner W. Crane, "Franklin's Marginalia and the Lost 'Treatise' on Empire," *Papers of the Michigan Academy of Science, Arts, and Letters* 49 (1957) : 169–71, offers a thorough study of Franklin's views of the authority of Parliament over America. Also see Crane, "Franklin and the Stamp Act," pp. 70–77. It is not clear from Franklin's writings that in 1766 he opposed Parliament's regulation of American commerce on constitutional grounds, as he later would. He termed the Navigation Acts, in his "Marginalia," p. 219, "selfish," but he did not say they were unconstitutional.

tained some statement on a constitutional union.[5] This period, after repeal of the Stamp Act and when Anglo-American relations were outwardly calm, was the time for these men to transform hazy plans into action.

Given their interest, it is somewhat surprising that neither Franklin nor Galloway developed any concrete plan of union at the time when the need for one was pressing and when both men were throwing out hints along this line. Franklin was an old hand at presenting plans of union—and seeing them rejected. His Albany Plan of 1754, which combined a British-controlled executive and an intercolonial council, had satisfied neither Britain nor the colonial assemblies. There was little likelihood that this scheme would be more satisfactory in 1766. The Declaratory Act certainly gave Franklin no indication that any British ministry would consider treating Americans on terms equal with Britons. Union of the colonies under the Crown was probably more palatable to Galloway than to most other colonial leaders. Yet he had his doubts on the subject; his "Political Reflections" was never published. One problem was that any union of the colonies with the mother country would cost local leaders some of their power; another was that Congregationalists and Presbyterians, whom Galloway blamed for Stamp Act violence and for his own political difficulties, might dominate such a union.[6] Both Franklin and Galloway, idealistically favoring a closer union, admitted by their inaction that in practice any union of Britain and America would be such a radical departure from past experience that only dire necessity could influence its acceptance and make it work.

If political union could not be achieved in 1766, a rea-

5. Galloway to Franklin, January 13, [1766], *Franklin Papers*, 13 : 36. Franklin told Galloway, September 27, 1766, ibid., 13 : 426, that he wanted to publish this piece in Britain, but he never did.

6. Probably Galloway feared, as did William Franklin, the domination of any general colonial legislature by "democratical" New Englanders and Presbyterians. His dislike of Presbyterians shows clearly in his *Historical and Political Reflections*. Also see Goddard, *The Partnership*, p. 16. William Franklin to Franklin, August 22, 1767, *Franklin Papers*, 14 : 238.

sonable facsimile, that is, closer economic ties, could be. Franklin still held to his paper money scheme, which he had suggested as an alternative to direct taxation before the Stamp Act went into effect and at the time that repeal was being considered. He had made and kept notes on the plan in the event that the home government should decide to adopt it. In April 1766, after repeal of the Stamp Act, Franklin consulted Charles Townshend on his paper money scheme, as he had earlier presented it to Grenville and to Rockingham. He did not, after the summer of 1766, press it on the new Chatham-Grafton ministry, for many of those who had seen the scheme before were still in office under the new government. Nevertheless, Franklin continued to hope that the plan would be adopted as he had presented it. To enable the colonists to pay their debts by mortgaging their land and to enable Britain to extract painlessly a moderate 6 percent for imperial purposes would greatly aid in promoting imperial reconciliation. As he wrote to Galloway in October 1766, he regarded the scheme as a "Matter of great Importance." [7] It might have utility if Parliament became inclined to attempt again to raise a revenue from America.

Galloway had not known of Franklin's paper money plan before October 1766, because Franklin feared that it might be misinterpreted if revealed in a Pennsylvania torn by political strife. But, independently, the partner remaining in Philadelphia concluded by late 1765 that the lack of paper money was one of the root causes of American economic discontent. If Americans had no money with which to pay their debts and taxes to Britain, they would, of course, be forced to resist paying and to struggle to free themselves of all burdens. Galloway believed that a stable paper currency would help quiet all unrest. If the home government would allow the colonies to issue legal tender once again, American opposition would

7. Franklin to Galloway, October 11, 1766, *Franklin Papers*, 13 : 449. Sosin, *Agents and Merchants*, p. 87. Ernst, in "Currency Act Repeal Movement," pp. 188–89, thinks that Franklin had by October 1766 given up the scheme. This seems contrary to what Franklin told Galloway.

decrease and, although real union would not be achieved, at least the possibility of further disunion would be minimized. Britain was concerned that Americans wanted to manufacture for themselves, but Galloway replied, "Let us have Money and we shall never think of Manufacturing or if we do, we shall never be able to perfect it to any Degree." [8]

In January 1766 he drafted for the Assembly a petition to Parliament requesting the repeal of the prohibition on legal tender. This petition drew heavily on the memorial of the merchants of Philadelphia of November 1765, which Galloway had helped to draft to protest the Stamp Act, and which devoted four pages out of eleven to complaining that the prohibition on legal tender was harmful to the colony. In both the memorial and the later petition Galloway noted that when the greatest quantities of paper money circulated in Pennsylvania the greatest amount of British merchandise was imported. The prohibition had forced Pennsylvanians to curtail purchases from Britain.[9] Lamenting to Franklin that "the Gold and Silver we may smuggle from the Spaniard, will like the Birds of Passage Continue but a small Time among us, and then take their Flight to the Mother Country in lieu of her Manufactures," Galloway insisted that "a Currency of our Own, permanent and fixt in its Value, seems therefore Necessary to our Commerce." [10]

It was in reply to Galloway's earnest requests that he work to obtain a paper currency for America that Franklin took his partner into his confidence about the paper money scheme. Galloway agreed with Franklin that a loan office established and controlled by the home government would provide a sound currency system. Yet, Galloway feared the plan would

8. Galloway to Franklin, January 13, [1766], *Franklin Papers*, 13 : 36–37.

9. Galloway claimed that since 1760, £30,000 had disappeared from circulation in Philadelphia yearly. *To the Merchants and Manufacturers of Great-Britain; The Memorial of the Merchants and Traders of the City of Philadelphia,* in draft, Franklin Papers, 57 : 5, APS. *Votes,* 7 : 5822. The petition is discussed in Ernst, "Currency Act Repeal Movement," p. 187.

10. Galloway to Franklin, June 16, 1766, *Franklin Papers,* 13 : 318.

be viewed by some of the more anti-British elements in Pennsylvania as another plot of the agent and the ministry to exploit and enslave the colonies. Having finally rehabilitated Franklin's reputation and his own, Galloway did not desire to expose himself to further scurrility from the proprietary faction. At first very cautious about revealing what Franklin had told him, Galloway asked William Franklin to keep his father's scheme between themselves and the Whartons, "as I have heard from many very warm objections against such a Plan, and in the present Temper of Americans, I think it wd. occasion great Clamours." [11]

Perhaps William Franklin ignored Galloway's injunction; perhaps Galloway decided to discover if there would be much adverse reaction to Franklin's scheme if the agent were successful in getting it adopted in Britain. At any event, in March 1767 a plan very much like Franklin's was made public in the party newspaper, the *Chronicle*. "Amicus," who was probably Galloway or William Franklin, proposed that the colonies issue paper money to be loaned out at 5 percent interest, each loan to be secured by the borrower's land. One-half the interest collected would be retained by the colonies, and one-half would be freely given to the Crown. Amicus strongly emphasized that the Crown's share was not to be collected as a tax, but donated by the generous colonials. This trial balloon for Franklin's scheme incurred no condemning reply, but it received no praise either.[12] The managers of the *Chronicle* did their part in testing what reaction Franklin's paper money plan might receive; it would have been opposed but it would not have met the resistance that the Stamp Act

11. Galloway to William Franklin, December 21, 1766, Franklin Papers, 58 : 36, APS.

12. *Pennsylvania Chronicle*, March 2–9, 1767. The only Philadelphia objection which has come to light is "Y.Z.," *Interesting Hints to the Inhabitants of . . . [sic]* (Philadelphia, 1767? [Evans no. 41724]), pp. 3–4, which opposed such a scheme because specie was better as money and because the bills might be "seized" by another "Grenville." Ernst, "Currency Act Repeal Movement," p. 189, n. 39, mentions objections that appeared in New York.

incurred or that would probably be arrayed against another tax.

The paper money scheme would have to await initiation by Parliament, at which time Galloway could attempt to obtain the approval of Pennsylvania for it. Yet, some local remedy for the lack of currency in circulation was needed immediately; by late 1766 the merchants of Philadelphia had almost no circulating medium of exchange with which to transact business. The old bills of credit which were being retired according to the provisions of the act of 1764 prohibiting legal tender paper money had to be replaced by something. Galloway was under heavy pressure to find some way to alleviate the currency shortage. He thwarted a plan of some Philadelphia merchants to issue scrip for local use, regarding this unauthorized circulation of nonlegal tender paper money as very dangerous economically. His advice to the merchants to drop the scheme popped what was known as the "Philad. Bubble," and left the problem as before.[13]

The Assembly of Pennsylvania, Galloway at first believed, could no more evade the act of 1764 than the merchants could issue scrip. Paper money which was not legal tender was, in Galloway's view, not really money and would neither be legal satisfaction for debts nor hold its value in commerce. Any attempt to wiggle around the parliamentary prohibition on legal tender might result in complete economic chaos, with debtors who held this nonlegal money pursuing creditors to pay them off without mercy, and with creditors resisting their settlement. Galloway's lawyer temperament, his belief in the sanctity of contracts, and his abhorrence of all that might lead to disorder caused him to be wary of such schemes. Through the last months of 1766 the merchants grumbled while the Speaker, whose political position depended in large part on merchant support, tried to figure out some solution.

13. The "Philad. Bubble" was planned by Abel James, a Quaker merchant who strongly supported Franklin and Galloway. Merchants who were not invited into the scheme objected to it; many agreed not to take the scrip. Galloway to William Franklin, December 17, 1766, Franklin Papers, 56, part i : 10, APS; *Pennsylvania Gazette,* December 11, 1766.

Economic pressure on the merchant backers of the Assembly party soon forced Galloway to reach a decision. In January 1767 he became convinced that the Assembly would have to authorize a paper money issue, legal tender or not, to meet government obligations and merchant demands. He consulted Franklin about his difficult position; he did not wish to stand idly by while the economy of Pennsylvania was ruined and his merchant supporters deserted him, but he did not want to bring down on Pennsylvania the wrath of the Board of Trade by disobeying an act of Parliament, especially not while Franklin's negotiations were in progress. There was little hope, Franklin reported to Galloway in April 1767, for any lifting of the paper money prohibition of 1764; the Board of Trade was opposed to it. Franklin was lobbying diligently for repeal, and he advised Galloway, for the meantime, to get the Assembly to vote a new issue which would not be a legal tender.[14]

Under the Speaker's influence, the Assembly prepared a bill which provided for the printing of £20,000 in indented bills to be "sunk" by an excise on liquor. The specific device utilized by Galloway and the Assembly to avoid issuance of a legal tender was the provision, stated on the bills, that these notes entitled the bearer to receive from the provincial treasurer a certain sum in bills of credit. Because, in practice, the government of Pennsylvania would accept these bills in payment of debts and taxes, Galloway hoped that the inhabitants would also be willing to accept this issue in payment for goods and services. The Speaker had to push the bill through the Assembly against the opposition of William Allen; it was passed and accepted by the governor May 20, 1767.[15]

14. Franklin advised Galloway, April 14, 1767, *Franklin Papers*, 14 : 123, to "give an interest on [the bills] till the Time of Payment." Galloway apparently decided that it would be uneconomical for the government to pay interest to the holders of the bills. The money would have to sink or swim on the demand of the people for a circulating medium.

15. William Allen offered some resistance, he reported to Thomas Penn, March 8, 1767, Penn Papers, HSP, for he believed that nonlegal tender "must depreciate in value." *Votes*, 7 : 6011, 6016–18, 6023. *The Statutes*

The Board of Trade also had to be convinced that this act, which was essentially an evasion of an act of Parliament, was admissible. Franklin apparently took it for granted that the Board would approve, although Galloway was probably not so sure. But since October 1766 Franklin had been talking up the hardships imposed on the colonies by restraints on legal tender and had won some sympathy. As a result, he probably believed that since the Pennsylvania money issue did not directly violate the prohibition on legal tender, it would not be opposed. Overall, he saw this act as in the interest of keeping the empire better bound together economically. The Penns made no opposition. Perhaps it was Franklin's lobbying that convinced the Board that there was no reason to oppose this paper money issue, for the act was not reported against.[16] The expedient proved satisfactory in Pennsylvania as well, for the bills held their value. The colony continued to em- the device of nonlegal paper money until the revolution. Galloway, who with Franklin saw the great utility of colonial paper money in keeping the colonies more closely attached to Britain, had been overcautious at first. After he saw no alternative solution, though, he joined with Franklin in solving one element of the complex paper money problem.[17]

---

at Large of Pennsylvania, 7 : 100–07, contains the provisions of this act. Ernst, "Currency Act Repeal Movement," p. 206, discusses the measure.

16. Franklin congratulated Galloway, August 8, 1767, Franklin Papers, 14 : 231, on his "trial of Paper Money without a legal Tender." The proprietors were evidently not much interested in this act, seeing no harm to them in it; they offered no comment. Journal of the Commissioners for Trade and Plantations from January 1768 to December 1775, 13 (London, 1937) : 7, 22. The Board would later object to a New Jersey act providing that the bills would "pass current," making them a legal tender. See Acts of the Privy Council, Colonial Series, vol. 5, 1766–1783 (London, 1912), pp. 196–97. Galloway neatly and shrewdly avoided this difficulty.

17. The importance of the issuance of nonlegal tender paper money by the colonies after 1766 is discussed by Ernst, "Currency Act Repeal Movement," and by Jack M. Sosin, "Imperial Regulation of Colonial Paper Money, 1764–1773," PMHB 88 (1964) : 174–98. Maryland, South Carolina, and New York were also attempting experiments with nonlegal tender

The temporary solution for Pennsylvania, of uncertain effectiveness in the long run, would perhaps keep that colony purchasing British manufactures, but it might not provide permanent relief nor have much relevance to the problems of other colonies. Throughout America, the commercial connection between Great Britain and the colonies was in danger of being loosened further if more thorough reform were not undertaken. Consequently, Franklin's endeavors to obtain repeal of the prohibition of 1764 remained important for Galloway even after the paper money issue of 1767. Very likely, Galloway encouraged Franklin in his attempts, since the agent reported in detail the elaborate steps he was taking and the *Chronicle* republished parts of letters that Franklin wrote to Galloway referring to this activity.[18]

Franklin's strategy was to collaborate closely with the mer-

---

money. For Maryland's emissions of nonlegal tender, see Charles A. Barker, *The Background of the Revolution in Maryland* (New Haven, 1940), pp. 292–93, and Sosin, *Agents and Merchants*, p. 92, n. 3. New York's Governor Moore blocked the Assembly from passing a paper money bill until he could determine whether the Board of Trade was willing to permit the colony to emit nonlegal tender. The Assembly objected to the Board's requirement that such an act include a suspending clause; no act was passed at this time. In April 1767 the South Carolina legislature ignored its obligation to submit legislation for review in Britain when it passed a bill providing for the emission of £60,000 in nonlegal tender. See Ernst, "Currency Act Repeal Movement," pp. 192–93, 207–08. Sosin, "Imperial Regulation," pp. 196–98, comments that Americans, by issuing nonlegal tender paper money, were tacitly admitting parliamentary authority over their internal affairs. In actuality, Maryland, Pennsylvania, and South Carolina were treading on thin ice in evading the intent, if not the letter, of the act of 1764. In the case of Pennsylvania, it was a workable evasion. Later Pennsylvania laws, none of which were challenged in Britain, provided for the issuance of £16,000 (1769), £15,000 (1771), and a daring £150,000 (1773). See *The Statutes at Large of Pennsylvania*, 7 : 204–11; 8 : 15–22, 284–300.

18. Several letters from Galloway to Franklin written during the early months of 1767 are not extant. Franklin reported faithfully to Galloway in letters of March 14, April 14, and May 20, 1767, *Franklin Papers*, 14 : 88, 123–24, 163–65; from these, one can trace the interest of both men in obtaining repeal.

chants of Britain, who saw the problem in much the same light as did the partners—and realized that consumption of British manufactures would be decreased under the present prohibitory policy. The agents of South Carolina and New York were also particularly active in seeking to remedy the lack of a circulating medium in their provinces, and they cooperated with Franklin in seeking a repeal. In March 1767 Franklin wrote for the merchants a detailed refutation of the report of the Board of Trade of 1764 which had been instrumental in getting Parliament to enact the prohibition on legal tender. The merchants adopted Franklin's refutation as their own position.[19] By May 1767 the agents and merchants could claim some success for their lobbying. Lord Clare of the Board of Trade and the Earl of Shelburne favored repeal of the act of 1764. Franklin reported to Galloway that the "Ministry had agreed to the Repeal." [20] Finally, after fighting the Penns since 1757, and after pursuing numerous ministers on varied matters since 1764, Franklin was on the verge of his first real victory in Britain. It was not as meaningful as subduing the Penns, on which he was still laboring, would have been, but it would remove a colonial grievance and perhaps lessen any tendency for the Americans to pull further away from the mother country.

Nevertheless, there were dark clouds in the bright sky. Anti-American sentiment was rampant in Parliament in the

19. This refutation argued, in opposition to the Board's report, that money did not need to have intrinsic value, that the policies of the British merchants and the British government were the chief causes of the depreciation of colonial paper money, and that bills of credit loaned out on land security were a practical money supply. *Pennsylvania Chronicle*, May 18–25, May 25–June 1, 1767; *Franklin's Letters to the Press*, ed. Crane, pp. 78–80; Ernst, "Currency Act Repeal Movement," pp. 197–99.

20. Franklin to Galloway, June 13, 1767, *Franklin Papers*, 14:180. Sosin, *Agents and Merchants*, p. 94. The terms of repeal would require colonial currency emission acts to contain a suspending clause, a condition at which New York balked. See Ernst, "Currency Act Repeal Movement," p. 201.

spring of 1767, owing partly to New York's refusal to obey the Quartering Act of 1765 and partly to a lingering feeling that colonials had gained too great an advantage over Parliament in getting the Stamp Act repealed. Chancellor of the Exchequer Charles Townshend had been talking since January 1767 of raising a revenue in America.[21] Besides his proposal for duties on glass, paint, paper, lead, and tea, Townshend appropriated Franklin's old paper money scheme, in a much modified form, for himself. The chancellor suggested that Parliament allow the colonies to print money and loan it out at interest. But, to Franklin's dismay, Townshend further recommended that the Crown use the interest revenue in the same way that it was planned to use the receipts from the customs duties he proposed: to pay the salaries of colonial governors, judges, and other civil servants.

While the form was much the same as Franklin's plan, the substance was far different. Franklin wanted the colonies to have the opportunity to agree to his paper money scheme, not have it forced on them. He planned that the interest revenue would be donated to the Crown as a free gift when requisitioned for necessary purposes. According to Townshend's proposal, the colonies would be forced to contribute to the subverting of their legislatures. Franklin got the ministry to drop this scheme by arguing that, while repeal of the prohibition of 1764 ought to take place, "no Colony would make Money on those Terms"; he thought "the Crown might get a great Share [of the interest revenue] upon occasional Requisitions, I made no doubt, by voluntary Appropriations of the Assemblies, but they would never establish such Funds as to make themselves unnecessary to Government." [22]

Franklin's old paper money scheme was still to haunt him. On May 13, 1767, when Chancellor Townshend formally

21. Ritcheson, *British Politics*, p. 92, discusses anti-American sentiment. Franklin commented on the "Clamours" raised by "Grenville's Party" to Galloway, April 14, 1767, *Franklin Papers*, 14 : 124–25, and reported that Townshend planned a salt duty.

22. Franklin to Galloway, June 13, 1767, *Franklin Papers*, 14 : 181.

presented to the House of Commons his plan to levy duties on colonial imports, he also announced that a paper money plan, which at first had "slipt his Memory," would be included and that a bill was being prepared to allow the colonies to print paper money, the interest from which would be applied to the civil list.[23] Townshend's espousal of this plan scotched the drive of the agents and merchants for repeal of the legal tender prohibition. If Parliament repealed the act of 1764 and then forced the colonies to contribute the interest revenue from paper money loans to support hated governors and other ministerial minions in America, the agents feared that they would be blamed for the whole idea—and the merchants feared that the colonists might institute boycotts against them. As Franklin put it to Galloway, these two groups would not "furnish the Chancellor with a Horse on which he would put what Saddle he thought fit." [24] The temper of Parliament in May 1767 was so anti-American, so intent on punishing the disobedience of the New York Assembly, that an effort to obtain the repeal of the legal tender prohibition, without promoting the plan for appropriating the interest revenue, was doomed to failure. At a meeting of the agents and merchants in early June, Franklin suggested that Pennsylvania might attempt to obtain repeal of the act of 1764 for herself alone. He believed that Pennsylvania would more likely receive such a concession from the home government than would any other colony, that Townshend would not levy his interest appropriation on this one colony, and that a restrained employment of legal tender in Pennsylvania would open the door to attaining complete repeal of the prohibition of 1764 when anti-American feeling abated.

23. Ibid. Grenville was evidently responsible for causing Townshend to restore his paper money scheme to his revenue program. The former minister claimed, when the chancellor presented his plan, that Townshend's duties were all "Trifles," and that a paper money scheme would be more profitable. Probably Townshend restored the old Franklin scheme to his program on the spot.

24. Ibid., 14 : 182–83.

The other agents and the merchants vetoed the idea and Franklin, for the sake of American unity in the face of British oppression, agreed to drop his proposal.[25]

Fortunately for Franklin's reputation, the paper money scheme was again dropped from Townshend's program; the duty acts passed Commons easily on June 15 and became law July 2, 1767. Probably the Board of Trade, especially Lord Hillsborough, was most instrumental in blocking a repeal of the prohibition of 1764, for the prejudice against paper money was still strong in that quarter. Without the support of the agents and merchants for repeal, Townshend had no foundation on which to build his own loan office plan.

The paper money scheme had been an adequate substitute at the time of the Stamp Act, even though it would probably not have been as lucrative or as certain as that measure. If the plan had been submitted to the colonial assemblies for their approval; if the interest money had been requisitioned and applied to defense purposes; and if the scheme had been put into operation in a constitutional manner so as not to subvert the right of colonial assemblies to control the salaries of royally appointed officials, it probably would have been much more palatable to Americans than were the Townshend duties, not to mention the preceding attempt at colonial taxation. It would also have been more profitable, for the customs duties were to raise £35,000–£40,000, or about two-thirds of what Franklin estimated his plan would produce.[26] Now that Townshend had twisted the plan into an oppressive tax, it was useless to Franklin and to America. A plan which would

25. Ibid.

26. Gipson, *Coming of the Revolution,* p. 174. Crane, *Franklin and a Rising People,* p. 125, and Sosin, "Imperial Regulation," p. 190, argue that the paper money scheme was an infringement on the rights of the colonists and that Franklin's reputation in America had a "narrow escape" when the scheme was not incorporated into the Townshend program. On the second point they are probably right, but only because Townshend had altered the scheme. Gipson, *The British Empire before the American Revolution,* 11 (New York, 1965): 263, n. 131, terms Franklin's paper money plan a wise one.

have been more in the British interest than those adopted failed because of the lack of perception of that interest. Neither Franklin nor anyone else had a workable alternative to Townshend's plan, so its passage could not be prevented.

Despite this defeat, Franklin persevered tenaciously throughout the remainder of 1767 and into 1768 in lobbying for the repeal of the paper money prohibition as well as for the change of government. Instructions from Galloway's Assembly ordered Franklin to keep pressing for repeal, yet to be cautious that such a repeal was not tied to the terms Townshend had proposed.[27] Thus Franklin, at the same time that he was doggedly seeking out ministers to try to persuade the Privy Council to hear his Pennsylvania petition, entreated the same ministers to get the Board of Trade to reverse its position of 1764. The agent won some allies, like Shelburne and Clare, but the Board remained firm.[28] Hillsborough, who had been president of the Board of Trade in 1764, was much less encouraging to Franklin on this matter than he was in regard to Pennsylvania's change of government. He remained unalterably opposed to colonial paper money; he tried to conciliate Franklin by stating that he would not officially oppose paper money for Pennsylvania, New Jersey, and New York, but he made it clear that the agent was wasting his time.[29] The meeting between the agent and the secretary of state on February 17, 1768, marks the end of Franklin's quest for paper money. On this iceberg of colonial administration, both the petition to make Pennsylvania a royal province and the cause of legal tender for the colonies finally foundered.

The perversion of Franklin's paper money scheme and the end of the movement to get the prohibition on legal tender repealed were for the partners much less bitter to swallow than the defeat of the change of government—yet perhaps more damaging in their long-run implications. Galloway was

27. *Votes,* 7 : 6069–70.
28. Franklin to William Franklin, August 28, 1767, *Franklin Papers,* 14 : 243.
29. Franklin to Galloway, February 17, 1768, *Writings,* ed. Smyth, 5 : 98.

able to put into circulation in Pennsylvania enough paper money to satisfy current needs, although his expedient was only a halfway measure of questionable legality. As long as Pennsylvania could emit nonlegal tender sufficient to provide a medium of exchange, Franklin's failure in Britain did little harm to his own colony. But it brought union with Britain no closer.

By late 1767 Franklin began to question whether paper money was really the solution for the economic and imperial problems of America that he and Galloway had thought it was. His earlier reliance on economic interdependence between Britain and America, founded on paper money that would bind the empire more tightly commercially, was replaced by the growing conviction that economic independence, founded on American natural and human resources, should be the policy for all patriotic Americans to advocate. "The mere making more Money will not mend our Circumstances," he advised Galloway, "if we do not return to that Industry and Frugality which were the fundamental Causes of our former Prosperity." [30] The Poor Richard strain of ideas, the belief that the virtuous, thrifty, hard-working and self-reliant Americans would prosper and should be allowed to prosper by following their own devices, rather than be subordinated to an imperial economic system, dominated Franklin's conception of empire by early 1768. In 1769, little more than a year after the repeal of the prohibition of 1764 had been finally rejected by Hillsborough, Franklin was to see his ideas of industry and frugality applied widely in America in efforts to make the colonies economically independent of Britain. The vehicle was a group of nonimportation agreements. Franklin then discarded his advocacy of paper money for the colonies and praised the manufacture of goods by Americans. "Whether the [Townshend] Acts are ever repeal'd or not [because of nonimportation], the Frugality & Industry

30. Franklin to Galloway, December 1, 1767, *Franklin Papers*, 14: 330–31. From November 1767 through January 1768 the *Pennsylvania Chronicle* carried many letters arguing that more paper money should be issued.

will work greatly to our Advantage, & make Money plenty among us, tho we should never be allow'd to issue Paper." [31]

The joint effort of Franklin and Galloway to obtain legal tender paper money was not precisely the same sort of partnership venture as was the quest for the change of government. Franklin did not at first take Galloway into his confidence about his paper money scheme. Because of the imperial nature of the effort for repeal of the act of 1764, the agent in London played a much greater role than the Speaker. Yet, the same sort of method of operation that the partnership employed in combatting the Penns was used to try to put new issues of paper money into circulation. In Pennsylvania, Galloway, advised by Franklin, did his part by successfully reinstituting paper money issues. Galloway also encouraged Franklin to press for repeal of the prohibitory act. Franklin lobbied in this cause much as he had to get his petition heard. Finally, the agent was offered essentially the same solution in both instances: he could obtain royal government and paper money on terms advantageous to narrow British concepts of colonial administration and harmful to American rights. In both cases, Franklin refused to compromise his principles, knowing that obtaining the change of government and paper money on these terms would seriously damage the power of the representative assembly.

Thus, in both cases the British government rejected plans advanced by the more moderate and compromising groups in America, only to encourage the more anti-British activists. Britain provided no support for those like Galloway, who were not adamant on the question of rights but who opposed the oppression of America, or for those like Franklin, who asserted that America deserved recognition of her rights but who were also anxious to conciliate differences. After these failures, Franklin and Galloway lost the initiative. They were unable to offer constructive suggestions leading to the solu-

31. Franklin to Galloway, March 9, 1769, William L. Clements Library, University of Michigan.

tion of imperial problems until, about six years later, they were driven to such solutions by desperate circumstances.

The partners kept the hope alive that some form of constitutional foundation for the empire that would prevent recurring disputes might still be built. Even though by 1769 Franklin was plumping for greater economic independence for America from British restrictions, he had no desire to see Britain and America go their separate ways. As he wrote to Galloway in 1770, "I am perfectly of the same Sentiments with you, that the old Harmony will never be restor'd between the two Countries, till some Constitution is agreed upon and establish'd, ascertaining the relative Rights and Duties of Each." [32] After Franklin's failures in Britain in 1768, the partners could only await developments. Greater and more serious crises loomed ahead; finally they both would be inspired to draft plans of union, but then it would be too late.

32. Franklin to Galloway, January 11, 1770, ibid.

7 The Split Widens

The problems of 1764–67 had not prepared Franklin and Galloway to meet future imperial crises. The partners had not developed any firm plan for solving the constitutional dispute. They both abhorred British taxation of America but were unsure how to prevent or combat it. Both wanted to avoid violent resistance. Moderate opposition had proved effective and had aided in the recovery of the political strength of the Assembly party after 1765. Their problem was, could a decent and respectful opposition to any given British action in the future be kept peaceful, or would this opposition probably lead to violence? Their uncertainty about the results of resistance made Franklin and Galloway slow to take the offensive against the Townshend duties. In time the partners were obliged to take stands on resisting the duties—stands which opened a wider split in their partnership.

Franklin first relied on reasoned argument to convince Britain of the error of taxing the colonies. In April 1767, when taxing America had become popular in Parliament and likely to be undertaken, Franklin tried to combat it in the press. He scathingly criticized British assertions that Americans were in revolt against Parliament, castigated British restrictions on American commerce, and hinted that Americans would not cheerfully pay taxes.[1] In one newspaper piece, Franklin

1. *London Chronicle,* April 9, 1767, reprinted in the *Pennsylvania Chronicle,* June 1–8, 1767; London *Gazetteer,* April 18, 1767, reprinted in *Franklin's Letters to the Press,* ed. Crane, no. 46, pp. 94–99. Franklin wrote to Galloway, April 14, 1767, *Franklin Papers,* 14: 124, that "I have written several Papers to abate a little if possible the Animosity stirr'd up against us, and flatter my self they may be attended with some Success."

recognized that the colonists had appeared to Britain to deny only the right of Parliament to tax within the boundaries of the colonies, where the local legislatures were supreme. The colonists had not clearly enunciated opposition to "external" taxes or import duties. Franklin reiterated the argument he had made in his examination before Commons—that import duties might be resisted by the colonial refusal to purchase the duties articles. Franklin did not state, as perhaps some Britons were led to believe, that Americans would accept duties on imports. They had not determined that these duties were unconstitutional; they had determined that they were not desirable.[2] As usual, Franklin's arguments had no effect on British policies.

After the Townshend Acts became law in July 1767, Franklin ceased his agitation temporarily, awaiting word from Galloway to find out what would be the reaction of Pennsylvania to the duties. What course he took in London would depend on what action his fellow Americans took. This time Franklin would not permit himself to be caught in a position different from that of his constituents; rather, he would follow their lead. He now evidently thought himself a much shrewder politician than in 1765; he intended to provide ideas around which his countrymen could rally, but he would not yet endorse specific action. Franklin anticipated that America would not approve the duties, and thus he did not attempt

2. *London Chronicle*, April 11, 1767, reprinted in the *Pennsylvania Chronicle*, June 1–8, 1767. Crane, *Franklin and a Rising People*, p. 124, notes Franklin's distinction between internal and external taxes and indicates that this may have influenced British policy. Franklin wrote, "an external tax or duty is added to the first cost and other charges of the commodity on which it is laid, and makes a part of its price: If I do not like it, at that price I refuse it. . . . If they are willing to pay *external* though not *internal* taxes, and we say they are the same, 'tis then the same thing to us, provided we get the same money from them." This hypothetical statement was an effort to be conciliatory and at the same time note that the colonists might refuse to purchase the duties articles. If Townshend was encouraged to propose his duties by Franklin's argument, then the minister was displaying his own obtuseness, not taking Franklin's advice.

to have any friends nominated as customs officers. Probably he foresaw a peaceful nonconsumption of British goods, as he had, in his examination, predicted Americans might undertake. He depended on his Pennsylvania partner to prevent any peaceful resistance from turning to violence.

Galloway, haunted by the memory of the Stamp Act crisis, was much less cognizant of the meaning of the Townshend Acts than was the agent in Britain. "I confess I do not like the Scheme, and wish it had never been thought of." But Galloway saw some advantage to be gained by it. "If Part [of the revenue] should be applied toward the Support of our Civil Authority will not the Crown name the Governor, or will it pay Men Who are Named by its Subjects? . . . Besides if the Governor and Judges are to be independant of the People, as they now really are, I think it would be infinitely better that they should also be independent of the Proprietors, whose Interest so often Clashes with that of the People." [3] Galloway disliked the duties because he feared they could be used as a political issue against the Assembly party, as the Stamp Act had been. He was not concerned about the rights of Americans or the economic disadvantage to the colonies but about the practical effect on his situation in Pennsylvania. Scurrilous broadsides and howling mobs could soon threaten the political stability he had so recently created and on which he depended. Dickinson and his friends, Galloway feared, would find some way to use the Townshend Acts against him.

Consequently, Galloway hoped that the duties were preliminary to the establishment of royal government in Pennsylvania. Thus, instead of leading to an erosion of authority, they might bolster it by bringing royal government. Galloway was ready to catch at any straw, even some form of British oppression, that might possibly bring the king's government to the colony. His main concern was yet local; his thoughts ran chiefly in the narrow channel of opposition to the proprietors. The imperial issue, that representative government in America was being undermined further by parliamentary

3. Galloway to Franklin, October 9, 1767, *Franklin Papers*, 14 : 277.

taxation and by parliamentary establishment of a civil list, passed over his head completely.

As Americanus, Galloway had at least recognized the need for colonial representation if America were to be taxed by Britain. By late 1767 he was willing to ignore the confrontation between parliamentary assertions of authority and the American right to meaningful representation, if this neglect would help bring about the change of government. Galloway forsook the most important common ground that he and Franklin had found up to this time—the primacy of the Pennsylvania Assembly in governing the colony—and made little objection when Parliament, in passing these duties, attempted to usurp some of the authority of the Assembly. Galloway was blinded by local concerns; Franklin had a wider perspective and saw that America and Britain would be driven further apart.

The Pennsylvania politician's strategy was to insure that the colony offered no overt opposition to the duties; any resistance might initiate a renaissance of the Proprietary party as well as discredit Pennsylvania in Britain. The Assembly party generally supported its leader's position, for the Quaker members wanted no violence and the White Oaks at first saw no reason to resist these indirect taxes. Franklin, Galloway, and the other Pennsylvania leaders of their party were undoubtedly pleased that after September 1767, when the new duties were published in the colonies, no recurrence of Stamp Act violence marred Pennsylvania's reputation. But Franklin, who had given Britain notice that Americans might refuse to consume the duties articles, must have been somewhat disappointed that his home colony was ready to pay the taxes almost cheerfully.

John Dickinson shattered the silent acquiescence of Pennsylvania with his "Letters from a Farmer in Pennsylvania." This famous series of newspaper pieces first appeared in the *Chronicle,* demonstrating that Goddard had a conception of a free press quite different from that of his silent partners. In the "Farmer's Letters," published from December 1767 to

February 1768, Dickinson pursued two objects: he attacked the British invasion of the rights of Americans; and he chided the Pennsylvania Assembly for doing nothing to protect those rights. He did concede to the home government the power to regulate trade, but Parliament, he asserted, had no right to levy duties for revenue because this was taking money from the colonists without their consent. He called on the colonial assemblies, especially the one directed by Galloway, to petition Parliament for the repeal of these duties. He declared that the assemblies should not shirk their obligation to their constituents because timid leaders feared possible riots and tumults. If petitions proved of no avail, Dickinson suggested that nonimportation of British goods, which had been successful in getting the Stamp Act repealed, should be instituted again.[4]

Reactions to Dickinson's arguments and proposals showed important divisions in American opinion, as well as differences between Franklin's and Galloway's views. In New England, hotbed of anti-British sentiment, Dickinson became famous rapidly, the movement for nonimportation gained strength, and Boston, which had adopted nonconsumption in October 1767, adopted nonimportation in August 1768. In Pennsylvania the "Farmer" was a prophet without honor in his own country. Galloway, always calculating how an issue might be turned to his political advantage, and believing that others usually did likewise, was convinced that the prime purpose of the "Farmer's Letters" was Dickinson's political advancement. He took little notice of the argument they contained. William Franklin reported to his father that Dickinson's style had made the letters "pass very well with great Numbers of the common People, and with some others," but for Galloway and himself they had little substance.[5]

4. John Dickinson, "Letters from a Farmer in Pennsylvania," *Pennsylvania Chronicle*, December 2, 1767–February 18, 1768. See letters 3 and 12 for recommendations of action.

5. William Franklin to Franklin, May 10, 1768, Franklin Papers, 2 : 126, APS.

The agent did not think, as did his son and probably Galloway, that the "Farmer's Letters" were "absurd & contradictory." Franklin was fair-minded enough to leave political considerations aside and view the series as it dealt with British policy. He contributed the preface to the British edition of his political opponent's work, cautiously commenting, "How far these Sentiments are right or wrong, I do not pretend at present to judge." [6] Franklin wished to allay any British opposition to the Americans that the series might stir up, and he wanted to avoid giving the impression that he endorsed the view that the American assemblies had not done enough in opposing the duties. Yet Franklin, unlike Galloway, approved of Dickinson's call to peaceful resistance. As well, he agreed with the "Farmer" that Parliament could not constitutionally raise revenue from America. But Franklin began to doubt Dickinson's assertion that Parliament could legislate concerning colonial relations with the empire. The vigorous reasoning of the "Farmer's Letters" inspired the agent to rethink his own position and privately to adopt doctrines concerning imperial relations that were much bolder than his rival's, not to mention his partner's.

Franklin's failure to get the ministry to allow the printing of legal tender without appropriating the interest revenue; his inability to get a hearing on the petition for the change of government; his dislike of British politics—in which he had no success at playing an effective role; his conviction that Parliament would for a long while remain unwilling to accommodate Americans in any way; and his reading of Dickinson's pamphlet crystallized his opinion that any parliamentary control over the colonies was unconstitutional and unjust. Since the time of the Stamp Act, Franklin had, in his writings,

6. Franklin, *Preface to the Letters from a Farmer in Pennsylvania*, in *Writings*, ed. Smyth, 5 : 128–29. The Earl of Hillsborough, believing that all defenders of America had the same opinions, was certain that Franklin had written the "Farmer's Letters," as Franklin reported to his son, March 13, 1768, ibid., 5 : 114. This provides some indication of the circulation of Franklin's defenses of American rights heretofore.

usually conceded the jurisdiction of Parliament over colonial trade, but he had previously not been perfectly clear in his views about parliamentary authority. By January 1768 he was unambiguous about the matter. In March he asserted to his son that no middle doctrine, as found in the "Farmer's Letters," could be maintained. "Something might be made of either of the extremes; that Parliament has a power to make *all laws* for us, or that it has a power to make *no laws* for us; and I think the arguments for the latter more numerous and weighty, than those for the former." To demolish Dickinson's nice distinction between taxation for revenue and regulation of trade, Franklin advanced a criticism of British commerical policy. Britain theoretically could levy export taxes on goods sold to the colonies, which would raise revenue in the same way as import duties collected in America. But such export duties would be as unjust as the Townshend duties—because Britain prohibited Americans from importing manufactured goods except from the mother country. "This she does, however," he continued to William, "in virtue of her allowed right to regulate the commerce of the whole empire, allowed I mean by the Farmer, though I think whoever would dispute that right might stand upon firmer ground, and make much more of the argument." [7]

Franklin's position on the unconstitutionality of parliamentary legislation affecting the colonies led him to alter his views on possible solutions for imperial controversies. His hopes and plans for imperial union, whether political or economic, which he had expressed since the Stamp Act crisis, were little mentioned after the first months of 1768. A political union, "like that with Scotland . . . is not likely to take place, while the nature of our present relation is so little understood on both sides of the water, and sentiments concerning it remain so widely different." [8] In January 1768, shortly before he disclosed his views to his son, Franklin, in his "Causes of the American Discontents Before 1768," de-

7. Franklin to William Franklin, March 13, 1768, ibid., 5 : 115–16.
8. Ibid., 5 : 115.

clared for the restoration of the pre-1763 imperial system, in which Parliament had legislated for the colonies only rarely and Britain had enforced this legislation even more rarely. He termed the requisition method of procuring revenue from the colonies happy and constitutional, meaning that all imperial legislation since 1763 had invoked something unconstitutional and unpleasant. Franklin also condemned the paying of the salaries of governors and judges from the proceeds of the Townshend Acts, for assemblies would then have no control over tyrannical or incompetent officials.[9]

Advancing beyond a mere attack on the duties, Franklin put himself on the firmer ground of criticizing British restrictions on commerce and manufacturing. He was angered that Britain was "not content with the high prices at which they sell us their goods, but have now begun to enhance those prices by new duties." It was unjust that Britain, by restrictions on manufacturing and by Navigation Acts, denied to Americans the "natural right . . . of a man's making the best profit he can out of the natural produce of his lands."

Franklin recommended united action. "Let us unite in solemn resolutions and engagements with and to each other, that we will give these new officers as little trouble as possible, by not consuming the British manufactures on which they are to levy the duties. Let us agree to consume no more of their expensive geegaws." [10] By nonconsumption of dutied articles and luxuries, Americans could force Britain to repeal the

9. Franklin, "Causes of the American Discontents Before 1768," *London Chronicle,* January 7, 1768, reprinted in the *Pennsylvania Chronicle,* April 18–25, 1768. Franklin here restated his balance theory of the judiciary, which he had expounded to Galloway, March 14, 1767, *Franklin Papers,* 14 : 122. See above, p. 152.

10. Franklin, "Causes of American Discontents," *Pennsylvania Chronicle,* April 18–25, 1768. Franklin claimed that he did not necessarily endorse these sentiments, but presented them as typical American views. Clearly they were much like his own opinions. He informed William Franklin, December 29, 1767, *Franklin Papers,* 14 : 349, that he wrote the piece to calm the clamors against Boston's nonconsumption resolutions of October.

duties and restore the imperial relationship to its proper, pre-1763 state. An economic boycott had worked before and would work again.

At the same time that Franklin was advancing his arguments against parliamentary authority over the colonies, he, having failed to get the act of 1764 prohibiting legal tender repealed, was also advocating that America establish greater economic independence from Britain through industry and frugality. Nonconsumption, he believed, was the means to encourage industry and frugality. Consequently, the lack of a sufficient medium of exchange and the necessity of resisting the Townshend duties combined to influence Franklin to recommend greater economic independence for America. "If our people should follow the Boston example in entering into resolutions of frugality and industry full as necessary for us as for them, I hope they will among other things give this reason, that 'tis to enable them more speedily and effectually to discharge their debts to Great Britain," he advised William Franklin.[11] Franklin had now molded the objectives and the method to which he would adhere until the outbreak of the revolution: no interference in American affairs by Parliament, a return to the pre-1763 imperial situation, and a loosening of economic ties between Britain and America—all to be achieved by the refusal of Americans to consume British manufactures.

The general agreement of Franklin and Dickinson that the Townshend Acts were unjust and that some form of nonconsumption or nonimportation was the proper resistance brought the two Pennsylvanians no closer together politically. Franklin's idea of nonconsumption, as adopted in Boston, might have the same effect on the British as nonimportation, but it was quite different in its operation and enforcement. Its

11. Franklin to William Franklin, December 29, 1767, *Franklin Papers*, 14: 350–51. Franklin also wrote to his son, March 13, 1768, *Writings*, ed. Smyth, 5: 116–17, and to Cadwalader Evans, February 20, 1768, ibid., 5: 101–02, that America could manufacture some items but could not easily replace imports from Britain. Franklin was playing both sides; he claimed that Americans would boycott British manufactures but also that they really needed them. The purpose was to enlist British merchants to take the Americans' part.

effectiveness depended on the willingness of a great majority of the people to observe their agreement, but the sight of the proscribed articles in merchants' shops would undoubtedly tempt many to cheat. If nonimportation agreements prevented British goods from entering the colonies, Americans would not be led into temptation. Dickinson advocated formal agreements among the merchants, such as the Stamp Act had engendered; Franklin would be satisfied with less formal and less enforceable agreements among the people at large. Dickinson, pointing to the inaction of the Pennsylvania Assembly, argued that colonial representative bodies had the primary responsibility to petition for colonial rights. In the case of Pennsylvania, Franklin apparently was content to leave to Galloway the decision on what action the Assembly should take. He relied on his old partner for wise and moderate leadership, for he must have known from experience that Dickinson might rush the province into hasty and ill-considered measures.

If Galloway was disturbed at the strong stand Franklin took against the duties, he never displayed his feelings. He probably was aware of Franklin's views, as expressed to his son, for William Franklin generally relayed information from his father's letters to Galloway.[12] He recorded no disagreement with the man on whom his own political stature depended so greatly; Franklin's views on parliamentary authority were far different from his, but Franklin's suggestions of industry and frugality were mild enough for him to accept. At any event, he saw the political utility of Franklin's patriotic position. With his blessing, the "Causes of the American Discontents Before 1768" was reprinted in the party newspaper.[13] Galloway was anxious to show that Franklin was

12. William Franklin and Galloway relayed information to each other about Franklin in 1766–67. See William Franklin to Franklin, August 22, 1767, *Franklin Papers*, 14 : 235; Galloway to William Franklin, December 21, 1766, Franklin Papers, 58 : 36, APS.

13. Franklin sent Galloway a copy of his "Causes" in his letter of January 9, 1768, *Writings*, ed. Smyth, 5 : 91. William Franklin reported to his father, May 10, 1768, Franklin Papers, 2 : 126, APS, that his "Causes"

continuing to defend America and to let all see that Franklin's defense was as well argued as, if not better than Dickinson's. Because Franklin had blasted British policy and had recommended nonconsumption of British goods, Galloway believed that the publication of his "Causes" would imply that the Assembly party held the same views and was firmly behind the agent in his defense of American rights. Because Franklin had not criticized Galloway's Assembly for inaction nor recommended any more than collective resolution not to buy British goods, his "Causes" did not really conflict with Galloway's policy of ignoring the Townshend Acts officially, nor did it support Dickinson's advocacy of nonimportation. As it had in 1766, the Assembly party would again cloak itself in Franklin's patriotism.

The anti-British halo that Galloway donned did not fit him very well. Although opposed to the new duties, the Speaker did not believe that the question of American rights was paramount. So fixed was he on bringing royal government to Pennsylvania and on preserving his own position that he could think of imperial issues only in terms of how his opponents might use them against him. During early 1768 the governor and the Assembly were locked in debate over who was to blame for Stump's escape and Indian unrest—to Galloway a more significant and less dangerous question than imperial problems.[14] If the Speaker could keep the attention of the House on local matters and thereby discourage it from taking action on the Townshend Acts, no harm would be done to himself or to the loyal reputation of Pennsylvania. If the duties were soon repealed, his inaction could not be held against him; if they endured, Pennsylvania might receive royal government as a reward for its loyalty. By the beginning of 1768, the differences in theory and tactics between Franklin and Galloway had greatly sharpened. Franklin had refined his position so that it more clearly reflected his long-held

---

was "thought by Many to be more to the Purpose than all the Farmer's Letters put together."

14. See chapter 5 for details of the Stump case.

principles; Galloway had neglected the principles to which
he had once firmly held and had become more determined
to use British policies for his own purposes.

The Stamp Act had done the Proprietary party little good;
the party's resistance to the Act was too violent for Pennsylvania, and Franklin and Galloway had outmaneuvered their
opponents. If Galloway remained cautious, ignored the
Townshend Acts, and permitted the violent opponents of
the Assembly party to discredit themselves, these new duties
would serve them no better. The "Farmer's Letters," the
example of Boston, and the proven effectiveness of nonimportation in getting the Stamp Act repealed inspired a
vocal group of activists, led by the Farmer himself, to raise
opposition to the duties in Pennsylvania. In February 1768
Dickinson and his supporters began to press the Speaker to
lead the Assembly on a course of resistance to the duties and
to petition king and Parliament for repeal.[15] Because the
duties were unpopular, Galloway had to make some gesture,
but he tried to avoid giving in to his political opponents. On
February 20, 1768, the Assembly drew up special instructions
to agents Franklin and Jackson in Britain, directing them to
cooperate with the other colonial agents in making "a decent
and respectful Application to Parliament, in case such Application is made by [the other agents] for a Repeal of the late
Acts imposing Duties on the Importation of Paper, Glass,
&c. into the *American* Provinces, which Act is looked upon
highly injurious to the Rights of the People, and our commercial Interest." [16] In comparison to this mild and condi-
tional method of protest, view the Assembly's denunciation,
a few days later, of "the feeble Hands of a Proprietary Governor," who would take little action in the Stump affair, and

15. In March, some Boston merchants adopted nonimportation in the
expectation that Philadelphia would soon join. See Arthur M. Schlesinger,
The Colonial Merchants and the American Revolution (New York, 1957),
p. 114; and Merrill Jensen, *The Founding of a Nation: A History of the
American Revolution, 1763–1776* (New York, 1968), pp. 270, 283.

16. *Votes,* 7 : 6168.

who was "too weak to support Order in the Province, or give Safety to the People." [17] By meekly sending instructions telling Franklin, in effect, to be cautious in protesting the duties, and by strongly condemning the proprietary government, Galloway believed that he had placed local and imperial problems in their proper perspective and had done his duty by his constituents.

The Speaker also dealt effectively with the pressures to take more positive action put on Pennsylvania by other colonies. The Massachusetts circular letter of February 11, 1768, which exhorted the other provinces to join with her in resisting taxation without representation, was a torch for the group led by Dickinson. Galloway's opposition attempted to get the House to act on the appeal of a sister colony, but Galloway outmaneuvered it. The Pennsylvania Assembly was not in session when the letter from Massachusetts arrived. When sessions resumed on May 10, 1768, Galloway could not avoid having the letter read, but he could avoid taking any action on it. The Speaker adjourned the House until September without permitting time for discussion of the Massachusetts appeal.[18] The man who had done the most to save Pennsylvania from riot in 1765 was not in any way going to associate his province with that most riotous of colonies. Adroitly, Galloway countered his opponents and played for time until, he hoped, the issue would be forgotten.

Dickinson and his allies in the agitation for stronger protests and resistance realized that Galloway was stalling until the duties were repealed or until American resistance faded away. Joining with Charles Thomson, a longtime associate of Franklin and Galloway, but also an advocate of firm opposition to Britain, Dickinson endeavored to persuade the merchants of Philadelphia to establish a nonimportation agreement in concert with Boston and New York.[19] After several

17. Ibid., 7 : 6179.
18. Ibid., 7 : 6181–84, 6187.
19. Dickinson and Thomson held meetings with the merchants in March and April, 1768. *Pennsylvania Gazette,* March 31, 1768; Robert

abortive attempts at winning merchant support, they began, in May 1768, a vigorous broadside and newspaper campaign to get the general public aroused against the timid merchants and the do-nothing Assembly.[20] Thomson drew on the reputation of his friend Franklin, just as Galloway attempted to do; the proponents of nonimportation announced one of their meetings with a famous quotation from Franklin: "Those who give up *essential Liberty* to purchase a little *temporary Safety*, DESERVE neither *Liberty* nor *Safety*." [21]

Franklin's opposition to the duties, the popular appeal of the "Farmer's Letters," and the successful application of nonimportation during the Stamp Act crisis were points for the advocates of a boycott not easily matched by Galloway. But the Speaker was more adept than his opponents in propaganda battles, having been case hardened by years of them. And he had control of a newspaper. Writing as "Pacificus" in the *Chronicle* in late July, Galloway explained the position of the Assembly. Pacificus did not, as did his alter ego, Americanus, attempt to justify British policy, for Galloway knew that this tactic would be far from conciliatory. In fact, he condemned Hillsborough's order to Massachusetts to rescind its circular letter. He argued only against immediate resistance, conceding that the Assembly would act when the time was ripe. Merchants and politicians should delay any resistance until September when the Assembly was to meet again; if the agents in Britain had not accomplished anything by that time, other action could be taken. He wanted no giving in to "ministerial mandates" but no "rash and premature" action; Galloway termed his way "moderation." [22]

L. Brunhouse, "The Effect of the Townshend Acts in Pennsylvania," *PMHB* 54 (1930) : 360–62.

20. *Pennsylvania Gazette*, May 12, June 2, July 21, 1768; [William Goddard?], *To the Public* (Philadelphia, 1768 [Evans no. 11018]).

21. *Pennsylvania Gazette*, July 28, 1768.

22. *Pennsylvania Chronicle*, supplement, July 25, 1768. David L. Jacobson, "The Puzzle of Pacificus," *Pennsylvania History* 31 (1964) : 406–18, straightens out the problem caused for historians because both Gallo-

Circumstances forced Galloway to give in to Dickinson and Thomson more than he had at first planned. Their mass meetings had much support; petitioning for repeal might easily become an election issue embarrassing to the Assembly party. The Speaker was perhaps most discouraged by the failure of the British government to act sensibly. The haughty Hillsborough circular letter, ordering colonial governors to prorogue or dissolve their assemblies if those bodies gave any attention to the Massachusetts circular letter, turned the Assembly party to a more anti-British tack. This attempt to interfere with its singular privilege of sitting on its own adjournments for extended periods enraged the House. When it met in September, it was anxious to petition king, Lords, and Commons; petitions were quickly drafted and brought in. Probably Galloway's influence kept these toned down. They complained about British denials of American constitutional rights and liberties but were couched in respectful and dutiful terms. Petitions of this nature, Galloway apparently believed, could do no harm to Pennsylvania's reputation in Britain and would satisfy the more anti-British elements in Pennsylvania. Moreover, the Speaker had already set in motion a plan to insure that his rivals would not benefit politically by his concessions.[23]

In the party newspaper, from mysterious origins, appeared extracts from a pamphlet, *An Address to the Committee of*

way's piece and *To the Public,* in n. 20 above, were signed "Pacificus." The authorship of the latter is attributed to Dickinson by the American Antiquarian Society in its Readex microcard edition. Jacobson attributes *To the Public* to Goddard. The writing seems to resemble Goddard's sarcastic style more closely than Dickinson's graceful one. Schlesinger, *Colonial Merchants,* pp. 116–17, credits Galloway with writing the pieces signed "A. B." in the *Chronicle,* July 18–25, and "A Chester County Farmer" in the *Gazette,* June 16, 1768. Galloway may have written the former, but its argument and tone is rather different from his other writings. He probably did not write the latter, which expresses more particular interests of a farmer.

23. *Pennsylvania Chronicle,* August 1–8, 1768, reports the instructions of Dickinson's and Thomson's mass meeting. Hillsborough's letter was printed in the *Gazette,* July 7 and July 14, 1768. *Votes,* 7 : 6271–77.

Correspondence in Barbadoes, written by Dickinson in 1766. This pamphlet was highly critical of the American agents in Britain, implying that Franklin, motivated by his corrupt nature and lust for office, had forged the chains of the Stamp Act, forcing Americans "with shackled hands *to drudge in the dark,* as well as we could, forgetting the *light* we had lost." [24] Dickinson certainly had nothing to do with publishing his pamphlet in the *Chronicle* at this juncture; the old charge about Franklin's complicity in the Stamp Act had hurt, not aided, the Proprietary party, and Franklin's arguments against the Townshend Acts were of use to the proponents of petitioning and nonimportation.

Most probably, Galloway had the *Address* printed as part of his devious strategy. For, a few weeks later, Dickinson's *Address* was attacked in the columns of the *Chronicle* by several pseudonymous contributors, all of whom pointed out Franklin's proven loyalty. The authors of these pieces, probably Galloway and William Franklin, naturally questioned the motives of anyone who would scurrilously attack Franklin's reputation and character. They laid bare Dickinson's designs, showing them to be as black as his unjust accusations against the Assembly party leader. According to the attacks on him in the *Chronicle,* the "Farmer" evidenced "Oliverian" tendencies and was attempting to incite riotous mobs so he could make himself dictator of America. The most mild accusation, that nearest the truth, charged Dickinson with using his pen to procure a seat in the Assembly.[25] Keeping up the fire for about a month, Galloway's party organ blasted Dickinson from

24. This piece was published in the *Chronicle,* June 27–July 4, 1768, with the headnote that "it may be proper at this time" to publish this earlier work of the Farmer. In the excerpt quoted, Dickinson satirized Franklin's letter to Thomson, July 11, 1765, *Franklin Papers,* 12 : 207–08, quoted above, p. 113.

25. *Pennsylvania Chronicle,* July 25–August 1, August 1–8, August 8–15, and August 15–22, 1768. Even though Goddard apparently opposed Galloway's views on resistance to the duties, he was still subject to the power of the party leaders and published their propaganda. This instance was the prime example of Galloway's use of the *Chronicle* to defame his opposition.

every possible side, in remarkable contrast to the high praise for the "Pennsylvania Farmer" that poured into the Philadelphia newspapers from other colonies.

Galloway had achieved one of the most cunning strategic moves of his career. By branding Dickinson as an iconoclast who had maliciously attempted to tear down the image of the great Franklin, whom all acknowledged a patriot, he showed his rival to be not identifiable with Franklin but a vicious schemer for power. Moreover, by identifying the "Farmer's Letters" with the more violent and partisan views that Dickinson had earlier expressed, Galloway suggested that the aim of the letters was to stir up riots. Because Dickinson had made rash and foolish statements against Franklin, the policies he advocated, especially nonimportation, were by implication rash and foolish. As he had done during the Stamp Act crisis, Galloway outmaneuvered his opponents by making them appear too radical for Pennsylvania. He also demonstrated that it was he, not Dickinson, who followed Franklin's lead; by sending the petitions to Britain, he showed that he was attempting to defend the rights of the colony in moderate and respectful ways, which was what Franklin and Pennsylvania desired.

The wisdom of Galloway's strategy was clear in the results of the election of 1768. *"No* Farmer *in the Assembly"* was the cry of the White Oaks.[26] The Assembly party again won a smashing victory. For the first time in his career, Galloway polled more votes than the Quaker stalwarts Richardson and Fox, and he led the ticket. Dickinson and his allies completely failed in employing the Townshend duties against Galloway's party. After the election, the Speaker could report quite proudly to his partner in London that although "great Pains have been taken in this City by some hot headed indiscreet Men, to raise a Spirit of Violence agt. the late Act of Parliament, . . . this Design was crushed in the Beginning by our Friends, so effectually, that, I think, we shall not have

26. Goddard, *The Partnership,* p. 18.

it soon renewed." [27] Until the results of the petitions were known there would be no more talk of resistance. Again, Galloway insured that, for the time being, Philadelphia would not imitate Boston. He thought he had done his duty by preserving both the peace of his province and the predominance of his party.

Franklin was moving too fast in Britain for Galloway to keep up in Pennsylvania, for by the last months of 1768 the agent began to assert the case for America in ways which undermined his partner's attempts to keep the colony loyal and inactive. Because it appeared that Parliament would not soon repeal the duties, Franklin's arguments in the British newspapers became more fervent. He tried to show that Britain would be greatly injured economically if Americans instituted widespread nonimportation; an American boycott would upset the favorable balance of trade that British merchants enjoyed. Franklin also advanced the sarcastic argument that Britain was on the way to a profitless war with America to force the colonies to import British goods.[28] His arguments had little impact, for the working alliance between agents and merchants had largely broken down after the failure to get the act of 1764 prohibiting legal tender repealed. The merchants feared a boycott much less in 1768 than in 1765, and they did not believe that all colonies would adopt nonimportation. Without much support in Britain for American appeals, colonial petitions stood little chance of acceptance

27. Galloway to Franklin, October 17, 1768, Franklin Papers, 2 : 143, APS.

28. Franklin claimed that Britain enjoyed a balance of trade advantage of about £2,000,000, which would be lost if the colonies adopted nonimportation. *London Chronicle*, November 3, December 6, 1768, reprinted in the *Pennsylvania Chronicle*, February 27–March 6, 1769. Another piece, in the London *Public Advertiser*, January 17, 1769, reprinted in *Franklin's Letters to the Press*, ed. Crane, no. 76, pp. 156–59, noted that an American war would cost Britain £108,500,000. Franklin contributed other pieces to the newspapers during this period, most of which restated his old arguments against unconstitutional taxation and faulty economic policy. See ibid., nos. 68–70, 77, pp. 134–41, 160–61.

by Parliament, which, after the summer of 1768, was determined not to give way to Bostonian lawlessness. One of Franklin's friends in the House of Commons attempted to introduce the Pennsylvania petition there, but a reading of the Declaratory Act prevented him from doing so. This decent and respectful petition, from which Galloway really expected results, got little further than did a strong remonstrance from the Virginia House of Burgesses, which no member of Parliament dared to introduce.[29]

Franklin's failures, from 1764 through 1768, to cause any shift in British policies by propaganda or by lobbying made him increasingly aware that American requests had little chance of getting a hearing. In Pennsylvania, where the society was small and relatively simple in structure and where the legislators were continually under the surveillance of the electorate, Franklin's organized attempts to publicize issues worked well at most times. In London, he believed he had little success in presenting the American case not because his methods were ill-conceived or unsuited, but because the political system was thoroughly corrupt. Parliamentary seats were bought and sold, much to Franklin's dismay and much in contrast to what he considered the honest and proper methods of electioneering in Pennsylvania. Franklin saw these corrupt practices as the direct result of the lack of a large electorate and the direct cause of misgovernment. "They are so hardened in this practice that they are very little ashamed of it," Franklin observed righteously to Galloway, conveniently for-

29. The petition to the king was presented, that to the Lords was not because no Lord would take it in. Franklin to Galloway, January 9, 1769, *Autobiographical Writings*, ed. Van Doren, pp. 187–88; *Pennsylvania Chronicle*, May 15–22, 1769. In February 1769 the agents seeking repeal selected Franklin to draw up a petition to Parliament that would avoid alienating that body by not mentioning the claim to rights of the colonies. But it was not presented because the agents also feared that to avoid mentioning the claim to rights would imply that they were relinquishing that claim. Franklin to Galloway, March 9, 1769, Clements Library, University of Michigan. Kammen, *Rope of Sand*, pp. 230–33, discusses how the refusal to hear petitions was a major difficulty for the agents.

getting that the partners had purchased votes for their party with treats for thirsty Germans.[30] Franklin fancied himself a Puritan in Babylon, vainly trying to get British officials and merchants to heed his prophecy while they blindly and corruptly led the empire to damnation.

Arguments had failed, petitions had failed, cooperation with the merchants had failed; economic pressure was the only weapon of proven previous success. By January 1769 Franklin had shifted his efforts, in the main, from persuading Britain to encouraging American resistance. He fully supported nonimportation as advocated by Dickinson and as established in Boston and New York. His earlier suggestion, nonconsumption, he now realized was not practical because it could be too easily ignored or violated, while a merchants' boycott would be more complete and put real strain on British merchants and manufacturers. To Galloway he explained the strategy thusly: "The House will probably sit till June or perhaps July, and it is thought here, that if News can come of all the Colonies having join'd in the Determination to buy no more British Goods, the Acts must be repealed before they rise." [31] Merchants would demand en masse that Parliament relieve their distress. The unemployed might riot, Franklin thought, if the boycott were not broken by repeal. The agent well knew that nonimportation was an extreme measure that might seriously injure his old allies, the Philadelphia merchants. Yet he had been amazingly patient before recommending drastic action; he had tried everything else to no avail. Now he put his trust in the determination of the American merchants to make Britain surrender.

Nonimportation was the Rubicon Galloway hesitated to cross. One can fairly accurately infer how he viewed this means of resistance. It would mean hardship and possible disaster for Pennsylvania's commerce. It would mean giving in to Dickinson. It might mean mob violence to enforce the boy-

30. Franklin to Galloway, February 17, 1768, *Writings,* ed. Smyth, 5 : 100.
31. Franklin to Galloway, January 29, 1769, Clements Library, University of Michigan.

cott. It would mean that America was declaring herself economically independent of British manufactures. Might not
greater economic independence, and even political independence, follow? Britain might take harsh reprisals. Galloway had, during the Stamp Act crisis, accepted nonimportation to get the terrible tax repealed. But duties on commerce,
he evidently thought, did not demand an opposition so extreme and so fraught with danger. Franklin apparently was
well aware of his old partner's reluctance to have Pennsylvania
adopt nonimportation, for he tried to reassure him of its
necessity. "Possibly they [Britain] may think of some equal
Means of hurting us; but something must be try'd and some
Risque run, rather than sit down quietly under a Claim of
Parliament to the Right of disposing of our Properties without our Consent." [32]

The essential difference between the partners was now
uncovered and recognized by both of them. Franklin was
determined to chance all the harmful effects of nonimportation because it had worked previously and because there
seemed to be no other way to get the duties repealed. Galloway
ignored these very powerful arguments, apparently because
the likely baneful effects of nonimportation outweighed, in
his mind, the need to establish American rights. In 1765 he
had seen a mob come close to "disposing of our Properties
without our Consent," and he did not wish to incur this
risk again. During the Stamp Act crisis, Franklin and Galloway had split on the question of American rights; Franklin
asserted them as primary and Galloway subordinated them to
imperial considerations. Then, however, they had easily disregarded these theoretical differences as irrelevant to their
practical partnership. In 1769, when they parted on the
question of the means by which to establish American rights,
the partners could not ignore their disagreement as they
had in the past. The issue of nonimportation had dealt the
long alliance between the two men its most disruptive blow.

Franklin, Dickinson, and the Pennsylvanians who had

32. Ibid.

grown weary of procrastination won. The Philadelphia merchants, encouraged by the local agitators and by Franklin,
adopted nonimportation on February 6, 1769, because Parliament had given no indication that it would repeal the duties.[33]
Galloway probably was distressed despite Franklin's justification of the action. Nonimportation in Philadelphia was the
worst in a series of disappointments for him. The failure of
the campaign to repeal the legal tender prohibition, the
failure of the change of government effort, and now the
institution of firm resistance against British policy all were
adverse to the program of loyalty and the principle of moderate, nonviolent resistance that he had espoused. Indeed,
Galloway's merchant friends may have been led to support of
nonimportation because there was no longer any rationale
for keeping Pennsylvania loyal and dutiful. But the Speaker
and party leader apparently did not change much. His in-
grained habits—seeking royal government, upholding the
principles of the British Constitution, abhorring measures
which might lead to violence and social disruption—prevented
him from taking an openly anti-British stance.[34]

Whatever Galloway's depth of feeling, he could not

33. The merchants agreed on this date to cease importing all goods,
except medical supplies and other critical items, from Britain by April 1
if no encouraging reports were received before that date. See Arthur L.
Jensen, *The Maritime Commerce of Colonial Philadelphia* (Madison,
1963), p. 179; and Schlesinger, *Colonial Merchants*, pp. 129–30.

34. Hutson, "Campaign, Part II," pp. 46–48, argues that the rejection
of the petition for the change of government by Hillsborough in August
1768 demoralized the Assembly party, made it angry with the ministry,
left its leaders passive toward nonimportation, and led it to abandon
leadership of the lower-class White Oak supporters to Dickinson and
Thomson. The party was certainly angry with the ministry because of
Hillsborough's rejection and his circular letter. But the failure of the
petitions against the duties and the problem of the effects of nonimportation seem to have been more important factors in the stance of Galloway and his colleagues at this time. The imperial issues were so much
more significant than the local issues that the party would have reacted
in pretty much the same way whether the change of government was alive
or dead.

openly oppose Franklin's support for nonimportation. He agreed with both Franklin and Dickinson that the duties were bad policy; but he had no alternative, acceptable suggestion for opposing that policy. Franklin was still the foundation stone of the Assembly party. To break with him was to invite worse trouble. Galloway apparently realized that if he kept quiet about nonimportation he would be regarded by the Philadelphia electorate as still in the Franklin camp and fundamentally a pro-American patriot. Perhaps to get further away from bothersome imperial affairs Galloway became more involved in local matters. During 1769 and the first half of 1770 he gave most of his attention to quarreling with Governor Penn over patronage and to reestablishing the loan office to issue more paper money.[35] The renewal of old battles with the proprietors was much more to Galloway's liking than was dealing with imperial controversies. He never lacked courage; rather, Galloway was a discreet sidestepper who avoided becoming entangled in matters distasteful to him. Fortunately, until mid-1770 Philadelphia under nonimportation was relatively peaceful, making it easier for the politician to keep out of any controversy.

Shifting the attention of the Assembly did not bolster Galloway's political position, nor did it have any effect on the observance of nonimportation. Smuggling of foreign goods, mob action against those who informed on smuggling merchants, threats against slacking merchants tempted to cheat on the agreement, and other anti-British behavior bordering on violence and mob control must have rankled the man who believed in law and order under the British system.[36] The political temper reverted to what it had been during the Stamp Act crisis. Outrageous mob violence was not permitted by the inhabitants, but resistance to the duties was firmly maintained. As anti-British sentiment grew, Galloway's popularity sank. An unfortunate case of sunstroke he suffered while

35. *Votes*, 7 : 6321–22, 6376–93.
36. Brunhouse, "Townshend Acts in Pennsylvania," pp. 366–68; *Pennsylvania Gazette*, October 12, 1769.

working in his father-in-law's fields weakened his hold on provincial politics still further.[37] In June 1769 he was forced to retire temporarily from the Assembly and consequently was unable to pursue his controversies with Governor Penn. His pet loan office bill failed of admission during his inactivity. After this time, illness continued to plague Galloway. By 1775 weak health may have figured largely in his serious political difficulties. As a result of his inactivity and his coolness toward nonimportation, he fell from the top position on the ticket to seventh place in the election of 1769, losing ground to those of his own party who were more outspokenly in favor of nonimportation.[38]

Galloway had indeed misjudged how he should act in regard to the Townshend duties. He could not see the distinction that Dickinson clearly outlined in his "Farmer's Letters" and that Franklin perceived—the distinction between firm resistance and mob violence. By remaining in the background while nonimportation ran its course, he believed he would be protected from the bad political consequences of his earlier opposition to resistance. By keeping silent he preserved for the time being his hold and that of his party on the Assembly.

In contrast to Galloway's reluctance to acknowledge that the Townshend Acts and nonimportation existed, Franklin maintained a keen interest in imperial developments after early 1769. After the boycott in Philadelphia had been in operation some four or five months, he began to view nonimportation as an end in itself, not merely as a weapon by which the colonists could win their rights. Perhaps it was nonimportation's failure to achieve immediate relief that led Franklin to point out its other virtues. If the duties were not repealed for some time, he argued, the colonists would be less dependent on British luxuries, the unfavorable balance of trade would vanish, and America would become wealthier by producing domestically what she needed.

37. Cadwalader Evans to Franklin, June 11, 1769, Franklin Papers, 2 : 180, APS.

38. *Votes,* 7 : 6386–87, 6447.

Franklin wrote to the merchants of Philadelphia a widely publicized letter to add his influence to maintaining the non-importation agreement.

> And in the mean time, the country will be enrich'd by its industry and frugality, those virtues will become habitual, farms will be more improved, better stock'd, and render'd more productive by the money that used to be spent in superfluities; our artificers of every kind will be enabled to carry on their business to more advantage; gold and silver will become plenty among us, and trade will revive after things shall be well settled, and become better and safer than it lately has been; for an industrious frugal people are best able to buy, and pay for what they purchase.[39]

Frugality, meaning nonconsumption of British superfluities, and industry, meaning expansion of domestic production as a substitute for importation, became Franklin's watchwords; he repeated them in nearly every letter he wrote in reference to nonimportation. The old Poor Richard, the self-reliant Franklin, reappearing first when the quest for an American legal tender had been defeated, continued to preach economic morality to America to justify and encourage resistance to Britain. Poor Richard seemed unconcerned that frugality and industry might lead Americans toward economic, and even political, independence from Britain. Franklin's advocacy of these ideas exemplifies his ability to adjust his position to the situation at hand and to forge into the forefront in defending American rights after previously hanging back at the rear.

Franklin maintained his interest in Galloway's struggles with Governor Penn over purely Pennsylvanian matters, but he was now much more interested in Pennsylvania as part of the united American front.[40] He saw that which Galloway

39. Franklin, *Letters, to the Merchants' Committee of Philadelphia, Submitted to the Consideration of the Public* (Philadelphia, 1769 [Evans no. 11658]).

40. Franklin's continuing interest in Pennsylvania politics during the nonimportation period is noted in letters to Galloway of January 11,

chose to ignore: that the nonimportation agreements adopted by the various colonies gave them all common cause and required them to remain united in order to make American resistance effective. Franklin identified himself with the growing intercolonial movement and considered himself in this struggle as not primarily a Pennsylvanian but an American. Other colonies reciprocated his attention; they viewed his spirited defenses of American rights as important, albeit unsuccessful, efforts in their behalf. Georgia recognized Franklin's abilities and labors by appointing him agent in 1768, and New Jersey followed in 1769.[41] The Reverend Samuel Cooper and James Bowdoin, with whom Franklin had long corresponded concerning scientific matters, began in 1769 to write him about the difficulties of Boston and of Massachusetts, which stood in the forefront of the resistance against Britain. In December 1769 the merchants of Boston wrote to add their encouragement to Franklin's efforts.[42] The agent, exploiting his growing importance and cognizant of rising American dependence on him, increased his endeavors to get the duties repealed. In early 1770 he mounted another concentrated effort in the British newspapers, as usual overstating the plight of the colonists in the face of parliamentary oppression. He was little heeded.[43] He exhorted his American

1770, Clements Library, University of Michigan; June 11, 1770, *Autobiographical Writings,* ed. Van Doren, pp. 193–95; June 26, 1770, Yale University Library.

41. Franklin never understood why Georgia appointed him, as he knew no one in that colony. Franklin to William Franklin, July 2, 1768, *Writings,* ed. Smyth, 5 : 146–47. William Franklin helped manage the New Jersey appointment, principally to get a paper money act by the Board of Trade. *New Jersey Archives,* 1st ser., *Documents Relating to the Colonial History of the State of New Jersey,* 10 (Newark, 1886) : 135–39 (hereafter cited as *N.J.A.*).

42. In 1769 Franklin exchanged three letters with Cooper and one with Bowdoin. The letter of the Boston merchants of December 29, 1769, is in Franklin Papers, 2 : 210, APS.

43. Franklin's major press contribution was "The Colonists' Advocate," which appeared in eleven numbers in the London *Public Advertiser,* January 4–March 2, 1770. *Franklin's Letters to the Press,* ed. Crane,

correspondents to "persevere in our schemes of frugality and industry." [44] They listened. Franklin did everything that could be expected of a patriot leader in Britain, and American admiration of him grew; Galloway did little that could be expected of a patriot leader in America, and Pennsylvania's admiration of him waned.

The widening split over policy between Franklin and Galloway did not discourage either man from continuing the long partnership. The two close friends still believed that they had to rely chiefly on each other. Galloway revealed that he needed Franklin desperately when he used Franklin's patriotic, anti-British position as a cover for the Assembly party and when he declined to oppose nonimportation vocally and openly. Galloway could only hold fast to the gunwales, hoping that Franklin would not rock the boat so violently that they would both fall overboard. By 1770 Franklin probably did not need Galloway's support. He had depended on him through the Stamp Act crisis and the campaign for royal government, but now his own popularity and position were most likely secured against any circumstances. Yet there was no one else in Pennsylvania whom Franklin felt he could trust as much as he trusted Galloway—not his old friend Thomson and certainly not Dickinson; only his son over in Burlington was equally in Franklin's confidence. If Galloway and his party were driven from power, it would be unlikely that Franklin would be recalled, but he would certainly feel himself less secure. Dickinson was not reconciled to Franklin; there was no communication between them. The proprietary group had too many old scores to settle with the Assembly party leaders to forgive Franklin. Galloway, Franklin thought, would be more

---

maintains from internal evidence that Franklin was the author of this series. It restates many of the arguments Franklin used against taxation without representation and against duties on colonial imports. Numbers 6 and 7, in ibid., no. 90, pp. 183–86 and no. 92, pp. 192–94, are most representative.

44. Franklin to James Bowdoin, July 13, 1769, *Writings*, ed. Smyth, 5 : 222.

reliable than anyone else in continuing to maintain his position in Britain and his prestige in Pennsylvania.

The friendship between the partners, which had grown out of their political partnership, was now more vital than their political cooperation. Franklin expressed great concern for the deviant course Galloway appeared to be taking. He invited his young partner to forsake the political wars for a time and come to Britain for a visit.[45] The change of scene might help Galloway recover his old fiery spirit, dampened by illness and adversity. Franklin very likely thought that if Galloway could see British politics first hand he would alter his views and recognize the need for strong resistance to parliamentary encroachments, which might do wonders for his political as well as his physical health. Because Franklin had arrived at his support for nonimportation partly as a result of his experiences in Britain, Galloway also might realize the need for drastic measures and the justice of the American cause if he were made aware how decadent Britain was in contrast to America. Unfortunately, Galloway never followed his partner's prescription.

The partnership was no longer either an offensive weapon against the proprietors or a defensive force against the home government. By 1770 it was dedicated chiefly to preserving the political positions of each partner. Yet the friendship between the two men had been too long and too close to permit a permanent breach to remain between them. As during the Stamp Act crisis, both men looked forward to the passing of this time of troubles; and both were fairly confident that all differences between themselves, and between Britain and America, would eventually evaporate and that their political cooperation could be revived.

45. Franklin to Cadwalader Evans, September 7, 1769, ibid., 5 : 226–27.

8   Facing in Opposite Directions

The repeal in March 1770 of all Townshend duties but one opened the possibilities that Anglo-American relations would resume a more benign course and that Franklin and Galloway could reconcile their differences. Now that Parliament had once again admitted its mistake, the partners were in a position to forget their disagreement on nonimportation. Franklin, and all America, could count the tea tax not worth the continuation of the boycott, thus adopting Galloway's expedient of backing out of imperial controversies. Yet the auspicious partial retreat of Parliament increased Franklin's determination to get Britain to recognize American rights fully—and turned Pennsylvania politics on a course which meant disaster for Galloway.

Franklin and the other colonial agents, together with some merchants, had, by their petitions, helped convince the ministry that the duties were uncommercial. Repeal indicated to Franklin that the British government had weakened; now America should press harder for a complete repudiation by Parliament of its assumed authority to tax the colonies. The remaining tea duty was not in his view a necessary concession to Parliament; rather, it was an aggravating declaration that Parliament was determined to exert its authority over America. The principle of the primacy of the colonial legislature in colonial affairs was still challenged. Unlike the situation in 1766, when Americans gratefully accepted repeal of the Stamp Act and ignored the Declaratory Act, Franklin refused to abandon the fight for his principles. He attempted to get British merchants to work for the repeal of the remaining duty. He encouraged the retention of nonimportation agreements in the colonies, for he believed it was the loss to Britain of some £700,000 in American trade during 1769 that had convinced Parliament that the duties were indeed uncommercial and should be at least partially repealed.[1] In his letters to American friends, especially to Charles Thomson, a leader of the Philadelphia boycott, he expressed confidence that America had Parliament in full retreat and that the colonists would establish their right to be free from parliamentary taxation if they held firm.[2]

Franklin was very influential in holding the colonial merchants to their agreements after the partial repeal. His faith in the effectiveness of nonimportation probably had much justification, for the ministry was sufficiently alarmed by this technique of American resistance to consider a bill punishing merchants who participated in nonimportation agreements. But Franklin had not fathomed that partial repeal was a stratagem of Lord North, the prime minister. North planned to break American resistance by giving way in part, and retaining the tea duty as an example of parliamentary authority. In continuing to advocate nonimportation Franklin both underestimated the resolve of the ministry and overestimated the resolve of his countrymen.[3]

1. Sosin, *Agents and Merchants,* pp. 123–27; Kammen, *Rope of Sand,* pp. 199–200. Franklin and other agents, according to Sosin, pp. 122–23, desired to make it appear that the British merchants, not the colonials, were leading the struggle for total repeal. Gipson, *Coming of the Revolution,* p. 197, and Jensen, *Founding,* pp. 354–64, explain the effects of the boycott. Schlesinger, *Colonial Merchants,* pp. 182, 190, 193, claims that nonimportation caused losses to British trade of over £200,000 in New England, over £400,000 in New York, and over £300,000 in Philadelphia by 1770. Both Schlesinger and Jensen, *Maritime Commerce,* pp. 184–85, conclude that the Philadelphia agreement was very effective.

2. Franklin to "An Unknown Correspondent," March 18, 1770, *Writings,* ed. Smyth, 5 : 253–54. The recipient, Charles Thomson, is identified by Crane in *Franklin's Letters to the Press,* ed. Crane, no. 99, pp. 209–12. Crane argues that Franklin's espousal of continued nonimportation marks a significant change in his political alignment. See also Franklin to Galloway, June 11, 1770, *Autobiographical Writings,* ed. Van Doren, p. 193.

3. The measure to punish boycotting merchants was never brought up

Galloway continued neutral and equivocal on nonimportation, as he had been since its institution. After repeal he did not publicly support either a continuation of nonimportation or an abandonment of the agreement. Because Hillsborough's anti-Americanism rankled him and perhaps because Franklin's predictions had thus far turned out to be correct, he was reconciled to the continuation of nonimportation. Privately, he termed nonimportation "the Cause of Liberty" and expressed to Franklin the hope that the ministry would see the error of its policy: "The M——y are much mistaken in imagining that there ever will be an Union either of affections or Interest betw. G. Britain and America untill Justice is done to the latter and there is a full Restoration of its Liberties." [4] But Galloway did not transform his private sentiments into action; he did not work in Philadelphia for a continuation of the agreement. His health perhaps limited his activity, and the city and his party were dividing on the question of nonimportation.

The dry goods merchants, many of them staunch supporters of the Assembly party, demanded an end to nonimportation almost immediately upon repeal of the duties. As traders primarily with Britain, who had had little to trade, they believed that they had sacrificed enough. Repeal had come in the main, so normal trade should be resumed, they argued.

---

partly because Franklin strongly opposed it. Franklin to Galloway, June 11, 1770, *Autobiographical Writings*, ed. Van Doren, p. 193. Miller, *Origins of the American Revolution*, pp. 279–81, discusses North's strategy in repealing all duties except that on tea. See also Jensen, *Founding*, pp. 325–26, 329. Sosin, *Agents and Merchants*, pp. 122–23, argues that Franklin's appeals to his Pennsylvania correspondents, Thomson and Galloway, to continue nonimportation were grandstand plays designed for the Pennsylvania political situation. This view hardly explains why Franklin also advised his Massachusetts correspondents to hold to the agreement or why he publicized his stand in Britain. See "On Partial Repeal," London *Gazetteer*, February 7, 1770, reprinted in *Franklin's Letters to the Press*, ed. Crane, no. 94, pp. 197–200. Franklin may have been naive concerning nonimportation—or he may not have been, for his theory was not tested—but he was not hypocritical in his advice to his American friends.

4. Galloway to Franklin, June 21, 1770, Franklin Papers, 3 : 18, APS.

The mechanics—those craftsmen who during the boycott had profited from increased demands for their products—and merchants who did not trade primarily with Britain, or who thought that the principle involved was more important than their economic interest, adopted Franklin's view that the agreement should be continued by all colonies until complete repeal was forced on Parliament.[5] Because both sides in this controversy, merchants and mechanics, were Assembly party supporters, Galloway feared giving offense to either group by taking a stand, and consequently he kept quiet. He predicted to Franklin that the merchants would be forced by economic pressures to break the agreement, perhaps hoping Franklin could offer more arguments for holding out. But he apparently took no active part in the discussions and meetings in Philadelphia in which both sides debated the issues.[6]

After the New York merchants broke their agreement in July 1770, the Philadelphia merchants became more anxious to break theirs. The threat of competition from New York and the prospect of economic ruin faced them; against these considerations the arguments of Dickinson, Thomson, and their mechanic supporters were very weak. In the newspapers and in more public meetings, advocates of American rights clashed with merchants defending their pocketbooks—and lost; the more anti-British element managed to hold off repudiation of the nonimportation agreement only until September 20, 1770, when the merchants voted to apply nonimportation to tea alone.[7] Galloway played little part in killing the

5. The *Pennsylvania Gazette* reported, January 25, 1770, that suspicions that the dry goods merchants were considering reneging on the agreement were unfounded. A meeting on May 23, reported in ibid., May 24, 1770, condemned Newport for breaking the agreement, showing that nonimportation still had strong support in Philadelphia.

6. Franklin to Galloway, June 26, 1770, Yale University Library. Franklin advised the merchants to alter the agreement to make it more uniform with those of other colonies and less hampering, but he remained opposed to breaking it.

7. *To the Public*, October 3, 1770 (Philadelphia, 1770 [Evans no. 11823]). The merchants claimed that they could no longer endure the competition from New York. The more anti-British committee on nonimportation

agreement. He presumably hoped that now imperial affairs would return to normal, that no residue of resentment would linger against the merchants for breaking the agreement, and that the controversy would do no harm to his political position.

The anti-British Philadelphians, especially the mechanics, were irate; they believed that giving up the boycott was in effect resigning to the claim of Parliament to tax America. That some merchants could sway the leaders of the colony and the general public to permit their breaking of the agreement especially angered and dismayed them. Certain merchants, they thought, had too much power. Merchants like Joseph Richardson, Joseph Fox, Abel James, and Thomas Wharton led the Assembly party, together with Galloway planned the ticket and the election strategy, and reaped the largest rewards. White Oaks and mechanics in general were ignored in the process of making party decisions, but courted when Galloway needed the rough work done at election time. The Speaker did not have the personality to charm the mechanics and small merchants as did their idol and ideal, Franklin, who had risen from lowly mechanic status himself.[8] Galloway could no longer induce them to view him as Franklin's alter ego in politics; while Franklin encouraged continued nonimportation from Britain, Galloway remained neutral in Philadelphia, careful not to alienate his merchant allies. The breaking of the agreement constituted final proof to the me-

---

was willing to modify the agreement to allow more imports, but it lost to the merchants. *Pennsylvania Gazette,* October 4, 1770. Schlesinger, *Colonial Merchants,* p. 231.

8. Before 1756, the major determinant of self-conscious group identification in Pennsylvania politics had been religion. Franklin and Galloway had to some extent broken this down by relying on Quakers, Anglicans, some Presbyterians, and Germans for political support. Of course, religious distinctions had not completely disappeared, as the attacks by propagandists on religious groups in 1764–66 testify. Imperial issues did the most to eliminate much of the remaining relationship between religion and politics in Pennsylvania and to substitute the anti-British issue as a major determinant.

chanics that the governing class of Pennsylvania and the rich of Philadelphia were antagonistic to the interests of the less wealthy and middling orders. Now the White Oaks and other mechanics realized that economic inferiority meant political subordination to the wealthy, that they were not equal within the Assembly party but were treated as an inferior group that should not have decision-making power. They vowed revenge on the leaders of the party that no longer represented their interests.

On September 27, 1770, four days before the election, "A Brother Chip," in a letter to the *Gazette,* questioned the ability of the party leaders and the method of establishing a ticket. Although mechanics, like Chip, possessed the right to vote, "a certain Company of leading Men [would] nominate Persons, and settle the Ticket, . . . without ever permitting the affirmative or negative Voice of a Mechanic to interfere. . . . Have we not an equal Right of electing, or being elected?" Chip inquired. "I think it absolutely necessary that one or two Mechanics be elected to represent so large a Body of the Inhabitants." [9] The mechanics had now identified themselves as a political group with special interests different from those of the assemblymen who were chosen for "Greatness and Opulence." They would make certain their voice would be heeded.

The dissatisfaction of the mechanics with the Assembly party ticket of wealthy merchants was not at first directed primarily at Galloway. The main target was Joseph Richardson, opulent Quaker merchant who had opposed continuing the nonimportation agreement.[10] Yet, a strange combination of circumstances entangled Galloway in this revolt and cost him his political support in Philadelphia.

The well-laid scheme of Speaker Galloway, Governor Franklin, and merchant Thomas Wharton—to employ the *Chronicle* to enhance the reputation of Benjamin Franklin and the Assembly party—exploded in their faces. Printer Goddard from

9. *Pennsylvania Gazette,* September 27, 1770.
10. Ibid.

the first believed that his should be a free press, open to all sides, but Galloway, of course, was determined to use it to blast Dickinson and other political opponents. When Goddard published the "Farmer's Letters" and other writings of the Farmer, which were implicitly critical of the Assembly's supine stand during the Townshend Acts crisis, the silent partners in the newspaper took him severely to task for giving aid to the enemy. Despite the fact that Goddard had always provided the Assembly party with the most space and had immeasurably helped Galloway defeat Dickinson in 1768, the Speaker and Wharton in 1769 refused to support their printer partner any longer. The silent partners defaulted on their share of the debts of the partnership and attempted to oust Goddard by making him take Benjamin Towne, his journeyman, as a partner. Goddard fought back, forcing Towne out and retaining control of his press. He vowed revenge on Galloway and Wharton for their betrayal of him; he prepared an exposé of the "corrupt junto" that had at first seduced his press and then deserted him. This denunciation, entitled *The Partnership: or the History of the Rise and Progress of the Pennsylvania Chronicle,* appeared the second week of September 1770, just at the time the controversy over nonimportation was inciting the mechanics against the merchants, and only a fortnight before the election.[11]

Purporting to trace the history of the *Chronicle* from the time Goddard was installed in Philadelphia, *The Partnership* was in reality a scathing attack on Galloway and Wharton. Goddard first criticized Galloway's lack of loyalty to the American cause, an issue that was politically crucial during the merchant-mechanic debate. Galloway, Goddard claimed, was enraged at the printing of the "Farmer's Letters." He reportedly stamped and stormed, ridiculed Goddard's notions of the rights of mankind, and called him a "damned republican." [12] Goddard's picture of Galloway's actions was probably

11. Miner, *Goddard*, pp. 87–98. Arthur M. Schlesinger, *Prelude to Independence: The Newspaper War on Britain, 1764–1776* (New York, 1958), pp. 120–22.

12. Goddard, *The Partnership*, p. 16.

fairly accurate, for the Speaker disliked Dickinson enough to throw a temper tantrum about the publication of his writings. Why was Galloway so angry, Goddard inquired? Because Galloway was Americanus, alleged friend of the Stamp Act and enemy of America. Goddard resurrected the old charges of the 1765–66 political campaigns—charges that Galloway and his friend Hughes had advocated the Stamp Act.

A second damning allegation by the printer concerned Galloway's prejudice against Germans. When the politician promised the colony's printing business to Goddard in 1766, the printer demurred until more equipment had arrived. Galloway insisted that Goddard commence the government printing that October. According to Goddard, he would not let the other English printers have it. Nor could he give it to and then take it from Heinrich Miller, a German printer, else he would have all the "damn'd Dutchmen upon my back." [13] All these accusations concerned events of several years before, were based on slender evidence, and did not reflect Galloway's present desire, as expressed to Franklin, that there should be a "full Restoration of [American] Liberties." Goddard, rather than displaying patriotism, showed chiefly a vindictive desire to ruin Galloway politically by coupling the Speaker's past actions with the then current dispute over nonimportation.

In 1766 Galloway triumphed over the Proprietary party even though it had accused him of favoring the Stamp Act. Goddard's blast, four years later, appears to have been just as petty and less threatening. Ordinarily, Galloway could have shrugged off these accusations, but September 1770 was an evil time for him to have his patriotism questioned and his role as Americanus reviewed. He had created no local issue which would overshadow the controversy surrounding the breaking of the agreement, so he could not turn the thoughts of the electorate away from imperial affairs. The mechanics were induced by *The Partnership* to believe that the leaders of the Assembly party had been betraying their interests all

13. Ibid., pp. 11, 65–72. Wharton seems to have been treated more harshly by Goddard than was Galloway.

along. The Germans, as well, were apparently reawakened.
They had not entirely lost their sensitivity to the insults of
the Franklin-Galloway group. Grievances against the Speaker
were summed up poetically by "A German Freeholder":

> Unjustly "damn'd" by him, who'd arrogate
> To his Great Self Knowledge of future Fate,
> Who to his Footstool would have People come,
> And act the Farce that Peter acts at—Rome,
> Make the deluded vulgar bow the knee
> To his supreme——infallibility.[14]

Philadelphia was tired of its "pope," who ruled the Assembly
and the party autocratically and had no thought for the aspirations of social orders lower than his own. No longer would
the White Oaks, other mechanics, small merchants, and Germans pay him homage.

A few days before the election, when Chip's letter was
printed in the *Gazette* and Goddard's recriminations had
widely circulated, the storm broke. The White Oaks and other
mechanics decided to desert Galloway, the rich merchants, and
the Old Ticket that they had so long supported.[15] Galloway saw his party dissolve in the acid of Goddard's invective,
the reaction accelerated by the catalyst of the nonimportation
controversy. The Assembly party, which Franklin had begun
and which Galloway had nurtured so carefully, was no more
in Philadelphia. Writing to Franklin about this catastrophe,
Galloway blamed Goddard and indicated his resolution to
stick it out. "So much [abuse and calumny] have fallen to
my Share, Since your Departure, that was it not for my Connections in Politics, Nothing woud induce me to Serve ye
Public." [16] He sensed immediately that he had no chance for
reelection from Philadelphia County, but his reluctance to

14. *A German Freeholder, to his Countrymen,* September 22, 1770 (Philadelphia, 1770 [Evans no. 11665]).
15. Galloway to Franklin, September 27, 1770, Franklin Papers, 3 : 28,
APS.
16. Ibid.

run from a fight, to abandon Franklin and his friends, and
his desire to continue to be politically prominent made him
determined to retain his Assembly seat and his Speaker's chair
by any means. The death of his father-in-law in March 1770
gave Galloway an opportunity to keep his office. Lawrence
Growden left to the Galloways a handsome inheritance, including Trevose, the family home in Bucks County. The politician thus received property and timely political influence
far from the madding Philadelphia crowd. Therefore, shortly
before the election, Galloway left his fine house at Sixth and
Market Streets in Philadelphia to campaign among the
bumpkins of Bucks County. Goddard rejoiced at and ridiculed
his flight, claiming that Galloway was admitting that the defection of the White Oaks had finished him in Philadelphia
when he stated that he would get into the Assembly via a
"back Door." [17]

Bucks County offered Galloway a quiet refuge from the
turmoil into which Philadelphia politics was now thrown.
It was a backwater as well as a back door—the most overrepresented county and a Quaker stronghold whose assemblymen had generally followed Galloway's lead in the House.
Growden had been influential in county politics, although
he was a proprietary officeholder, and Galloway inherited this
influence as well as the estate.[18] It was not, however, so easy
for the refugee to wiggle onto the county ticket only a few
days before the election. The nominees had already been
picked, and at first none wanted to defer to the outsider.
Finally, on election day, one of the Old Ticket candidates
declined, undoubtedly induced somehow by Galloway to do
so. Meanwhile, Galloway's friends busied themselves writing
up tickets with his name on them and distributing them to
voters. Reportedly, German voters demanded that the name of

17. *Pennsylvania Chronicle*, September 24–October 1, 1770.

18. Growden died March 29, 1770, and was buried in a Friends' burial
ground. *Pennsylvania Gazette*, April 12, 1770. The combination of Quaker
and proprietary officeholder was unusual; Growden was not a very active
supporter of the Penns.

him who had damned them be struck from their tickets; but, since many of them could not read English, they were tricked into voting for Galloway. Some voters present at the election site in Newtown were heard to say, *"If Galloway was voted in, they would believe and declare he was crammed down their throats against their wills."* [19] The county swallowed the immigrant but almost choked; he was eighth in the race for eight seats.[20]

In an era when elections were frequently manipulated, Galloway, master of the political craft, would not be outdone. But the defection of his Philadelphia supporters and his forced political exile made a great difference in the kind of campaign Galloway now conducted. He and Franklin had fought hard but reasonably honest and fair electoral battles, and they had depended on a free choice of the electorate for their support. After 1770 Galloway was no more than a rotten borough member of the Assembly. Unable to win an honest election in a more sophisticated urban community, he had had to flee to a rural area where he could manipulate voters more easily. He kept the Speaker's chair but lost much respect throughout the province.

Philadelphia experienced a political revolution in 1770. Some of those elected from the city and county were long-time Galloway supporters, but the mechanics and small merchants made certain that all their representatives, including Galloway's allies, were suitably anti-British—even if they were associated with the "corrupt junto" of rich merchants and crafty politicians. Dickinson was elected for the first time in six years. After 1770 the machinery by which the Old Ticket had rolled over the opposition in previous elections remained

---

19. "A Bucks County Man" [pseudonym for either Goddard or William Hicks], *A True and Faithful Narrative of the Modes and Measures pursued at the Anniversary Election, for Representatives, of the Freemen of the Province of Pennsylvania, held at Newtown, in and for the County of Bucks, on Monday the first Day of October, Anno Domini 1770* (Philadelphia: William Goddard, 1771 [Evans no. 12253]), p. 5.

20. *Votes*, 7 : 6582.

broken beyond repair. The White Oaks did not attach themselves to any new politician or political organization. Dickinson and Thomson had no success in building up an organization comparable to Galloway's old one, as evidenced by the fact that they were not always elected to the Assembly after 1770. The word "party" ceased to have any real application in Philadelphia for six years.

After 1770 various groups banded together to put up candidates, but these groups were not parties with the organization or election machinery of the sort the Assembly party had once possessed. A "Patriotic Society" was formed by the mechanics in 1772, which claimed as its main objective the ouster of the old "corrupt Junto," meaning Galloway and his associates, from the Assembly.[21] In the election of that year, this society aided in the defeat of Abel James and Joseph Fox, who apparently were thought too pro-British, but it attempted no reorganization of Philadelphia politics and apparently became inactive in 1773. Consequently, in the period 1770–74 Galloway's opponents in Philadelphia were unsuccessful in gaining control of the Assembly and instituting a more anti-British policy. The Speaker, with support from most of the Assembly, controlled the House without much regard for politics in Philadelphia. The city and county remained in impotent political anarchy. Not until 1776, when adept politicians who were also patriots and democrats rebuilt the old organization and appealed to the mechanics and lower classes even more effectively than had Franklin and Galloway before 1770, did Pennsylvania politics regain its vitality and at the same time further the objectives of the revolution.[22]

Goddard stood guard on the road from Bucks County to Philadelphia, blocking Galloway's return permanently. The

21. *Pennsylvania Gazette*, August 19, 1772. *Fellow Citizens and Countrymen*, October 1, 1772 (Philadelphia, 1772 [Evans no. 12387]).

22. David Hawke, *In the Midst of a Revolution* (Philadelphia, 1961), pp. 101–02, points out that, in the revolutionary crisis of 1776, a new group of political leaders, building on the work of the old, began the democratic movement culminating in the constitution of 1776.

controversy between the former partners in journalism raged on throughout the early 1770s, becoming more and more of a personal vendetta. Goddard blasted Galloway with merciless invective every autumn at election time, as Galloway each year placed his name on the Philadelphia ticket in hopes that he might return from his exile. During the election campaign of 1771 this compliment appeared:

> Who would not rather be a FRANKLIN, gloriously defending the liberties and honour of his distressed country, before a BRITISH SENATE, than the first Minister of State endeavoring to enslave and ruin his countrymen?—And who would not rather be a DICKINSON, in a private station, . . . nobly exerting his talents for the preservation of the invaded rights of his country, than a GALLOWAY, asserting the cause of slavery, reviling *American* honour, treacherously undermining the capital pillars of the Constitution of his NATIVE COUNTRY, and slandering one of her ablest Advocates? [23]

When Galloway read this odious comparison, claimed Goddard, he "staggered" to the Statehouse to persuade the Assembly to declare the statement "false, scandalous, and malicious, a daring Insult to, and a Breach of the Privileges of this House." [24] Goddard, already imprisoned in default of the debts his partners had left him with, suffered no punishment in consequence of this resolution; it only made Galloway appear to Philadelphia as an enemy of freedom of the press. The Speaker won neither the controversy with the printer nor any votes. He was not among the first twelve on the Philadelphia ticket, and again he had to come into the Assembly by the back door.[25]

The election of 1772 saw Galloway again pitted against

23. *Pennsylvania Chronicle,* September 16–23, 1771 (original in italics).

24. Ibid., September 23–30, 1771. *Votes,* 8 : 6684.

25. Miner, *Goddard,* pp. 101–03. Election return, Philadelphia County, 1771, enclosed in a letter of William Franklin to Thomas Wharton, September 12, 1771, William Franklin MSS, Society Collection, HSP.

Goddard, this time in the Strange Affair of the Threatening Letter. Galloway received a demand from an anonymous extortioner: put fifty pounds under a milestone on the Chester Road or take the consequences. Quick-tempered Galloway too hastily concluded that only one of his enemies could be guilty of such criminality, and he swore out a complaint against Goddard before Chief Justice Allen. The printer, certainly innocent, was angered and outraged beyond bounds; he now had more reason than ever to defame Galloway in his newspaper.[26] When Galloway, after some sober thought, declined to press charges, he showed Philadelphia that his rashness and hot temper had once again made him play the fool. Inspired to retaliation by Galloway's renewal of the feud, Goddard stepped up his attack on the Speaker. He criticized an excise act that gave officers the power to search without specific warrants.[27] He forecast quite accurately and acidly Galloway's fate in the Philadelphia election of October 1772. The *Chronicle* published a cartoon showing Americanus, bearing on his back the milestone under which the extortion money was to be placed, trudging back to Bucks County again to return by the "back Door," and incidentally trampling on Liberty, the Pennsylvania Charter, and the Bill of Rights.[28]

Throughout his controversy with Goddard, Galloway evidenced an inability to comprehend the reasons for the political changes in Philadelphia or the relation which these changes

26. Goddard declared that Galloway's evidence against him was provided by one Evitt, the town drunk. Galloway had reportedly "run pimping and sneaking up a dirty Alley to the House of such a Wretch as *Evitt,* to SOLICIT Evidence against me, and then dance Attendance until *Evitt's* drunken Fit could be far enough over for him to awake, and be capable of talking." *Pennsylvania Chronicle,* April 13–20, 1772. The real extortioner was never discovered, nor was the threat carried out.

27. A correspondent to the *Chronicle,* February 17–24, 1772, inquired in reference to the excise act, "If, when we consider the situation of *Americanus,* who would have entailed misery and vassalage over this free country, we have not reason to think ourselves indebted to him for bringing *another* monster into the world?"

28. Ibid., September 19–26, 1772.

bore to imperial issues. He saw no reason why he, Speaker of the House and a devoted public servant who had done a competent job on local problems such as paper money, should be called to account for his Americanus piece of 1765, which was generally misinterpreted, or be criticized for opposing the publication of the "Farmer's Letters" in 1767, or be censured for blocking proposals for anti-British action in 1768, or be chastised for his alliance with the rich merchants in 1770. He did not seem to understand the patriotic fervor that had inspired his former supporters to reject him. Galloway's interpretation of the reason for his loss of popularity was evidently the one he had called on before and would employ later to explain away his failures. He was, he thought, faced with a devilish Presbyterian conspiracy which had, through its agent, Goddard, maliciously alienated the members of his party. The results of the elections after 1770 confirmed Galloway's conviction that anti-British Presbyterians were the chief enemies of order and good government. They had ruined his party and nearly ruined his political career.[29]

Galloway had rebounded from his 1764 defeat, but after 1770 he realized that, with no strong political organization to support him, he could not so easily recoup his losses. In 1764–66 the party machine had turned out 3,000–4,500 voters in Philadelphia County; in 1771 Galloway observed about 1,300 come to the polls, almost all of whom voted against him.[30] The situation was equally sad in 1772, he reported to Franklin. "Men of Property and Character," meaning Joseph Fox, Abel James, and himself, were rejected by the electorate. "The very Dregs of the People," meaning Goddard, who as a candidate of the Patriotic Society received a large number of

29. From Galloway's letter to Franklin, [November 1765], *Franklin Papers*, 12 : 377–78; in Goddard's account of Galloway's views in *The Partnership*; and in Galloway's *Historical and Political Reflections* of 1780 this attitude can be seen.

30. Election return, Philadelphia County, 1771, in a letter of William Franklin to Thomas Wharton, September 12, 1771, William Franklin MSS, Society Collection, HSP.

votes but failed of election, had popular appeal which could not have existed if the Old Ticket had still been active. Even stranger to Galloway was that many of those on the proprietary payroll had cast ballots against Dickinson, Thomson, and Goddard in 1772, "while those whom we used to call ours would not take the Trouble to walk to the State House" because there was no party organization to get them out to vote.[31] It was ironic that Galloway's old opponents, the pro-British part of the proprietary faction, now constituted part of the support of his moderate policy against the anti-British agitators. The situation was not improved in 1773; Galloway continued his failure to win back to the Assembly party any of its former adherents.

The only advantage remaining to Galloway was that his rotten borough seat gave him a nearly unbreakable hold on the Speaker's chair. He was retained in this post by his long-time backers from Bucks and Chester counties, on whom Goddard had no influence. Only a revolution involving all Pennsylvania could move him out of his seat. Goddard tried, caustically declaring in 1773, "The noted Joseph Galloway, is, to the Disgrace of Pennsylvania, again elected Speaker of the Assembly! Perjury, Subordination, and the basest Treachery, we may see, thro' blind Party Rage, are sometimes no Disqualifications to a Place of Trust." [32] Tirades like this did not diminish Galloway's support in the House. He awarded his followers the important posts at his disposal, and they repaid him with their allegiance.

His position, Galloway recognized, was indeed precarious. To hold it, he believed that he had to use the Speaker's post to instill a spirit of calm into Pennsylvania politics. He threw a sop to the anti-British faction by permitting Dickinson to

31. Galloway to Franklin, October 12, 1772, Franklin Papers, 58 : 38, APS.

32. *Pennsylvania Chronicle*, October 11–18, 1773. This was Goddard's valedictory attack on Galloway. He soon closed down the *Chronicle* in order to concentrate on his plans for an independent post rider system. Miner, *Goddard*, pp. 114–15.

draft and put through the Assembly, in March 1771, a petition to the king against the tea duty.[33] After this, Galloway successfully led the Assembly to ignore imperial questions and to take a conciliatory part in local affairs. For the first time since 1766, and for the last time, the Speaker and his friends staged a celebration of the king's birthday in Philadelphia in June 1772. This festival was much less elaborate than the one of six years before and was received with much less enthusiasm; repeated crises had dulled loyalty to Britain.[34]

Galloway also went out of his way to remain at peace with the proprietary group. He still hoped for the day when Pennsylvania would become a royal province, but he also recognized that in his political nadir he needed to make as many friends as possible. When Connecticut squatters invaded the Wyoming Valley in northeastern Pennsylvania, on the basis of the sea-to-sea charter of that colony, Galloway and the proprietors joined forces against them. He identified the Connecticut effort to grab Penn lands with the general conspiracy of New Englanders and Presbyterians to stir up trouble. Galloway took the opportunity to deal his enemies a blow, focus attention on something besides imperial issues, and prove that he was not an inveterate foe of the proprietary interest. The Assembly responded to the calls of Governors John and Richard Penn in February and October 1771 for legislation to suppress these wild Yankees.[35] Galloway also began working closely with James Tilghman, proprietary land officer, on legal matters affecting the Penn estate and on certain legisla-

33. *Votes,* 8 : 6628, 6658–59. Presumably, Franklin presented this petition through Lord Hillsborough, with no result. Galloway kept Dickinson from interfering in other ways by not appointing him to important committees. Ibid., 7 : 6585–86.

34. *Pennsylvania Gazette,* June 11, 1772.

35. *Votes,* 8 : 6628–36, 6732–35. At first, Thomas Penn, believing Galloway and the Assembly to be completely unscrupulous, feared that they might use the Wyoming controversy as a lever against the proprietors. He was very pleased to have his former enemies on his side against the squatters. Penn to John Penn, May 28, 1771, Thomas Penn Letter Book, Penn Papers, HSP.

tion. In return for these moves toward reconciliation, the Penns made no objections to the revival of the loan office and the emission of £150,000 in paper bills in 1773.[36]

For battle with any faction, proprietary or mechanic, Galloway now had little heart. He began to lose touch with the original aims of his party as well as with the popular mood. In 1772 Edward Biddle, a prominent western assemblyman, brought in a bill to have judges appointed on good behavior. This bill was supported by a letter in the *Chronicle* quoting such diverse authorities as Blackstone and Galloway on the advisability of appointing judges subject to removal only by the Assembly. In 1759 Galloway had exerted all his power to get such an act passed to curtail the proprietary prerogative. In 1772 he gave Biddle no support whatsoever and the attempt failed.[37] Galloway clearly displayed a despondent and resigned attitude toward politics by 1773. Except for the paper money emission he had little to count as accomplishments. Bad judgment and bad health had stymied him; personal troubles compounded his difficulties. A local scoundrel attempted to run off with his daughter.[38] Political activity and prominence had provided him with none of the rewards the vigorous, ambitious, and talented young Galloway had expected when he entered politics at Franklin's side in 1755.

Galloway considered two possible courses of action to relieve his misery. After 1771 he began to think of retiring from

36. Edmund Physick to Thomas Penn, June 11, 1770; James Tilghman to Thomas Penn, March 1, 1773, Penn Papers, HSP. The act for the emission was approved on February 26, 1773. *Votes*, 8 : 6913, 6914, 6919, 6928, 6965.

37. *Pennsylvania Chronicle*, January 20–27, 1772. In practice, the Assembly carried its point about the removal of an unfit judge. One Charles Jolly, a justice of the peace, was accused by petitioning citizens of criminality in office. The House addressed the governor on this matter, and Jolly was left out when new commissions were issued. *Votes*, 8 : 6823; *Minutes of the Provincial Council of Pennsylvania*, 10 (Harrisburg, 1852) : 45–46.

38. John Penn to Lady Juliana Penn, October 28, 1773, Penn Papers, HSP.

politics, ending his career and all his troubles while only in his early forties. "I am again returned to a Seat in the House," he wrote Franklin after the 1772 election, "but whether with or against my Inclination I really cannot inform you. The Opposition I met with was the only Matter which gave rise to a Wish to be elected." [39] Keeping his Assembly seat was a habit, a necessity born of political loyalty, a method of countering hated adversaries like Goddard and Dickinson, and a burden because of his unpopularity. At long distance, Franklin attempted to dissuade his old partner from quitting and to bolster his low spirits. "You are yet a young man," wrote the eternally youthful philosopher, "and may still be greatly serviceable to your Country. It would be, I think, something criminal to bury in private Retirement so early, all the Usefulness of so much Experience and such great Abilities." [40] In the same vein the agent wrote to Cadwalader Evans, "I do not see that [Galloway] can be spared from [the Assembly], without great detriment to our affairs and to the general welfare of America." [41]

Goddard's attacks an Galloway did not affect Franklin's relations with his old partner, for Franklin had seen this tactic before and thought it generated only by political animosity. He used Goddard's 1771 comparison of Dickinson and Galloway as a firelighter and advised Galloway that "we must not in the Course of Publick Life expect *immediate* Approbation and *immediate* grateful Acknowledgement of our Services." [42] Despite the differences between the old partners that the nonimportation controversy accentuated, and despite the collapse of the Franklin-Galloway party machine in Philadephia, Franklin encouraged and supported his old ally because he believed that, in this calmer period of imperial relations, Galloway was the best equipped to prevent violent action from flaring up.

39. Galloway to Franklin, October 12, 1772, Franklin Papers, 58 : 38, APS.
40. Franklin to Galloway, January 6, 1773, *Writings*, ed. Smyth, 6 : 6.
41. Franklin to Cadwalader Evans, July 18, 1771, ibid., 5 : 337.
42. Franklin to William Franklin, January 20, 1772, ibid., 5 : 380; Franklin to Galloway, December 2, 1772, ibid., 5 : 458.

Putting public service before private affairs, as he usually did, Franklin advised Galloway to retire from his law practice so he would be able to throw himself into politics more wholeheartedly and perhaps recover his losses. The agent's prescription was worthless; Franklin did not comprehend how sick Pennsylvania's political situation was. "I do not at this Distance understand the Politics of your last Election," he wrote to Abel James after the campaign of 1772.[43] It was of no use to advise his Pennsylvania friends to work harder, because his party had broken up beyond their ability to repair it. Galloway ignored Franklin's advice and resigned himself to his Bucks County rotten borough. To know that in spite of all his difficulties Franklin had not lost faith in him helped Galloway to bear the burden of unpopularity and the slanders of Goddard, and to continue his post. The partners no longer had a common issue, nor a party, nor a coordinated cooperation spanning the ocean, but neither wanted to see the end of their long-standing influence over the Pennsylvania Assembly.

Franklin in London, unaware of what was occurring in Pennsylvania politics, was little aid to Galloway; Galloway's second solution to his problems was to have the agent return to Pennsylvania. Knowing that Franklin believed himself needed in Britain, Galloway did not directly request his return, but he hinted strongly that he desired his partner at his side. Franklin alone could provide the inspiration that the broken Assembly party sorely needed, regain the allegiance of the White Oaks, and cloak his friend Galloway with that aura of patriotism that continually surrounded the foremost defender of American rights.[44] The year 1771 would have been an opportune time for Franklin to return, for anti-American sentiment in Britain had quieted down. "All Views or Expectations of drawing any considerable Revenue to this

43. Franklin to Abel James, December 2, 1772, ibid., 5 : 461.
44. Galloway to Franklin, September 27, 1770, October 12, 1772, Franklin Papers, 3 : 28, and 58 : 38, APS; these letters imply that Galloway believed the deterioration of Pennsylvania politics could have been reversed by Franklin's return.

Country from the Colonies are, I believe, generally given over, and it seems probable that nothing of that kind will ever again be attempted," he reported with relief and optimism.[45] During 1771–72 Franklin contributed almost nothing to the newspapers in defense of America; he prepared five articles but published only three of them. Nor did the colonial agents' lobby meet to plan any further activities to get the tea duty repealed.[46] Franklin was homesick, and he found his duties much less demanding than in previous years, but he could not return home.[47] He believed that his tasks in Britain had not been satisfactorily completed, and he took on added responsibilities in connection with these. He also had private business in Britain that directly concerned Galloway, William Franklin, and others of the old Assembly party. Galloway's problems in Pennsylvania politics, which Franklin did not believe were too serious, paled before the major responsibility of presenting the case for American rights in London.

Franklin took on what became his greatest burden in defending America when he was made agent for the Massachusetts House of Representatives in October 1770. It was no accident that Franklin received this appointment; he did not apply for the agency, but he cleverly managed to make himself the best available candidate. Perhaps he had his sights on this Massachusetts agency in the summer of 1768 when, as nonimportation began in America, Franklin discovered that his views were similar to those of the Boston leaders. In August of that year he accused the incumbent agent, Dennys De Berdt, an aged London merchant, of "screening a minister [Hillsborough]" and implied that De Berdt had failed to present the petition of the Massachusetts House against the

45. Franklin to Thomas Cushing, June 10, 1771, *Writings*, ed. Smyth, 5:323.

46. *Franklin's Letters to the Press*, ed. Crane, nos. 103–07, pp. 221–24. Kammen, *Rope of Sand*, pp. 145–46.

47. Franklin to William Franklin, January 30, 1772, *Writings*, ed. Smyth, 5 : 381–82.

Townshend duties as forcefully as he should have.[48] In June 1770, two months after De Berdt's death, Franklin submitted to his Boston correspondent, Samuel Cooper, a full statement of his position on the constitutional situation of America, which concluded that "by our Constitution [the king] is, with his plantation Parliaments, the sole Legislator of his American Subjects, and in that Capacity is, and ought to be, free to exercise his own Judgment, unrestrained and unrestricted by his Parliament here. And our Parliaments have right to grant him Aids without the Consent of this Parliament." In addition, while the Massachusetts House was without an agent, Franklin opposed a move by the ministry to alter the charter of the province.[49] By word and deed, Franklin demonstrated that he substantially agreed with the Bostonians, that he wanted Massachusetts to have adequate representation in London, and that he was willing to assume the responsibility for this. His reputation and activities, and Cooper's support, won for him this "unsolicited" post. The agent for Pennsylvania, Georgia, and New Jersey was probably not too surprised when House Speaker Thomas Cushing notified him of his newest appointment.

The prestige Franklin stood to derive in Britain by representing the House of this troublesome province was nil; the financial reward was also nil because Governor Thomas Hutchinson refused to approve his salary. Franklin assumed the post apparently because he wanted to represent by himself a united front of four colonies; such authority would enhance his bargaining power with the ministry. However, the Earl of Hillsborough refused to bargain at all. Franklin had an-

48. De Berdt alleged that Hillsborough had not refused to deliver the Massachusetts petition to the king in 1768, but that the minister had not seen the petition. Franklin claimed that the reason Hillsborough had not seen the petition was that De Berdt was refused permission to deliver it. *Public Advertiser*, August 31, 1768, reprinted in *Franklin's Letters to the Press*, ed. Crane, no. 65, pp. 125–28.

49. Franklin to Samuel Cooper, June 8, 1770, *Writings*, ed. Smyth, 5 : 261. Franklin to Thomas Cushing, December 24, 1770, ibid., 5 : 284. Prospects of war with Spain forced the ministry to drop this drastic plan.

noyed him with his petition for the change of Pennsylvania's government, his plans for repealing the act of 1764 prohibiting legal tender, and his advocacy of nonimportation; the secretary of state soon formed the opinion that the agent was "a factious turbulent Fellow, always in Mischief, a Republican, Enemy to the King's Service, and what not." Hillsborough used Hutchinson's refusal to concur in Franklin's appointment as an excuse to refuse to receive him on Massachusetts business. By 1772 he was avoiding Franklin's solicitations on all business. Consequently, Franklin had during this period no opportunity to present Massachusetts's complaint against the payment of Governor Hutchinson's salary by the Crown, nor to work for the repeal of the tea duty.[50]

Under these conditions, Franklin's agency was of little help to his constituents in Massachusetts, but he was not easily discouraged. He suspected that Hillsborough was not in favor with other ministers and might soon be forced out. Ever the optimist, Franklin was confident that any replacement would be more favorable to America and to her agents. Franklin also felt a great obligation to work for the repeal of the tea duty despite all obstacles, for he believed that "no harmony can be restored between the two countries, while these duties are continued." [51] Overall, even though calm prevailed in imperial relations, mainly because Hillsborough would permit the agents to accomplish little and because the ministry

50. Franklin to William Franklin, January 30, 1772, August 19, 1772, ibid., 5 : 378, 380–81, 413. Franklin to Samuel Cooper, February 5, 1771, January 13, 1772, ibid., 5 : 298–304, 354–57. Franklin to Thomas Cushing, April 13, 1772, ibid., 5 : 392. Kammen, *Rope of Sand*, pp. 280–81, notes the systematic way in which British officials attempted to obstruct colonial agents. Despite his rupture with Hillsborough, Franklin kept busy with more routine matters on behalf of Pennsylvania, Georgia, and New Jersey. Franklin to William Franklin, April 20, 1771, *Writings*, ed. Smyth, 5 : 314–15; Franklin to Noble Wimberly Jones, July 3, 1771, ibid., 5 : 330.

51. Franklin to Thomas Cushing, June 10, 1771, *Writings*, ed. Smyth, 5 : 322–23. Franklin to the Committee of Correspondence of Massachusetts, January 13, 1772, ibid., 5 : 351.

avoided stirring up America, nothing was really settled. "We govern from Hand to Mouth. There seems to be no wise regular Plan," Franklin wrote his son early 1773.[52] Overcoming strong desires to return to America, Franklin remained in Britain because he could not predict when his services might be required or useful.

Franklin's increased responsibilities also included a private venture. He, Galloway, William Franklin, Thomas and Samuel Wharton, other Pennsylvanians generally associated with the political schemes of the Franklin-Galloway group, and numerous important British dignitaries, including Lord Camden, other ministers, and Franklin's friends Richard Jackson, Thomas Pownall, and William Strahan, formed in 1769 the Grand Ohio Company, or the Walpole Company—so called after banker Thomas Walpole.[53] These investors planned to enrich themselves in the accepted colonial manner: land speculation. They eyed a large tract on the Ohio River where they proposed to found a new colony. Prime movers behind the quest for a land grant were the Whartons. Samuel Wharton came to London in 1769 to join with Franklin in seeking backers and government authorization.[54] Franklin's and Galloway's financial interests in this project were not large; Franklin aided Wharton in his lobbying because he had always been interested in projects for new colonies. Galloway gave legal advice to the speculators in Pennsylvania because some of them were his political allies.[55]

52. Franklin to William Franklin, April 6, 1773, ibid., 6 : 31.

53. Currey, *Road to Revolution,* pp. 248–52, discusses in detail the formation of the company. Currey also explores Franklin's earlier activities in land speculation.

54. Ibid., p. 252. Also see Thomas P. Abernethy, *Western Lands and the American Revolution* (New York, 1937), pp. 43–46.

55. Franklin held two of seventy-two shares. Currey, *Road to Revolution,* p. 334. The grant was to cost £10,460 7s. 3d., the cost of the land purchased from the Indians at the Treaty of Ft. Stanwix in 1768. Franklin could then anticipate an outlay of about £291 as his share of the purchase price, plus incidentals. He paid £600 for shares for Galloway, Wil-

In the summer of 1769 Franklin and Samuel Wharton petitioned the Privy Council for 2,400,000 acres. Hillsborough at
first encouraged the petitioners, as he had at first encouraged
Franklin in his quest for the change of government. He advised them to apply for about eight times as much land, sit-
uated west of Pennsylvania and north of Virginia from the
Ohio River to the Cumberland Gap. In reality, the secretary
was opposed to the extension of colonization beyond the Ap-
palachians and to the encouragement of emigration from
Great Britain to underdeveloped colonies. He thought that
an application for 20,000,000 acres would be rejected by the
Treasury out of hand and so finish the Walpole group's plans;
but, surprisingly, the grant was approved. Then Hillsborough
stalled the Board of Trade from reporting on the grant for
about two years, until April 1772, when finally the Board,
because of the secretary's influence, reported against it. Franklin helped Wharton prepare a refutation of this report to
submit to the Privy Council; this document more than adequately defended the grant from Hillsborough's criticism.
The Privy Council accepted the refutation of the Board's report and rejected Hillsborough's objections to the grant. The
Franklin-Wharton refutation was not accepted on its merits,
however, but because, behind the scenes, Hillsborough's enemies, the Bedford faction, had used the Walpole grant question to get rid of the colonial secretary. Just as his opponents
planned, Hillsborough resigned when the Privy Council rebuffed him and approved the grant. Franklin congratulated
himself that he had had some small part in contributing to
this obstinate man's forced resignation.[56]

---

liam Franklin, and himself, he reported to William Franklin, July 25,
1773, Franklin Papers, Library of Congress. Galloway's task as legal advisor
came to be pacifying William Franklin and the Whartons, who had sharp
differences with each other in matters concerning the grant.

56. Currey, *Road to Revolution*, pp. 290–93, rightly credits both
Franklin and Wharton with preparing the report, and he summarizes its
arguments. See also Van Doren, *Benjamin Franklin*, pp. 396–98; Ritcheson, *British Politics*, pp. 145–46; George E. Lewis, *The Indiana Com-*

The Walpole grant, which was never finally confirmed, was much less important to Franklin than getting rid of the biggest stumbling block that he had faced during his British missions. Hillsborough's ouster was to him a sign of better things to come. The ministry had justified Franklin's optimism by both getting the secretary out and acting favorably on an American petition. Imperial affairs seemed to take an even more propitious turn when Franklin, in the summer of 1772, was asked his opinion on a possible successor to Hillsborough. He recommended the Earl of Dartmouth, and Dartmouth was appointed. To Franklin, Dartmouth was the best possible choice because he had supported the repeal of the Stamp Act and because he opposed, in practice if not in principle, parliamentary exertion of authority over America. Dartmouth was chosen, however, not because Franklin approved but because Lord North wanted Dartmouth, a strong supporter of his ministry, in this post.[57] The new colonial secretary soon justified Franklin's recommendation. He discarded Hillsborough's unfriendly practice and now recognized agents appointed solely by colonial Assemblies. As agent for four colonies, Franklin found the new minister much more willing to talk to him than was the old one. By August 1772, after these favorable changes, Franklin believed that his influence and prestige were greater in Britain than they had ever been. He puffed out his chest in pardonable pride and bragged that even the king "has lately been heard to speak of me with great regard."[58] Yet, he received little evidence that British attitudes were basically changed, for when Massachusetts sent a petition to the king complaining about the payment of

---

pany (Glendale, Calif., 1941), pp. 111–12; Franklin to William Franklin, August 17, 1772, *Writings,* ed. Smyth, 5 : 410–11.

57. Franklin to William Franklin, August 19, 1772, *Writings,* ed. Smyth, 5 : 413–14. B. D. Bargar, *Lord Dartmouth and the American Revolution* (Columbia, S.C., 1965), pp. 56–58.

58. Franklin to Thomas Cushing, November 4, 1772, *Writings,* ed. Smyth, 5 : 448. Franklin to William Franklin, August 19, 1772, ibid., 5 : 414.

Hutchinson's salary by the home government, Dartmouth in November 1772 advised Franklin not to present it at that time. Because ministers were reasonably accommodating, but had not yet seen the light, Franklin believed that he could be useful in the near future in settling colonial affairs; he could not now leave his posts.[59]

The disgraced and despondent Galloway and the influential and confident Franklin were, by 1773, facing in opposite directions. The old partners seemed to have nothing in common except their close friendship. On public and private matters they continued to correspond, but as friends, not as political allies working toward the same goals. Franklin trusted Galloway completely with information about his own views—as he had done for years.[60] But he and Galloway no longer depended on each other for political support. To some degree, Galloway's association with Franklin gave him power within the Assembly, whereby the old Assembly party members from Philadelphia and the surrounding counties kept him on as Speaker, but outside the House it meant little. Galloway's base of popularity narrowed to small Bucks County, where sharp political maneuvering preserved his seat. His manipulation of elections in his rotten borough appears akin to the "corruption" in parliamentary elections that Franklin decried. Meanwhile, Franklin broadened his base of support to include the four colonies for which he was agent. After 1770 his tenure in London was certainly independent of whatever political shifts might occur in Pennsylvania, although he probably did not fully appreciate this and continued to favor his old friends like Galloway over the more anti-British political leaders.

The intellectual positions of the old partners were divergent

59. Franklin to Cushing, September 3, 1772, December 2, 1772, ibid., 5 : 435, 448–51. Franklin to Galloway, January 6, 1773, ibid., 6 : 6. Bargar, *Lord Dartmouth,* pp. 83–84.

60. For examples of Franklin's trust in Galloway, see Franklin to Galloway, January 29, 1769, Clements Library, University of Michigan; Franklin to Galloway, June 26, 1770, Yale University Library.

but not yet entirely contradictory. Both opposed British policies—Franklin, because they violated his principles; Galloway, because they were oppressive, unpopular, and, stirred up trouble for him in Pennsylvania. Franklin had won high honor defending America and encouraging American resistance; moreover, he thought by the beginning of 1773, his principles might soon receive some recognition from a slightly more friendly ministry. Galloway's failure to take a strong stand in Pennsylvania and his association with opponents of nonimportation won him only the condemnation of the zealot Goddard. He may deserve credit for his private opposition to the duties, and for not openly opposing nonimportation after 1769, thus not giving the local firebrands reason to undertake the kind of radical activity practiced in Massachusetts, but he did not enhance his political control by his actions. The period of calm since the end of nonimportation, unlike the period following the repeal of the Stamp Act, gave no impetus to an intellectual reconciliation of Franklin and Galloway. Their differences had become somewhat similar to British-American differences. That so far they had failed to reconcile these differences portended that Britain and America might also in the end fail to solve their dispute amicably.

Character changes were more subtle. Age had by this time reduced Franklin's earlier strong ambition, but there was no change in his devotion to public service. If anything, in the discharge of his Massachusetts agency duties he was less restrained. He was fast dropping the qualities of the politician and assuming those of the elder statesman.[61] Galloway also felt his earlier ambition dissipate, but in his case it was because of his political failures. He became more withdrawn, more timid, and more intent on preserving his power by questionable methods, rather than concerning himself with the welfare of the province.

61. Franklin was afflicted by gout and, according to William Strahan, by "natural inactivity." But he does not seem to have slowed down much. Kammen, *Rope of Sand*, pp. 130–31.

The partnership was dormant, but the friendship endured. Letters between the Speaker and the agent were more affectionate and exhibited more regard for personal affairs than heretofore, as if both men realized that, because their political alliance had lost much of its meaning, their personal attachment had to be strengthened. False rumor circulated in Philadelphia in late 1773 that Galloway feared Franklin's possible return would deprive him of his little remaining political power, but Franklin was quick to deny that he could ever believe ill of his old partner. "No insinuations of the kind you mention, concerning Mr. G—— have reached me," he wrote to his son, "and, if they had, it would have been without the least effect; as I have always had the strongest reliance on the steadiness of his friendship, and on the best grounds, the knowledge I have of his integrity, and the often repeated disinterested services he has rendered me." 62

Friendship and mutual trust were the foundations on which to rebuild their old partnership, but it could not be rebuilt unless Galloway could regain the political initiative from his opponents and recapture Philadelphia. In the past the partnership had thrived on crises. The defense crisis of 1755–56, the wartime situation of 1757–59, the Paxton Boys' march and the change of government controversy in 1764, and the Stamp Act crisis all had contributed to the increase in political cooperation between the two men. Would a new crisis reawaken Galloway and revive the partnership, or would it complete the work of the nonimportation controversy, finally destroying the alliance as well as the empire?

62. Franklin to William Franklin, January 5, 1774, *Writings*, ed. Smyth, 6 : 174. See also Franklin to Galloway, December 2, 1772, January 6, 1773, ibid., 5 : 458–60, and 6 : 5–7.

9 Plans of Union and Disunion

Franklin and Galloway showed more determination to meet the third great crisis in imperial relations head-on than they had shown in previous crises. Their partnership and the empire, each badly split after the Townshend duties controversy, could endure no more strain. Both Franklin and Galloway feared that the Tea Act of 1773 and its consequences would result in more violence and a further break; their fears impelled each man to take more concrete and positive action than either had dared to take previously. Finally and belatedly, individually and collectively, the old partners turned their efforts toward the salvation of Anglo-American unity.

Franklin's first reaction to the troubles of the East India Company in late 1772 was to smile; the British government had now discovered that the tea duty was encouraging Americans to smuggle their favorite beverage from the Dutch and helping create a surplus in the East India warehouses. North's "wise Scheme" of May 1773, to lower the British duty, eliminate the vendue, and permit the company to consign its tea to selected licensed merchants in America, was not very alarming to the agent at first. Franklin was confident that the British view that a tax of "3d in a lb. of Tea, of which one does not drink perhaps 10 in a Year, is sufficient to overcome all the Patriotism of an American" would be proved mistaken by American resistance to the scheme.[1] The Tea Act, the

1. Franklin to Galloway, December 2, 1772, *Writings*, ed. Smyth, 5 : 459–60. Franklin to Thomas Cushing, June 4, 1773, September 12, 1773, ibid., 6 : 57, 124–25. Benjamin W. Labaree, *The Boston Tea Party* (New York, 1964), has most thoroughly studied the tea crisis. He concludes that smuggling had increased after 1770 (p. 52) and that the plan of the

May 1773 refusal of two Massachusetts petitions against the payment of Governor Hutchinson's salary by the Crown (which Franklin had finally presented to the Earl of Dartmouth), and Franklin's growing suspicion that "the late Measures have been . . . very much the King's own" encouraged him to renew his attack against British oppression of America.

Employing a more sarcastic vein than before, Franklin in September 1773 drew up the two most effective press contributions of his British mission: "An Edict by the King of Prussia," and "Rules by Which a Great Empire May Be Reduced to a Small One." The argument of the former, that the bellicose Frederick the Great would presume to tax and regulate the manufactures of Great Britain because that nation was originally settled by migrants from Germany, was almost believable, and Franklin reported with glee that his little joke put across his point most effectively. The "Rules" Franklin cited included taxation without representation, appointment of unfit officials, harassment of assemblies, and other grievances that particularly plagued Massachusetts.[2] Neither of these pieces dealt directly with the Tea Act; Franklin was attempting to get the British government to reconsider all its unjust policies affecting the colonies.

There was no need for Franklin to take the lead in stirring up opposition to the Tea Act in America, and there was every reason to anticipate that resistance would be automatically forthcoming, for precedents and techniques abounded. The agent contented himself with writing to Galloway his

North ministry would not necessarily have driven the smugglers out of business (p. 77).

2. Franklin to William Franklin, July 14, 1773, *Writings*, ed. Smyth, 6 : 98. Franklin, "An Edict by the King of Prussia," ibid., 6 : 118–24; Franklin, "Rules By Which a Great Empire May Be Reduced to a Small One," ibid., 6 : 127–37. The "Edict" article appeared in Britain in the *Gentleman's Magazine*, September 1773. Both pieces were republished in the *Pennsylvania Gazette*, December 15, 1773. Two other short newspaper pieces opposing British policy in a less biting way are reprinted in *Franklin's Letters to the Press*, ed. Crane, ons. 112, 114, pp. 232–33, 235.

thoughts on the effects of resistance. "If [the tea] is rejected, the act will undoubtedly be repealed, otherwise I suppose it will be continued; and when we have got into the use of the Company's tea, and the foreign correspondences that supply us at present, are broken off, the licenses will be discontinued, and the act enforced [that is, the price raised to pre-1773 levels]." [3] American freedom from parliamentary taxation depended on the American refusal of the tea.

The rejection that Franklin desired was probably that sort that occurred in most colonial seaports; the consignees were persuaded to resign and, with no one to accept the tea, it was turned back without landing or stored in the customs house and not permitted to leak out. The obstinance of Governor Hutchinson and the fear of the Boston town leaders that the tea, if landed, would be surreptitiously distributed in the province, resulted in the destruction of the tea by the "Mohawks." [4] This reaction was not to Franklin's taste, although when the event was reported in Britain, he felt himself obligated to defend the colony. But he could do nothing to abate the uproar against Massachusetts—perhaps no one could have —because he had also been discredited, by the affair of the Hutchinson Letters.

In some way never fully revealed, Franklin, in late 1772, had procured letters from Governor Hutchinson and other Massachusetts officials to Thomas Whately, George Grenville's secretary, written in 1767–69 when Boston had adopted non-importation and rioted against the customs commissioners. [5]

3. Franklin to Galloway, November 3, 1773, *Writings*, ed. Smyth, 6 : 152.

4. Jensen, *Founding*, pp. 439–53; Labaree, *Boston Tea Party*, pp. 126–45.

5. The mystery surrounding Franklin's acquisition of the letters is a deep one. Franklin, in the London *Public Advertiser*, December 25, 1773, printed in *Writings*, ed. Smyth, 6 : 284, admitted that he alone "obtained and transmitted" the letters to Boston. Franklin reported to Thomas Cushing, July 7, 1773, ibid., 6 : 82, that the letters were probably given by Whately to Grenville, who "lent them to another, & dying before they were returned gave an Opportunity for their falling into [our hands]." To Galloway, February 18, 1774, in draft, Franklin Papers, 45 : 76, APS, Franklin wrote that the letters were produced by someone during an

Franklin sent the letters to Speaker Cushing of the Massachusetts Assembly, advising him that "there might be a Use in showing them to some Friends of the Province, and even to some of the Governor's Party, for their more certain Information concerning his Conduct and Politicks." To Franklin, Hutchinson's letters indicated that the governor wanted Britain to adopt firm measures, even revise the Massachusetts charter, to deal with riotous Boston. The people of that colony, including perhaps some of Hutchinson's erstwhile supporters, would, if they saw the letters, blame their own governor, not the British ministry, for sending troops, for precipitating the consequent Boston massacre, and for causing all their other troubles, and "by that means promote a Reconciliation" with the mother country.[6] What Franklin meant by a reconciliation was, probably, a move in Massachusetts to place all the blame on Hutchinson and to petition the king for his recall.

---

argument in which Franklin claimed that the home government had initiated the sending of troops to Massachusetts. His opponent showed him the letters to prove that Hutchinson, Lieutenant Governor Andrew Oliver, and Charles Paxton (then customs commissioner) were responsible. Franklin requested permission from his source to send the letters to Massachusetts. Van Doren argues, in *Franklin*, pp. 458–61, that John Temple, of the customs office and friendly to America, was directly involved in obtaining the letters. Whoever it was, Franklin was not guilty of actually stealing the letters. See also Franklin's *Tract Relating to the Affair of Hutchinson's Letters*, in *Writings*, ed. Smyth, 6 : 258–69; Crane, *Franklin and a Rising People*, pp. 142–43; Currey, *Road to Revolution*, pp. 308–15.

6. Franklin to Cushing, July 7, 1773, *Writings*, ed. Smyth, 6 : 81. Franklin to Galloway, February 18, 1774, Franklin Papers, 45 : 76, APS. Hutchinson called for "some further restraint of liberty rather than the connection with the parent state should be broken." While the Massachusetts governor was not guilty of calling the British troops to Boston, his suggestion, from the colonists' point of view, was an inaccurate statement of the alternatives and might encourage Britain to use force. *Copy of Letters Sent to Great Britain, by his Excellency Thomas Hutchinson, the Hon. Andrew Oliver, and Several other Persons, Born and Educated Among Us* (Boston, 1773 [Evans no. 12818]), p. 16.

Indeed, the Massachusetts House charged Hutchinson with producing *"the severe and destructive measures,* which have been taken against the province," and sent to Franklin a petition for his recall, which the agent presented to Dartmouth in August 1773. But, contrary to Franklin's instructions, the House also made the letters public. The agent, to prevent the renewal of a duel between Thomas Whately's brother and John Temple, whom William Whately had accused of stealing the letters, confessed publicly that he had procured them and transmitted them to Boston. Although the letters were private and were used without permission, Franklin did not regard his conduct as unethical. It was more important, he judged, for the activities of Hutchinson to be exposed and the disputes with Massachusetts to be smoothed over than it was to observe the proprieties.[7] A breach of privacy was, for Franklin, excusable, just as deception and overstatement had been excusable earlier in his political and diplomatic career, when the end was justifiable.

The ministry, however, seized on the purloining of the letters as the weak point in Franklin's case. The Privy Council held a hearing on the Massachusetts petition which, after a postponement, took place on January 29, 1774, two days after official reports of the drowning of the tea in Boston harbor had arrived in Britain. Consequently, at the hearing both the scheming Franklin and the rebellious colonists of Massachusetts were put on trial. Before the full Privy Council, Solicitor General Alexander Wedderburn recounted the riotous be-

7. In the *Public Advertiser,* August 31, 1773, reprinted in *Franklin's Letters to the Press,* ed. Crane, no. 111, pp. 231–32, Franklin argued that the secret correspondence of colonial governors should be made public to show their falsehoods and that Hutchinson and Oliver should be punished for trying to start a war. Franklin, *Tract Relating to the Affair of Hutchinson's Letters,* in *Writings,* ed. Smyth, 6 : 276–81. Israel Mauduit, *The Letters of Governor Hutchinson, and Lieut. Governor Oliver, &c. Printed at Boston, and Remarks Thereon. With the Assembly's Address, and the Proceedings of the Lords' Committee of Council. Together with the Substance of Mr. Wedderburn's Speech Relating to those Letters* (London, 1774), pp. 67–70.

havior of Boston ever since 1765 and then for about an hour castigated Franklin as a thief, plotter of riots, and schemer who was seeking the governorship of Massachusets for himself. The Council apparently agreed; Franklin's petition was thrown out and, the next day, Franklin was thown out as deputy postmaster general. He lost in two days nearly all the prestige and influence he had attempted so diligently to cultivate.[8] His stock fell just at the time when his conciliatory influence was most needed. Everything turned sour in colonial affairs; Franklin's effectiveness as an agent was destroyed, and Boston's action primed Britain for severe measures in retaliation.

While Franklin meddled deeply in relations between Britain and Massachusetts, Galloway declined to assert any leadership. He must have looked on in dismay, unsure what course to adopt, as the final scenes of the drama unfolded in Britain and America. Wisely, he made no opposition to the movement in Philadelphia to reject the tea. That the anti-British elements organized a "committee for tarring and feathering" to command unanimous boycotting of the tea probably portended to him violence, revolution, and the political rise of his opponents. Yet Philadelphia was comparatively quiet as the tea was not permitted to land, and the ship sailed away.[9] But the Boston events, not those in Philadelphia, would determine the course of imperial relations.

In reaction to the almost inevitable British retaliation, Franklin was powerless to do anything, and Galloway continued to avoid the controversy as much as possible. Franklin, "at a loss to know how peace and union are to be maintained or restored between the different parts of the empire," hoped that Boston would immediately pay for the drowned tea,

8. Mauduit, *Letters of Governor Hutchinson,* pp. 98, 110–11. Franklin, "Account of the Massachusetts Petition," *Boston Gazette,* April 25, 1774, reprinted in *Franklin's Letter to the Press,* ed. Crane, no. 120, pp. 240–44. Bernard Donoughue, *British Politics and the American Revolution: The Path to War, 1773–1775* (New York, 1964), pp. 27–34.

9. The *Pennsylvania Journal* from September 29 to December 25, 1773, and the *Pennsylvania Gazette* from September 29 to December 24, 1773, carried numerous reports on the boycott in Philadelphia.

worth about £10,000, but he was not confident that restitution would satisfy Parliament.[10] He was confined to ineffective unofficial action against the Coercive Acts, passed in March-June 1774. In the newspapers he argued that Britain would surely create a war in America; he also helped to draft a petition for reconciliation.[11] But, in disgrace, he could do little more.

The reaction to the Boston Port Act in Pennsylvania was at first ignored by Galloway. In May 1774, after word of this harsh punishment for Massachusetts had arrived, citizens of Philadelphia requested the Committee of Correspondence of the Pennsylvania Assembly to write to other colonies to discover what action they planned to take to aid the blockaded city. Samuel Rhoads and Thomas Mifflin, prominent anti-British assemblymen from Philadelphia, wrote to Galloway to ask him to consult with the committee on the propriety of taking this action. Galloway was hesitant about being associated with an activity that would perhaps contribute to a united colonial resistance to Britain. He informed Rhoads and Mifflin that he would be out of town on business, conveniently, and that the committee should deliberate without him and do as it thought best.[12] While Galloway neglected responsibility, the committee wrote to Boston to express Pennsylvania's sympathy and requested Governor Penn to call the Assembly into special session. The moderate course that these underlings ventured was much more than their chief would undertake.

10. Franklin to Cushing, February 2, 1774, February 15, 1774, *Writings,* ed. Smyth, 6 : 179, 190–91. He later changed his mind about Boston's making amends. Franklin to William Franklin, September 7, 1774, ibid., 6 : 241.

11. Franklin claimed that a blockade would force America to become self-sufficient, that military government in the colonies would be impossible to maintain, and that castration was probably the only method that, in the long run, would stop American agitation. London *Public Advertiser,* April 15, May 21, 1774, reprinted in *Franklin's Letters to the Press,* ed. Crane, nos. 131–32, pp. 258–64. Sosin, *Agents and Merchants,* pp. 179–85.

12. Galloway to Samuel Rhoads and Thomas Mifflin, May 30, 1774, Society Collection, HSP.

Galloway soon discovered that he could not shirk his duty so easily. Governor Penn, who feared possible rash measures, refused to call the Assembly, yet only the governor had the authority to issue the call. Since the House could not legally meet, Dickinson and Thomson seized the initiative. In Philadelphia and the surrounding counties, they and other more anti-British spirits organized mass meetings and established local committees to prepare the colony for any emergency, even invasion. They also proposed to call a provincial convention to which delegates from the local committees would be elected. Resolutions from meetings in Philadelphia and Chester County demanded that Speaker Galloway call an Assembly, which Dickinson and Thomson believed would be influenced by the provincial convention.[13] If he refused, as the governor already had, the convention would assume control in the absence of the Assembly and direct Pennsylvania on a more active and patriotic course. Galloway's views on these developments were probably best expressed by a "Freeman" (perhaps a pseudonym for the Speaker), who maintained that organizing extralegal committees and conventions was "THE BEGINNING OF REPUBLICANISM." [14]

Galloway was in a quandary. If he called an Assembly on his authority alone, that body's legality would be no greater than that of the projected provincial convention, and Dickinson and Thomson might persuade it to adopt extreme anti-British measures. If he refused to call an Assembly, he would automatically hand control of the province over to his enemies in the provincial convention. In either event, duly constituted authority might disappear in Pennsylvania. Galloway shuddered to think what might take its place.

13. John Penn to Lady Juliana Penn, May 31, 1774, Penn Papers, HSP. *At a Meeting at the Philosophical Society's Hall on Friday, June 10 [1774]* (Philadelphia, 1774 [Evans no. 13534]). *Pennsylvania Gazette,* June 15, June 22, 1774. Schlesinger, *Colonial Merchants,* pp. 342–50. Jensen, *Founding,* p. 480.

14. "A Freeman," *Advices from Philadelphia, dated July 23, 1774* (New York, 1774 [Evans no. 13096]).

The potentially dangerous political situation apparently forced Galloway to take a long view of the possibilities. All the colonies, including Pennsylvania, were beginning to discuss the holding of an intercolonial or continental congress. The Stamp Act Congress of nine years before had produced nothing that suited Galloway's desires for closer union with Britain, but it had acted more responsibly than most colonial assemblies and the Sons of Liberty. An intercolonial meeting held on the eve of possible separation and war might, out of desperation, adopt some palatable and positive remedy for imperial ills. A continental congress directed by men of moderate sentiments seemed the last best hope to preserve the empire and promote union. Galloway probably decided that if the governor did not call the Assembly he would. Moreover, in late June he and the Committee of Correspondence of the Assembly wrote to the Massachusetts House that "a congress of Delegates . . . appears to us the first proper step to be taken. . . . In the Congress . . . something might be produced, by their united wisdom, to ascertain our rights, and establish a political union between the two countries, with the assent of both, which would effectually secure to Americans their future rights and privileges." [15] Whether Galloway had by this time prepared a plan of union to be introduced in this intercolonial congress is not known, but at least he finally saw the absolute necessity of such a plan and committed himself to formulating one. More significant is that he pulled his head out of the sand in this crisis, abandoning equivocation and boldly proclaiming the need for some definite solution to the Anglo-American disputes.

A second consideration influencing Galloway's decision to

15. Galloway, Samuel Rhoads, William Rodman, and Isaac Pearson to the Committee of Correspondence of Massachusetts, June 28, 1774, printed in the *Pennsylvania Gazette*, July 13, 1774. This letter was apparently printed to head off criticism of Galloway's inaction, but it was attacked by a New York writer for asserting that the legislatures, not the people directly, were the proper bodies to act in this crisis. *American Archives, Fourth Series*, ed. Peter Force, 1 (Washington, 1837) : 486.

present a plan of union to the congress was his political situation in Pennsylvania. As Speaker, he had held the Dickin-
son-Thomson group at bay since his exile from Philadelphia
in 1770; but, now that the province was gripped with anti-
British fervor of unprecedented intensity, the old political
order seemed in graver danger than before. Galloway saw
for the first time, as he should have seen in 1765 and 1768,
that his previous strategy of delay and inaction would not
suffice to maintain him in office. A plan of reconciliation and
union, if presented by him and adopted by the congress,
would restore his lost political prestige. It would give him
an intercolonial standing like Franklin's; it would give him
honors outshining those of his rival, the "Pennsylvania
Farmer"; it would provide him with a rallying point for the
re-formation of the Assembly party; and it would preserve
the power of the moderate group while frustrating the disloyal
element. Local political affairs were, perhaps for the first time
in Galloway's career, secondary to finding an imperial solution, but he hoped that he could solve two problems with one
bold stroke.

Galloway's probable intention to call the Assembly did
not need to be carried out. Governor Penn believed, much
as Galloway did, that the Assembly "will be more moderate
in their Resolves than the people in their Town Meetings";
he saved Galloway a burden by calling the House to meet in
the middle of July.[16] The provincial convention, led by Dickinson and Thomson, met simultaneously; it sent over to the
Assembly some fairly mild resolutions and a request, as Galloway might have predicted, that the House appoint Dickinson
and two of his colleagues in the convention, Thomas Willing
and James Wilson, together with four assemblymen, as delegates to the projected Continental Congress. Galloway ignored
this request and prevailed on the Assembly to choose himself
and four close associates, Samuel Rhoads, Thomas Mifflin,

16. John Penn to Lady Juliana Penn, June 24, 1774, Penn Papers, HSP.
Penn cited Indian unrest, stirred up by the activities of Virginians, as
the principal reason for calling the Assembly.

John Morton, and John Ross. The "Freeman" broadside, attacking REPUBLICANISM, was distributed to assemblymen to get support for Galloway's move to block the nominees of the convention. Under the Speaker's direction, the House instructed the delegates "to form and adopt a Plan, which shall afford the best Prospect of obtaining a Redress of *American* Grievances, ascertaining *American* Rights, and establishing that Union and Harmony which is most essential to the Welfare and Happiness of both Countries." [17] Again, at this most crucial hour, Galloway outmaneuvered his opposition and committed his province to constitutional union.

The hardest task, to persuade the delegates from other colonies of the necessity and feasibility of a constitutional union, was yet to come. Moderation triumphed in Pennsylvania because of Galloway's influence, but he had no standing, or even acquaintances, of much consequence outside his own colony. The more anti-British leaders—Sam Adams, Patrick Henry, and of course the Pennsylvania Farmer—had intercolonial reputations and some intercolonial contact. Committees of correspondence in the various colonies had already generally agreed on the course of action the Continental Congress should take. Nonimportation, the tried and true cure for British oppression, was certain to be recommended by the congress and perhaps would be complemented by a boycott on exports to Britain. Galloway therefore had no illusions about the difficulty in substituting a plan of constitutional union for the probable attempt to make an economic break with the mother country. By early August he was quite pessimistic about his chances, wrote to Richard Jackson that he hoped both Britain and America would back down, and began to cast about for some strategy that would turn the Continental Congress toward moderation.[18]

17. *Votes,* 8 : 7100. Schlesinger, *Colonial Merchants,* pp. 351–56.

18. Galloway to Richard Jackson, August 10, 1774, precis, *Historical Manuscripts Commission, Fourteenth Report* (London, 1887), appendix, part 10, MSS of the Earl of Dartmouth, p. 242. William H. Nelson, *The American Tory,* p. 19, argues that the lack of intercolonial contact be-

The first step was to have ready a concrete plan for the delegates to consider. By the end of August 1774, Galloway had probably thought out his plan of union; about this time he told William Franklin that he intended to propose one.[19] The second step was to unite moderate sentiment throughout the colonies behind the idea of a plan of union. To reveal his plan before the congress met would give those who wanted sterner measures an opportunity to attack it. Galloway believed it would be more fruitful to rally support by showing the need for a plan of union without revealing what the plan actually was. In August 1774 he printed a pamphlet, *Arguments on Both Sides in the Dispute Between Great Britain and Her Colonies,* which pointed out that "to preserve the Persons and Estates of the *Americans* from the absolute Power of the Mother State, from the Tyranny of a Foreign Yoke, or from the horrible Consequences of a Civil War among ourselves, it is become indispensably necessary that there should be formed and established between the two Countries some *political Union* founded on the Principles of the *British* Constitution." [20]

The *Arguments* pamphlet was never distributed, for Galloway apparently had some second thoughts on the advisability of showing his hand.[21] Plans of union, notably Franklin's Albany Plan, had been invariably rejected or ignored heretofore. Adroit handling and careful timing were of the essence in getting this plan adopted. Galloway finally determined that his best strategy was a surprise attack on the anti-British position. If the congress deadlocked between those who wanted a boycott and those who wanted conciliation, or if a fervently

---

tween the opponents of the extreme anti-British group greatly hampered their chances to block the more radical measures.

19. William Franklin to the Earl of Dartmouth, September 6, 1774, *N.J.A.,* 1st ser. 10 : 474–75. Franklin thought that the plan proposed American representation in Parliament.

20. Galloway, *Arguments on Both Sides in the Dispute Between Great Britain and Her Colonies,* in ibid., 10 : 491.

21. William Franklin to the Earl of Dartmouth, September 6, 1774, ibid., 10 : 474.

anti-British majority slightly outnumbered a moderate minority, then Galloway would spring his plan as a workable middle way. Taken by surprise, the more anti-British group would have difficulty raising objections, and the plan would sweep through the congress on a wave of conciliation.

When the delegates arrived in Philadelphia at the end of August 1774, Galloway, knowing nothing about most of them, cautiously attempted to sound them out to discover which ones would be most receptive to his plan. The hearing given to his moderate ideas by Edward Rutledge of South Carolina and by the New Hampshire delegates was encouraging.[22] The Massachusetts General Court had in its resolves of June, which were sent to the other colonies, called for the "restoration of Union and Harmony between *Great Britain* and the Colonies," but Galloway perceived little of this moderate mood in the attitudes of the brace of Adamses and the other Bay Colony representatives.[23] Sam Adams, whom Galloway later described as one who "eats little, drinks little, sleeps little, thinks much, and is most decisive and indefatigable in the pursuit of his objects," was more interested in consulting with the Pennsylvania Farmer than with Americanus.[24]

To Galloway's dismay, it was "privately settled by an Interest made out of Doors," between the Adamses, Dickinson, and Thomson, that the delegates would meet in the home of the provincial convention—Carpenters' Hall—not in the Statehouse.[25] This arrangement signified that the delegates thought the Pennsylvania Assembly too lukewarm toward resistance to Britain, but Galloway was still confident that he could win over enough support for his scheme. Each side sized up the other when Galloway, on September 1, dined with the Massachusetts delegation. He had to endure the New Englanders' discouraging hints about nonimportation and nonexportation, which certainly confirmed his determination

22. Galloway to William Franklin, September 3, 1774, ibid., 10 : 476.

23. Ibid., 10 : 475–76. *Votes*, 8 : 7088.

24. Galloway, *Historical and Political Reflections*, p. 67.

25. Galloway to William Franklin, September 5, 1774, extract, *N.J.A.*, 1st ser. 10 : 477.

to offer an alternative. John Adams as well saw in Galloway a worthy adversary. He noted with disdain that the Pennsylvanian was, politically, "just where the Hutchinsonian Faction were in the Year 1764 [1765] when We were endeavoring to obtain a Repeal of the Stamp Act." Galloway's "Air of Reserve, Design, and Cunning" indicated to Adams that attempts to make a strong stand against Britain would meet with resolute and clever opposition in the congress.[26] Each side now understood the other's general viewpoint, and each suspected the other of the worst motives and principles. Galloway enjoyed a slight advantage. He knew that the Adamses and their allies were planning to sever America from Britain commercially; his plan would take them by surprise and frustrate their schemes.

Because the Adams-led faction was suspicious of his moderation, Galloway attempted to allay their doubts about his patriotism by taking a firm and positive stand on the question of American rights in the debates in the congress. Although as Americanus and during the Townshend Acts crisis he had equivocated on the question, he could no longer evade the issue. In the discussions of the congressional committee charged with declaring the rights of the colonists and exploring ways by which these rights might be guaranteed, Galloway had to take a firm stand before the influential leaders from the other colonies, else he would be counted an enemy of American aspirations and his subsequent proposals would be disregarded. In the committee meetings, some delegates asserted the natural rights of the colonists, cited Locke to substantiate these, and declared that America ought to force Parliament to acknowledge them. More legalistic delegates believed that America should base its case on the British constitution, which Parliament had violated. To Galloway, the first argument was dangerous and the second was faulty. A reliance on natural rights as a justification for denying the authority of Parliament appeared to deny that the colonists were fundamentally Englishmen; moreover, such

26. John Adams, *Diary and Autobiography*, ed. Butterfield, 2 : 119–21.

an argument might be used as a justification for separation from Britain. Galloway admired the British "constitution" as protection for the rights of the British nation, but he realized that this constitution was changeable by parliamentary statute, while Americans went unrepresented in Parliament. Thus, the constitution could not really apply to the colonies.[27]

Galloway presented a third viewpoint, which neatly avoided the objections against these other arguments, probably astounded those who thought him too moderate, and laid the groundwork for his plan of union. He asserted that "we might reduce our Rights to one. An Exemption from all Laws made by British Parliament, made since the Emigration of our Ancestors." In this view, all legislation prior to 1607, including the Magna Carta, would be binding on America. All laws passed by Parliament after the Jamestown settlement, including the Navigation Acts, manufacturing restrictions, and duties, would be void and of no effect in America because America was not represented in Parliament and not part of the realm.[28] Galloway's position possessed little logical consistency and little historical reality. Colonial charters, in prohibiting the enactment of colonial laws contrary to the laws of England, had established a legal relationship between mother country and colonies. Americans might not believe that the Navigation Acts governed them, but they generally did believe themselves entitled to the protections of the Bill of Rights of 1689. Whether Galloway really adhered to this theory himself is doubtful, for he had never previously intimated that he thought that America and Britain had had no legal connection after 1607. Americanus had refused to oppose the Stamp Act and the Townshend duties on such grounds; now he boldly proclaimed that these acts and others like them

27. Ibid., 2 : 129–30. Page Smith, *John Adams* (Garden City, N.Y., 1962), 1 : 172–74. Jensen, *Founding*, pp. 493–94.

28. Adams, *Diary and Autobiography*, ed. Butterfield, 2 : 130. Galloway further argued that American rights should be stated on the basis of the rights of Englishmen. Americans had not clearly had these rights extended to them heretofore.

never were binding on America. His theory was apparently constructed on the spur of the moment in order to identify him as a defender of American rights and prepare the way for the introduction of his plan of union.

Galloway went beyond the conclusion that Franklin had reached in 1768 and that John Adams was soon to propound in his *Novanglus*—that the king, not Parliament, was the bond between Britain and America. For him, there was no present bond. "I am well aware," he announced to the congressional committee, "that my Arguments tend to an Independency of the Colonies, and militate against the Maxim that there must be some absolute Power to draw together all the Wills and Strength of the Empire." [29] Galloway did not desire the other delegates to draw the conclusion that America should therefore separate; he was intent on convincing them that America was truly in a state of anarchy which should be remedied. Because there was no formal connection between mother country and colonies in 1774, a plan providing for a constitutional union was essential to join them and form a legal and binding relationship. The theoretical basis for the introduction of his plan of union, to be presented when he believed the time was ripe, was now prepared.

Galloway's unconventional theory perhaps made John Adams revise this earlier estimate of his fellow delegate, but it was not well received. The declaration and resolves agreed to by the congress on October 14 were a compromise of the major points of view, reiterating the claims of Americans to natural and constitutional rights. Galloway opposed four of the resolutions but probably agreed with the other six; he particularly opposed the fourth resolution, that Americans could be represented only by their own colonial legislatures, for this proposition clashed with his projected plan of union.[30]

29. Ibid.

30. *Journals of the Continental Congress, 1774–1789,* ed. Worthington C. Ford (Washington, 1904), 1 : 63–73. Galloway, *Examination,* pp. 56–57, claimed that he did not remember whether he opposed or approved many of the resolutions, but this seems a deliberate equivocation.

In the Continental Congress, the majority of delegates, as one might expect, were firmly in support of nonimportation as the most effective remedy for American difficulties. The southern colonies, New York, and New Jersey had instructed their delegates to vote for nonimportation, and the New England representatives generally favored the measure. Galloway had neither inclination nor opportunity to oppose nonimportation, which was adopted unanimously, after considerable warm debate, on September 27.[31] He hoped to take advantage of the opposition to nonexportation, which the anti-British group sought to push through the congress next. The delegations were more widely split over this extreme step; Massachusetts and the southern colonies were in favor, although in disagreement over when it should begin, but the other colonies were reluctant to declare so boldly that they did not need British markets. This split accorded with Galloway's strategy. Those who regarded nonexportation as impractical and dangerous would, he thought, probably be willing to grasp at any reasonable alternative. On September 28 at the opening of the session, Galloway took the floor and proceeded with the most important task of his life.

Galloway, described by John Adams as a sensible, learned, but cold speaker, courageously summoned his oratorical powers in a passionate plea for conciliation and the adoption of a more moderate course. "I am as much a friend of Liberty [as] exists—and No Man shall go further, in Point of Fortune, or in Point of Blood, than the Man who now addresses you," he declared in an effort to convince the congress of his fervent patriotism.[32] He reminded the delegates that, despite their feelings toward Britain, they all had instructions to find a way to restore union and harmony. Nonimportation and nonexportation, Galloway argued, would not achieve this result. Nonimportation would not work its havoc on the British

31. *Journals of the Continental Congress*, 1 : 43. Jensen, *Founding*, pp. 496–97. Schlesinger, *Colonial Merchants*, pp. 324–79, notes the instructions to the delegates.

32. Adams, *Diary and Autobiography*, ed. Butterfield, 2 : 142.

economy fast enough to effect the relief of Boston. Nonexportation was an "indigested proposition"; Galloway conjured up visions of ruined planters and prostrate merchants who depended on the sale of goods to Britain. Severing commercial ties with the mother country would make the colonists too weak to fight "another Struggle [with France] which I fear is too near." [33] These were bold and well-chosen words. Galloway demonstrated his agreement with the more anti-British members and asserted his readiness to take up arms to defend his country; but he criticized the more radical methods as self-defeating.

Now, at the optimum moment, the plan of union was revealed. Galloway proposed that the Continental Congress petition the king for a redress of grievances and submit to the king and Parliament his plan, amended as the congress thought advisable. The plan provided that a "British and American" legislature be established in the colonies. A president-general, appointed by the king, and a grand council, composed of representatives elected by each colonial legislature for three year terms, would make laws applying to intercolonial affairs. The grand council would be guaranteed all rights and privileges of the British House of Commons. The president-general would have veto power over the actions of the grand council. The legislature could not interfere in the internal affairs of any colony. All acts of the grand council, approved by the president-general, would be submitted to Parliament for ratification. All legislation in any way affecting the colonies that was passed by Parliament would have to be approved by this intercolonial legislature.[34]

33. Ibid., 2 : 141. Adams is the best source for Galloway's speech, as he certainly had no reason to portray Galloway as more of a patriot than he actually was. Galloway's version of his speech, in his *Historical and Political Reflections*, pp. 70–81, omits his remarks about fighting the British. This later version also praised parliamentary supremacy extravagantly, because Galloway hoped to get favorable treatment from Parliament.

34. *Journals of the Continental Congress*, 1 : 49–51; Boyd, *Anglo-American Union*, pp. 112–14. Galloway left several gaps in the plan for

Galloway drew inspiration from the Albany Plan presented by his old political partner in 1754. He used the same terms for the executive and the council as did Franklin. Three-year tenure and the election of councillors by the colonial legislatures were also features of Franklin's plan. Both plans contained a federal scheme that admitted a wide latitude of interpretation, for they gave the intercolonial legislature jurisdiction over all matters affecting more than one colony. The American check on Parliament and the parliamentary check on America were original with Galloway.[35] Unlike Scotland, the individual colonies possessed legislatures that controlled their purely local affairs. Unlike Ireland, America could determine what parlimentary legislation would be in force in the colonies. Galloway hoped that the features of colonial autonomy and colonial review of British imperial legislation would sell his plan to the congress—and that the feature of parliamentary review of American legislation would sell it to Britain.

Caught completely by surprise, as Galloway intended, many delegates reacted favorably to his proposal. It was quickly seconded by James Duane of New York. John Jay supported it; Edward Rutledge of South Carolina called it "almost a perfect Plan." [36] The Adams-Henry faction was dismayed at what it believed was purely a temporizing measure designed to kill support for nonexportation. Despite Galloway's criticism of boycotts, the chief of the Boston "Mohawks" believed that economic pressure on Britain was the only way to relieve Boston. A petition to the king accompanied by a plan acknowl-

---

the congress to fill in: the apportionment of representation on the council, the particular powers of the legislature, and the site of the capital city. He hoped to obtain adoption of the main outline and resolve these other matters later.

35. The Virginia Company in 1618 had provided for a similar relationship between it and the House of Burgesses in Jamestown, but this was only temporary. Whether Galloway had this rather obscure precedent in mind is doubtful.

36. Adams, *Diary and Autobiography*, ed. Butterfield, 2 : 143.

edging parliamentary authority over the colonies was for Sam
Adams a show of weakness. The chief Virginia radical might
allow that Caesar had his Brutus, but America would not
have her Galloway. Quickly he rose to speak against the plan,
claiming that the American legislature, appointed not by the
people but by the assemblies, would be susceptible to the same
bribery and corruption that diseased Parliament. Henry's
criticism was overstated yet typically American; Franklin had
compared "honest" American politics with British "corruption" on numerous occasions.[37]

After the congress recessed that day, Adams put mighty
pressures on the other delegates to reject the Galloway plan.
As Galloway in 1779 related the story:

> Mr. Adams and his party left no means in their power
> unessayed, to prevail on the Members of Congress to re-
> ject it on the second reading, and lest this step should
> fail of success, to incense the mob of Philadelphia against
> it. At that time, the minds of the lower ranks of people
> in Philadelphia, who were governed in a great degree
> by Mr. Adams, being prepared for the most violent
> measures, Mr. Galloway and his friends thought their
> personal safety depended on not renewing the motion.[38]

Perhaps fear of violence impelled Galloway to drop his plan,
as it had influenced him to preach moderation and practice
inaction in past crises. But it is unlikely that Adams's demagoguery defeated Galloway; he offered this explanation because he refused to admit that the Adamses and Henry had
powerful arguments on their side. They persuaded a majority
of the delegates to reject the plan probably on the grounds
that America had to force Parliament to recognize her rights
by coercive measures and thus could not offer union to

37. Ibid. One might compare Henry's objections to the Galloway plan
with his attack on the Federal Constitution in the Virginia ratifying
convention fourteen years later. His views have both consistency and
shallowness.

38. Galloway, *Examination*, p. 48, note.

Britain until the offensive legislation was repealed. On September 29 the congress postponed consideration of the plan by a close vote—six colonies to five. About a month later it was rejected finally. Probably by a vote on October 22, Galloway's motion and plan were obliterated from the minutes to preserve an illusion of unanimity.[39] Galloway had almost timed the introduction of his plan perfectly. It looked like a workable middle way. Yet, most delegates were in no mood to be accommodating toward Britain, and they were reluctant to try a new cure for imperial ills when more orthodox and tested remedies seemed in order. In reality, Galloway's plan came too late in the continuing breakdown of Anglo-American relations to do much good.

Rejection of his plan crushed the Pennsylvania delegate. He had placed all his hopes on it as a means of saving the empire from disruption and civil war. He could not comprehend how the Continental Congress could vote down this most reasonable of proposals for insuring political and social stability. Broken by his failure, Galloway was at first lost in confusion. He did not immediately quit the congress, perhaps because he thought he yet could do some good. Although detesting the prospect of nonexportation, but unable to oppose it effectively, he stuck out the debates. He signed the Continental Association, which established the boycott, although he later claimed that he never approved of it and signed only because all the delegates had agreed to act unanimously. More to his liking was the petition to the king, which he also signed, which detailed American grievances and humbly and dutifully prayed for relief. As well, Galloway had the onerous duty of revising the minutes, so he was forced to stare at the blank

39. William Franklin to the Earl of Dartmouth, December 6, 1774, *N.J.A.*, 1st ser. 10 : 504. *Journals of the Continental Congress,* 1 : 102. Galloway, *Examination,* p. 48, reported that his opponents feared the effect of the plan. "Conscious that it would be approved of by the people at large, if published, and believing Mr. Galloway would not venture to make it public, they procured a majority, who ordered it, with the introductory motion, to be erased from their Minutes."

from which his plan was expunged.[40] Defeat seemed to strip him temporarily of all creative capacity.

A second result of the rejection of Galloway's plan was his political demise. Adoption of the plan would have insured his control of Pennsylvania. Its presentation and defeat, however, showed the growing anti-British element in the colony that the Speaker was not sympathetic enough to their views. The election of 1774 in Pennsylvania, coming while the Continental Congress was meeting, was a distinct triumph for the anti-British faction. Dickinson was elected from Philadelphia County and Thomson from the city. To be confronted in the Assembly by his chief enemies at such a critical time was painful enough for Galloway; worse yet, many others who opposed his views were also elected. The newly organized county committees helped to place anti-British representatives in the Assembly; new faces who were not under Galloway's powerful influence looked up coldly at the Speaker's chair. The Speaker himself easily won in his rotten borough, but without his old supporters in the House he was lost. John Adams reported to his wife, "[the election] will change the Ballance in the Legislature here against Mr. Galloway who has been supposed to sit on the Skirts of the American Advocates." [41] Adams was an accurate analyst. The more anti-British assemblymen led in unanimously unseating the Speaker of the last eight years and installing Edward Biddle, a Quaker patriot from the western county of Berks. The revolution begun against Galloway in 1770 was now completed.[42]

Lost were Galloway's chances for both restoring Anglo-American harmony and rebuilding his own political prominence. It was small consolation for the broken politician that he still retained some influence in the Assembly and was

40. Galloway, *Examination*, p. 51. *Journals of the Continental Congress*, 1 : 80, 101, 113, 121.

41. John Adams to Abigail Adams, October 7, 1774, *Adams Family Correspondence*, ed. Butterfield (Cambridge, Mass., 1963), 1 : 165.

42. *Votes*, 8 : 7148. Craig Biddle, "Edward Biddle," *PMHB* 1 (1877) : 100–03, is barely adequate on the new Speaker.

named to important committees. His defeats made Galloway view his position in Pennsylvania as quite desperate, and they encouraged him to leave the colony for more congenial climes. In November 1774 he departed for a short visit to New York, the colony whose delegates had seconded his plan of union. Here he hoped to encounter more sympathetic ears and perhaps be able to take the case for his plan of union directly to the people, bypassing the congress.

The calling of the Continental Congress was a clarion to action for Franklin as well as for Galloway. Because he had lost all opportunity to lobby in Britain, Franklin directed his efforts toward encouraging united American resistance. In contrast to his slow and halting adoption of a position of resistance during the Stamp Act and Townshend Acts crises, Franklin now wasted no time in forwarding advice to the anti-British side in America. His plan was the same as it had been in 1769. "All who know well the State of things here, agree, that if the Non Consumption Agreement should become general, and be firmly adhered to, this Ministry must be ruined, and our Friends succeed them, from whom we may hope a great Constitutional Charter to be confirmed by King, Lords, & Commons, whereby our Liberties shall be recognized and established, as the only sure Foundation of that Union so necessary for our Common welfare," he advised Cushing in September 1774.[43] Franklin repeated his formula of nonconsumption, meaning nonimportation, in all his correspondence during the fall of 1774 and through early 1775. To encourage Charles Thomson, he wrote that "wise Observers are confident, that if America can hold strictly to its Non-Consumption Agreement another Year, it is impossible [the ministry] can stand the universal Clamour which begins to thicken round their Heads"; and, perhaps to reassure Galloway, he confidently asserted that if "we are steady till another Session

43. Franklin to Thomas Cushing, September 3, 1774, *Writings*, ed. Smyth, 6 : 239. Franklin to William Franklin, September 7, 1774, ibid., 6 : 240–42. William Franklin was by now showing Loyalist sympathies; his father called him a "thorough Courtier."

[of Parliament], this Ministry must retire, & our Points will be gained." [44]

The efficacy of economic pressure and the possibility of an overturn of the North ministry were probably not only Franklin's views but also those of his friends associated with the Rockingham opposition in Commons. Both predictions were really faint hopes of the minority. Perhaps the British economy could have been badly injured by a boycott, but Franklin received little support from the merchants, who showed scant fear of the Continental Association. By 1774–75 British merchants were less dependent on American trade, having found new markets in Spanish America, and were consequently less willing to support colonists who were questioning the power of Parliament to regulate trade.[45] The possibility that the Rockingham group would come to power very soon was even more chimerical. Franklin expressed some doubt that parliamentary change offered much hope; to Galloway he wrote, "I begin to think a Parliament here of little Use to the People: . . . being a very expensive Machine, that requires a vast deal of oiling and greasing at the People's Charge, for they finally pay all the enormous Salaries of Places, the Pensions, and the Bribes, now by Custom become necessary to induce the Members to vote according to their Consciences." [46] The agent optimistically remained in London to present whatever results the congress sent over and to try by means of newspaper pieces to generate some sentiment among the merchants for the American cause.[47]

44. Franklin to Charles Thomson, March 13, 1775, ibid., 6: 316. Franklin to Galloway, February 5, 1775, *Autobiographical Writings*, ed. Van Doren, p. 346.

45. Donoughue, *British Politics*, pp. 152–56; Sosin, *Agents and Merchants*, pp. 188–89, 199.

46. Franklin to Galloway, October 12, 1774, *Writings*, ed. Smyth, 6: 253–54.

47. Franklin published three newspaper pieces between November 1774 and February 1775 in which he attempted to appeal mainly to the British merchants. *Franklin's Letters to the Press*, ed. Crane, nos. 136, 139, 141, pp. 268–76 and pp. 279–83. He also republished the "Causes of the American

Like Franklin, others in Britain, even in the North ministry, hoped that reconciliation might yet be achieved. Although he was persona non grata with the ministry, and it abhorrent to him, it was not too difficult for ministers interested in reconciliation to coax a plan out of the agent. The Earl of Dartmouth and Thomas Villiers, Lord Hyde, two ministers who were much less hostile to America than most, decided to approach Franklin by two indirect lines. Dartmouth worked through his physician, Dr. John Fothergill, Quaker and longtime friend of Franklin; Hyde employed Lord Richard Howe and David Barclay, a Quaker merchant and friend of both Fothergill and Franklin.[48] In December 1774 Howe's sister, at Howe's instigation, challenged Franklin to play chess. During these sessions, she praised and flattered the old man, trying to draw from him his views concerning the basis for a reconciliation of Britain and America. She hinted that the ministry might make use of his services. Franklin replied that he doubted that he could do anything, but evidently Howe's sister set him to thinking.[49] The same day, December 4, that his chess partner had suggested he could help solve the crisis, Franklin met with Barclay and Fothergill at their request. They asked the agent "with great Earnestness" to draw up

---

Discontents Before 1768," ibid., no. 137, pp. 277–78, apparently because he believed that his previous arguments were as valid in 1774 as they had been in 1768.

48. The origin of this attempt to draw from Franklin some scheme of reconciliation is obscure. Almost certainly the initiative came from the ministers, not from Howe, Fothergill, or Barclay. Because of his favorable attitude toward America, Dartmouth seems most likely to have originated the idea of working with Franklin, but Bargar, *Lord Dartmouth,* p. 134, is uncertain on this point. Barclay and Fothergill were included because of their associations with Franklin and America. Howe was sympathetic toward America, according to Troyer S. Anderson, *The Command of the Howe Brothers During the American Revolution* (New York, 1936), p. 338. See also Van Doren, *Franklin,* pp. 495–96.

49. Franklin, *An Account of Negotiations in London for Effecting a Reconciliation between Great Britain and the American Colonies,* in *Writings,* ed. Smyth, 6 : 326–27.

some plan for solving the crisis. Moved by these varied solicitations, Franklin prepared what he called "Hints for Conversation," which he read to Barclay and Fothergill on December 6.

These seventeen "Hints," agreed to with minor changes by the Quaker gentlemen, did not consititute any real plan of union. Franklin did not see how a plan of union presented at this point would fare any better than his Albany Plan had. His "Hints" suggested that the best approach was first to restore the status quo ante 1763. The drowned tea would be paid for. Parliament would repeal the tea duty. The Coercive Acts and the extension of the Treasons Act to the colonies would be repealed. Castle William would be restored to Massachusetts. To guard against future disunion, Franklin suggested reforms of the commercial relationship and the imperial constitution. The American Vice-Admiralty courts would be reformed. All customs officers would be appointed by colonial governors, not directly from England. The colonial legislatures would enact the Navigation Acts, making them binding on the colonies by their own decision. All revenue from the operation of these acts would be applied to American expenses. Royal naval officers would enforce them. The acts that restricted manufacturing in America would be reconsidered by Parliament. The colonies would support their own militias in peacetime; no requisitions would be levied by Britain during peacetime. In wartime the colonies would contribute to the Crown upon requisition; the size of each colony's contribution would be determined by the proportion of peacetime taxation the colonies levied. No troops could enter a colony, and no forts could be built, without consent of the assembly. Governors would be paid by assemblies only. Judges would be appointed on good behavior; or, if appointed at pleasure, they would be paid a salary appropriated yearly by the assembly. Finally, and most important, Parliament would renounce all power to make laws affecting the internal affairs of the colonies.[50]

50. Ibid., 6 : 328–41. Barclay and Fothergill persuaded Franklin to substitute "reconsidered" instead of asserting that the acts restraining manu-

The "Hints" were not really new, for they restated Franklin's persistent argument that Britain should return the imperial situation to the good old days of salutary neglect, when Anglo-American relations had been peaceful and demands on the colonies at a minimum. They reflected rather accurately the rights that the Continental Congress and colonial writers were demanding from Britain. They also provided for a constitutional arrangement, which, although not a union, better defined the imperial relationship.

Having copied down the "Hints," the intermediaries forwarded them to Dartmouth and Hyde. But even these pro-American ministers found that the "Hints" demanded too much; on December 22 Barclay informed Franklin that "Lord H. [yde] tho't the Propositions too hard." Not recognizing that the "Hints" constituted that which Franklin and other colonial leaders had been demanding since about 1768, Dartmouth and Hyde apparently believed that the agent was raising the price of peace artificially high in order to strike a bargain. Howe, intimating that a reward might be in store for Franklin if his efforts were successful, requested him to draw up another plan, which Franklin did the last week of December 1774. This plan, based on the "Hints," was forwarded to Howe by his sister, Franklin's chess opponent. It provided that the laws to which the Continental Congress' petition to the king objected—the revenue acts and the Coercive Acts—would be repealed, that all troops and fleets would be withdrawn from America, that other grievous legislation would be repealed or altered, and that Britain would recognize the Second Continental Congress by appointing "a person of Weight and Dignity of Character" as president of it and by requisitioning it for supplies.[51] On January 19, 1775, Howe informed Franklin that these terms were also unacceptable.

---

facturing should be "repealed." One "Hint," that America would supply requisitions in peacetime if Britain gave up her commercial monopoly, was struck out.

51. Ibid., 6 : 344, 353–56, 358–59.

Franklin now requested that the ministry supply some indication of what it would accept. This he received in a meeting with Fothergill and Barclay on February 4. They informed him of Dartmouth's opinion of the "Hints": the ministry refused to repeal the Coercive Acts, except for the Boston Port Act; would not permit the reenactment of the Navigation Acts by the colonial legislatures; would not admit that colonial legislatures had to grant approval before troops could be dispatched to a colony; and would not renounce parliamentary authority over American affairs.[52] In rejecting the most important of Franklin's "Hints," while accepting the others with qualifications, Dartmouth made the error of assuming that Franklin would counter with a less demanding proposal. But the "Hints" were statements of the basic rights that Americans claimed, and Franklin declared "that while the Parliament claim'd and exercis'd a Power of altering our Constitutions at pleasure, there could be no Agreement; for we were render'd unsafe in every Privilege we had a Right to, and were secure in nothing." [53] Franklin knew that Americans would not accept parliamentary supremacy, while Parliament would apparently accept nothing less. The treatment of the petition of the Continental Congress showed this. Dartmouth accepted it and the king submitted it to the House of Commons, but there no attention at all was given it.[54] Reconciliation on the basis of the recognition of American rights by Britain was unwisely rejected by the ministry.

Some pro-American British leaders desired, as did Galloway, that both sides back down. The Earl of Chatham drew up a plan whereby America and Britain would each relinquish some claims; on January 29, 1775, he brought it to Franklin for his suggestions. It was not as strong as the "Hints"; Chatham resisted Franklin's attempts to improve it. The plan recognized the right of Parliament to make laws for the colonies but suggested that those laws to which the colonists

52. Ibid., 6 : 371–74.
53. Ibid., 6 : 373–74.
54. Franklin to Charles Thomson, February 5, 1775, ibid., 6 : 304.

particularly objected be temporarily suspended. The Continental Congress would be made legal and permanent and would be obliged to make free grants to the Crown for imperial purposes. Three days after their meeting, Franklin watched in disgust in the House of Lords as the ministerial faction, arguing that the agent was the real author of this plan, rejected even this mild proposal.[55]

Another plan of reconciliation was conceived by David Barclay and submitted to Franklin on February 16. It was essentially those "Hints" of Franklin to which the ministry responded affirmatively. The first step in this plan was for the Massachusetts agents, Franklin and Arthur Lee, to engage that the tea would be paid for; then, a commissioner would be sent over to open the port of Boston. Franklin thought this plan much inferior to his own, but he agreed to it if the ministry would repeal all the Coercive Acts. Barclay reported Franklin's reaction to Lord Hyde and Lord Howe, who received it with enthusiasm at first. But when Franklin met with Lord Hyde on March 1, the latter had cooled considerably; the ministry refused to repeal the Coercive Acts under any conditions. The determination of the home government to preserve and exert parliamentary authority over America completely blocked all Franklin's attempts at negotiation.[56]

The Galloway plan of union came to Franklin's hand

55. Franklin, *Account of Negotiations,* in ibid., 6: 360–71. Donoughue, *British Politics,* pp. 235–38. Van Doren, *Franklin,* pp. 511–13.

56. Franklin, *Account of Negotiations,* in *Writings,* ed. Smyth, 6: 375–87, 391–95. Hyde was more interested in discovering what Franklin and America thought of Lord North's "conciliatory" motion. Introduced on February 20, but apparently planned since January, the plan offered the colonies freedom from parliamentary taxation if they would tax themselves to contribute to the common defense. Donoughue, *British Politics,* pp. 224, 244, 250–51; Jensen, *Founding,* pp. 575, 580–82. Franklin, writing to Galloway, February 25, 1775, *Writings,* ed. Smyth, 6: 313–14, regarded it as at best a highwayman's demand and at worst a trick to split the united colonial front. The chief service of this plan was that it enabled the ministry to reply to Franklin and others who opposed its American policy that it had offered America reconciliation, and the colonists should accept these "generous" terms.

sometime in January 1775, while the agent was waiting for a reply to his proposals.[57] Now Franklin saw more clearly than ever before how much he and his old partner had split apart in repeated crises. Galloway wanted to allow Parliament a limited authority over the colonies, but his mentor believed this unacceptable and unjust. He replied to Galloway that he had now given up his hopes for any constitutional union; a legislative junction of Britain and America was unwise and probably impossible to maintain, if any regard were to be paid to American rights. Union between corrupt Britain and virtuous America would ruin the latter. In Britain "Numberless and needless Places, enormous Salaries, Pensions, Perquisites, Bribes, groundless Quarrels, foolish Expeditions, false Accounts or no Accounts, Contracts and Jobbs, devour all Revenue and produce continual Necessity in the Midst of natural Plenty," Franklin charged in the manner of Tacitus recounting the vices of imperial Rome. American frugality and industry would soon succumb to corrupt British profligacy when combined in any legislative union, he claimed—much as Patrick Henry had argued against Galloway's plan. This was not a very valid objection to the plan; a colonial union linked to Britain would not be inherently corrupt.

Franklin raised a more telling point: Britain's interests were not the same as imperial interests. "[Britain] may drag us after them in all the plundering Wars, which their desperate Circumstances, Injustice, and Rapacity, may prompt them to undertake."[58] Americans never thought that Britain's wars on the Continent were much of their concern, Franklin argued. The results of European expeditions were the draining

57. Galloway probably sent Franklin a copy of his plan in a letter of October or November 1774. Franklin to Galloway, February 5, 1775, *Autobiographical Writings*, ed. Van Doren, p. 345. William Franklin sent a copy to Dartmouth and suggested that it might be used as a basis for settlement of the Anglo-American dispute. William Franklin to the Earl of Dartmouth, December 6, 1774, *N.J.A.*, 1st ser. 10 : 503–04. Dartmouth acknowledged its receipt on January 6, 1775, to William Franklin, January 7, 1775, ibid., 10 : 535.

58. Franklin to Galloway, February 25, 1775, *Writings*, ed. Smyth, 6 : 312.

of the resources of the whole empire and the heightening of friction between the British colonies and their French and Spanish neighbors. Franklin did not advocate that America aim for complete independence from British foreign policy; he believed that the British Empire should be an instrument for the defense of the mother country and colonies, not an offensive alliance against the powers of Europe. Here he hit upon a basic weakness of Galloway's plan; it did not provide America with any voice in determining the overall policy of the empire. The plan was wise in its proposal for a new imperial constitution, but it preserved some of the defects of the old one.

Objections notwithstanding, Franklin saw that Galloway had made a genuine and honest effort to bind up the widening wound. In this grave crisis no possible solution could be cast aside. Believing that Britain might accept the plan even though the Continental Congress had not, at the end of January the agent showed it to Lord Chatham and Lord Camden, hoping that it might "bring on some Negociation and stay their Hands from Blood; of which I grieve to say there is but little Prospect. . . . I would try any thing, and bear any thing that can be borne with Safety to our just Liberties," he confided to Galloway, "rather than engage in a War with such near relations, unless compelled to do it by dire Necessity in our own Defense." [59]

Milder and more conciliatory plans like Chatham's had been rejected. There seemed no hope for Galloway's plan in Britain. Chatham and Camden never made use of it. Dartmouth ignored it, never encouraging his colleagues in the ministry to try the plan. Before April 1775 it received little notice in Britain; then, a printed version circulated in London. Samuel Wharton reported to Franklin from London that his old partner's scheme was not well received. The "Courtiers" treated "with ineffable Contempt, the Plan of

59. Franklin to Galloway, February 5, 1775, *Autobiographical Writings*, ed. Van Doren, p. 345; Franklin to Galloway, February 25, 1775, *Writings*, ed. Smyth, 6 : 312.

Union proposed, and which they say, by *not* being adopted,—offended the Authors Pride, and has been the happy Means, of their being satisfactorily *confirmed* in their Idea, of the Weakness and Division of the Colonies; And that by Perseverance,—they shall unquestionably obtain a perfect Submission." [60] Parliament pushed on toward the destruction of the empire, deriding attempts to save it, rather than repeal offensive legislation or permit Americans to reject laws affecting the colonies. Galloway's plan, like Franklin's Albany Plan, offered more to Britain than Americans in general would concede, but it was deemed too republican by the British. The last and most important efforts of the partners had failed.

All opportunities for peace seemed lost, and the empire appeared doomed; in March 1775 Franklin had no alternative but to return to Pennsylvania. His position in Britain was not only useless but also precarious, for he feared that if revolution broke out in America he might be seized.[61] As well, although of less significance, his wife Deborah had died in December 1774, leaving business matters to be settled in Philadelphia. Probably the loss of his wife made him feel guilty about deserting his family and his friends for so long. As he prepared to depart, Franklin could see that his long years as an agent had been to little purpose. The best man Pennsylvania had to offer had achieved little of his program. Britain gave him no opportunity to accomplish anything.

60. Samuel Wharton to Franklin, April 17, 1775, Franklin Papers, 4 : 50, APS. Wharton was still angling in vain for the Walpole grant.

61. William Franklin wrote his father, December 24, 1774, ibid., a separate letter: "If there was any Prospect of your being able to bring the People in power to your Way of Thinking, or of those of your Way of Thinking being brought into Power, I should not think so much of your Stay. But as you have had by this Time pretty strong Proofs that neither can be reasonably expected and that you are look'd upon with an evil Eye in that Country, and are in no small Danger of being brought into Trouble for your political Conduct, you had certainly better return to a Country where the People revere you, and are inclined to pay a Deference to your Opinions."

Agents like Franklin were the only representatives the colonies had in London, yet they were generally ignored. Britain thereby demonstrated that it had a calculated policy of treating the colonists as inferiors. The agents were forced to lobby for what crumbs they could obtain as if they represented not parts of the political state but some minor business interest. The American colonists expected fair treatment as a matter of right; in London their agents were compelled to beg for fair treatment as a favor. Under these circumstances the colonies could never attain what they deserved.[62]

Franklin's departure from Britain on March 21, 1775, and his crossing to Philadelphia must have been among the lowest moments of his life. Rejected, powerless to stop the coming catastrophe, he was now returning to a scene where the part he would play was unclear. Where would he, almost seventy years old, fit in among the younger men who were directing his colony on its course of resistance? Of those most opposed to Britain, Franklin was really friendly with only his old supporter Thomson. His son and his old partner had opposed the programs of the congress, which he had supported. Would he likewise be out of tune with the revolutionary movement once he arrived home?

Franklin probably intended to make the transition from the British to the American scene as smoothly as possible. Because he had continually corresponded with Thomson, he would probably not be ignored by the supporters of the Continental Congress and the Association. He had also written to Galloway that he believed he could iron out the differences between his old partner and himself. "In the calm Retirement of Trevose," he wrote to Galloway at the beginning of the crisis, "perhaps we may spend some hours usefully, I am sure they will be spent agreeably." [63] He apparently intended to explain to Galloway face to face how through the last ten trying years

62. Kammen, *Rope of Sand*, pp. 314-18, draws somewhat different conclusions about the agents' reasons for failure.

63. Franklin to Galloway, February 18, 1774, in draft, Franklin Papers, 65 : 76, APS.

he had at every turn been confronted by ministerial duplicity, parliamentary unwillingness to listen to American grievances, and a general belief that colonies and colonists were inferior and subordinate. Straight talk might win Galloway over to his point of view. If they could not patch up the split empire, at least they might patch up the split partnership. An old aim of the partnership, the preservation of peace and harmony between Britain and America, was now impossible to maintain. Franklin had chosen sides. What side would Galloway, who throughout his career had wavered, now choose?

10 The Final Break

During the six months preceding Franklin's return to Philadelphia in early May 1775, Galloway's political views became more estranged from those of his old partner than they had been before the crisis. The two men had previously disagreed on the authority of Parliament and the propriety of boycotts. Now they parted further on another important question concerning imperial relations: the meaning and effect of the actions resolved upon by the First Continental Congress. From London, Franklin endorsed the union of the colonies in a congress and encouraged that body's proposals for both reconciliation and resistance. Galloway went to New York in November 1774 to find support for his plan of union outside the congress and the extralegal committees. It was a greatly changed Galloway, a Galloway who seemingly had lost his rationality, his political poise, and the pro-American determination he had displayed in the congress. He let his unstable temper take command of his reason. Stubbornly and illogically he blamed for the defeat of his plan and for his failures in Pennsylvania politics a conspiracy of "Presbyterians" who had their eyes set on independence. He convinced himself that this "malevolent sect" had captured control of the congress, and of many colonial assemblies and extralegal conventions, to achieve its aim of separating America from Britain. Rejection of Galloway's plan to restore union and harmony proved to him that this "Presbyterian" group did not want union and harmony.[1] Now Galloway was determined that his plan should perform a different function. With it, he would lash out at the Continental Congress and its supporters, deriding their

1. Galloway to William Franklin, March 26, 1775, *N.J.A.*, 1st ser. 10: 585.

republicanism and calling attention to his plan as the only way to save America from a horrible fate.

Galloway's experiences and his emotional state compelled him to reject Franklin's view, which, by the end of 1774, he knew to be approval of the congress' actions. In New York, where the Assembly failed to approve the Continental Association but separately petitioned the Crown for redress, he found more congenial intellectual company: James Duane, Samuel Verplanck, and John Jay. He also found a printer, James Rivington, who operated the "free press" that Galloway wanted to use to "recall the deluded people to their senses." [2] He was soon convinced that there was a majority who opposed the extreme measures of the Association and whom he could reach by anticongress propaganda. Once he had presented his plan to the public, this majority would, he thought, rally around his alternative to nonimportation and nonexportation, overturn the anti-British leaders, and demand that the congress and the colonial assemblies institute his scheme.

Hot off Rivington's press, Galloway's *Candid Examination of the Mutual Claims of Great Britain, and the Colonies: with a Plan of Accommodation, on Constitutional Principles* appeared in February 1775. Not candid in the slightest, it was a vindictive tirade against the "illegal, motley" congress which, among other crimes, incited the "unthinking, ignorant multitude" to ravish the wives and daughters of the loyal element.[3] Certain that the Presbyterians were plotting independence, Galloway warned of the consequences of such a move. Britain would very likely crush with severity an attempt to break away. If she did not oppose American independence, Americans would not, anyhow, long enjoy their freedom.

2. Galloway to Samuel Verplanck, February 14, 1775, "Some Letters of Joseph Galloway," *PMHB* 21 (1897) : 481. Rivington was publisher of what was later called the "royal, loyal, lying Gazette."

3. Galloway, *A Candid Examination of the Mutual Claims of Great Britain, and the Colonies: with a Plan of Accommodation, on Constitutional Principles* (New York, 1775 [Evans no. 14059]), pp. 32–33, 50.

> The ambition of France is still alive and active. . . .
> What can America expect, while she still denies the
> authority of the mother-state? . . . She must in all proba-
> bility soon become the slave of arbitrary power,—of
> Popish bigotry and superstition.[4]

Or, Galloway predicted, there would be a horrible civil war
among the independent ex-colonies. America needed the imperial connection to preserve herself.

Galloway attempted to justify continuing the union with
Britain not only by predicting dire consequences but also by
building a legal case. He asserted that the colonies were in
truth subordinate to Parliament and that American firebrands,
not oppressive British ministers, were chiefly responsible for
the crisis. In lawyer's terms he explained the nature of the
imperial relation: it was to him like a contract between two
merchants. Governor and governed, king in Parliament and
colonists, had agreed to a "mutual covenant . . . including
a consideration perpetually to be performed on both sides,
upon which the validity of the covenant rests, if either party
refuse the performance on his part the other is discharged
of course, and the party refusing loses his right and claim to
the performance of the other." [5]

Galloway's assertion that the king in Parliament, not the
king alone, had final authority over the colonies was directly
opposed to the view of Franklin, John Adams, and other
patriots, who held that the king and Parliament were separate
and that Parliament had no American authority.[6] American
writers sometimes argued that a sort of compact bound Britain
and America. For them, it was obvious that Parliament had
broken the agreement; thus it was right for America to resist
parliamentary oppression. Galloway, the "candid examiner,"
admitted that Americans had "grievances to complain of," but

4. Ibid., p. 46.
5. Ibid., p. 23.
6. Ibid., pp. 15–21, 26–27.

he asserted more pointedly that the "American demagogues," by their independent behavior—by sending over to king and Parliament petitions that "conveyed to the royal ear, nothing but the language of independence," were most responsible for the break between the two countries.[7] The solution to the crisis was the Galloway plan of union. It would place the colonies in their proper and subordinate relationship to Parliament, safeguard Americans from arbitrary government, and avoid the leap into the dark that independence would bring.

Only Galloway's fervent desire for revenge on the Continental Congress for the rejection of his plan could have given birth to this inconsistent and emotional presentation. The *Candid Examination* is not as well reasoned a Tory argument as are those of Daniel Leonard and Samuel Seabury, because its author had, within a few months, made many intellectual reverses that robbed his work of any conviction. Before 1774, Galloway had gained little experience in writing polemics on imperial affairs because, having burned his fingers on this hot subject, he had tried to keep out of controversy. Lack of commitment and practice led him to make errors and inconsistent statements. Having told the congress only a few months previously that after 1607 Parliament had no authority over America, he now broadcast that Parliament could demand the obedience of the colonists. To the congress he proposed his plan as a means of both providing a constitutional imperial relationship where none had heretofore existed and avoiding war with Britain. To his supposedly large moderate audience, the candid examiner explained that his plan would accord Parliament its deserved sovereignty and frustrate the drive toward independence by the extreme anti-British plotters. His reversals of view expressed in this pamphlet were ploys to gain Tory support; he was also willing to offer a different opinion and agree with William Franklin that American representation in Parliament was the best form of union. At

7. Ibid., pp. 48–50.

this point, Galloway would have agreed with anyone who supported his stand against the Continental Congress. Because those of Tory sentiment would enjoy reading irresponsible slurs on the congress, he included these, discarding his remarks about American liberty that had introduced the presentation of his plan to the congress. Because rational discourse had not been effective, he allowed his short temper and arrogant disposition to dominate the public presentation of his plan.[8]

Reports indicated to Galloway that three-fourths of the people were opposed to the measures of the congress and were rallying to his plan. After returning to Philadelphia in December 1774, he wrote to Samuel Verplanck that it "has not wanted friends to support it in this Province." [9] In reality, the moderate majority did not exist. Sentiment in favor of his plan was probably restricted to his acquaintances in New York and to some merchant supporters, such as Thomas Wharton, in Philadelphia; but, it was strong enough to encourage Galloway to return to the Pennsylvania Assembly. Here, in the House he had for so long dominated, he would make his final stand for conciliation. The ex-Speaker still had the respect of and even some support from his old colleagues; they

8. William Franklin to Galloway, March 12, 1775, extract, *N.J.A.*, 1st ser. 10 : 578; and Galloway to William Franklin, March 26, 1775, ibid., 10 : 585. Both men mention the idea of American representation in Parliament. Werner, "Joseph Galloway," pp. 289–90, argues that Galloway did have a developed political philosophy, that his ideas were legally correct, and that they were much the same as those that formed the basis of the nineteenth-century British Empire. Jensen, *Founding*, pp. 512–13, suggests that the *Candid Examination* is an introduction to the *Federalist Papers*. These views do not fully consider all of Galloway's shifts and inconsistencies. Robert M. Calhoon, " 'I Have Deduced Your Rights': Joseph Galloway's Concept of His Role, 1774–1775," *Pennsylvania History*, 35 (1968) : 375–78, depicts Galloway as believing that he could lead America away from Whig "sophistry" by using his intellectual powers and the force of persuasion because only he had the truth.

9. Galloway to Verplanck, April 1, 1775, "Some Letters of Joseph Galloway," p. 482. Thomas Wharton noted to Samuel Wharton, November 16, 1774, Thomas Wharton Letter Book, HSP, that the proceedings of Congress "are not satisfactory to abundant Numbers."

nominated him to attend the Second Continental Congress scheduled for May 1775, despite his failure at the first.[10]

In the Assembly, Galloway was eager for battle, for he suspected that his old enemies, the proprietary faction, had joined with the "Independents" in plotting to separate from Britain. The opportunity came when, on February 21, Governor John Penn suggested to the Assembly that it petition the Crown for redress separately from the congress, as New York had done. Two days later, when debate began on the governor's proposal, Galloway was alone in supporting it. By magnificent oratory and the exertion of all his remaining influence, he managed to persuade fourteen members of the Assembly to join with him. Throughout the debate, "I kept my Temper unruffled & firm which gave me no small Advantage," he bragged to William Franklin; for Galloway this was an accomplishment worth boasting about. All that he could achieve, however, was a postponement of further consideration until March 8. By that time, Galloway hoped to win over public sentiment so that a majority of the Assembly would vote to petition separately.[11]

The Pennsylvania revolutionaries realized the immediate need of thwarting Galloway's renaissance, else he might succeed in breaking the united front of the colonies and in restoring himself to political power. To frighten him out of his obstructionism, some patriots threatened his life; shortly after the Assembly debate he received a box containing a halter.[12] Dickinson and Thomson were less crude and more effective. They attacked Galloway in the newspapers in a piece entitled "To the Author of a Pamphlet, entitled *A Candid Examina-*

10. Galloway to Verplanck, January 14, [1775], [dated 1774 by Galloway], "Some Letters of Joseph Galloway," p. 478. *Votes,* 8 : 7167. Galloway to William Franklin, March 26, 1775, *N.J.A.,* 1st ser. 10 : 586, notes that he refused the appointment in December; he officially resigned later.

11. Galloway to William Franklin, February 28, 1775, March 26, 1775, *N.J.A.,* 1st ser. 10: 573–74, 580–81. *Votes,* 8 : 7185–86, 7192–93.

12. Galloway to William Franklin, March 26, 1775, *N.J.A.,* 1st ser. 10 : 584–85.

tion." This refuted Galloway's contentions that a supreme legislative authority had to exist for America and that king and Parliament were inextricably linked in the legislative process. The inconsistencies between the patriotic anti-British view stated in the congress by the planner of union and the pro-British criticisms of that body made by the candid examiner were noted by his opponents.[13] Galloway published a defiant reply to Dickinson and Thomson, asserting that his plan "stands, like an impregnable bulwark, in the path to your independence; and you know not how to remove it." [14]

The plan of union proved not so impregnable to the attempts of Dickinson and Thomson to keep Pennsylvania united with the other colonies in resistance to Britain. To his dismay, Galloway found, on the day when further debate on the governor's proposal resumed, that public sentiment had not sufficiently changed and that his powers of persuasion had not been effective; he was four votes short of a majority. Because the Assembly would shortly adjourn, Galloway, hoping that more delay would change sentiment in his favor, moved for further consideration of the governor's proposal sometime before the Second Continental Congress was to meet in May. The House at first agreed to further consideration, and Speaker Biddle appointed a committee to draw up an answer to the governor's proposal, stating that the Assembly would delay its decision until later. The next day, March 9, when the committee reported back, Galloway discovered that the draft of the reply to the governor, prepared in his absence, probably by Dickinson, rejected the idea of the separate petition. He screamed that he had been tricked—although his opponents' strategy was no more devious than his own had been on occasion—and he implored the House to vote down the committee draft. The arguments of Dickin-

13. *Pennsylvania Journal,* March 8, 1775.

14. Galloway, *A Reply to an Address to the Author of a Pamphlet, entitled A Candid Examination . . . .* (New York, 1775 [Evans no. 14060]), p. 35.

son and Thomson had more weight; by a vote of 22–15 the Assembly approved the committee report against a separate petition. For Galloway this was the final political defeat.[15]

The vanquished leader retired from politics on May 12, when he submitted his formal resignation as a delegate to the Second Continental Congress. He did not attend the Assembly again. The next month he wrote to Verplanck, "I hope I have retired in Time from the distressing and ungrateful Drudgery of Public Life. The want of Health was one great motive, but I had many others, which united to become too powerful to resist." [16] The chief reason, which Galloway was reluctant to state, was that he had been stripped of all his power and prestige because of his unpopular stand. For twenty years he had devoted his life to politics. Losing his ability to continue in this role successfully, he could only give up.

It seems incomprehensible that Galloway, who throughout his career was always so careful to preserve his public image and his political influence, should lose both at such a critical time. For many years he had been fairly accurate in assessing his chances for political success in any specific endeavor. The plan of union and the *Candid Examination* were calculated risks which he believed he had to take. Much of his motivation for taking them was his conviction that he had the only solution to the imperial crisis; much was his hope that the acceptance of his solution would restore his waning political prominence. His career on the downgrade since 1770, Galloway relied on his plan of union to save himself. Even more desperate a gamble was his *Candid Examination*. Here Galloway wagered all or nothing; either his bitter tirade against the Continental Congress, his critical view of the whole campaign to achieve American rights, and his newfound theory of par-

15. *Votes*, 8 : 7210–13; Galloway to William Franklin, March 26, 1775, *N.J.A.*, 1st ser. 10 : 581–84. Galloway, *A Reply to the Observations of Lieut. Gen. Sir William Howe, on a Pamphlet Entitled, Letters to a Nobleman* (London, 1780), p. 127. Jensen, *Founding*, pp. 529–30.

16. Galloway to Verplanck, June 24, 1775, "Some Letters of Joseph Galloway," p. 483.

liamentary supremacy would turn America to his plan, or
these arguments would turn his colony and the Assembly he
had dominated for so long squarely against him. He had
calculated that his old supporters, the Quakers and the merchants of Philadelphia, would back him because they opposed
boycotts and violence. A meeting of Quaker representatives
adopted a formal stand against the Association and the "illegal
assemblies," but this was probably ignored by many Friends
and was no help to Galloway. The conservative merchants
had been outmaneuvered by the more numerous anti-British
merchants and mechanics.[17]. The *Candid Examination* did
Galloway little good in demonstrating the reasonableness of
his plan, since it showed that its author was quite the opposite.

Galloway believed that independence was the only alternative to his plan, but the popular view perceived that this was
the case only if Britain remained obstinate and initiated hos-
tilities. When news of Lexington and Concord came, the
Pennsylvania county committees called out their militias, and
the Assembly, in May 1775, voted money for defense while
rejecting Lord North's conciliatory proposals. Galloway saw
all hope of restoring the empire melt away. Now, more than
ever, he was certain that his angry outbursts were justified
and that the Continental Congress would lead America to
independence and disaster.

A faint glimmer of light yet cut through Galloway's gloom.
Franklin was returning home. The younger member of the
decayed partnership would soon be reunited with his mentor,
leader, guide, and friend. He must have awaited Franklin's
ship anxiously, hoping to discuss with Franklin the tragic
situation and believing that, once again working together, they
could do something—Galloway was not certain what—to
calm the terrible crisis. Only Franklin could rescue Galloway now.

17. *The Testimony of the People Called Quakers, given forth by a
Meeting of the Representatives of said People, in Pennsylvania and New
Jersey, held at Philadelphia the twenty-fourth Day of the first Month,
1775* (Philadelphia, 1775 [Evans no. 14052]). Jensen, *Founding*, pp. 526–28.

In 1764, when Franklin left Philadelphia, Galloway had envisioned quite a different set of circumstances attending the former's return. Franklin would bring home royal government. Galloway, the office-seeking Assembly party members, and the White Oaks would greet him. The partners would be reunited in triumph. Part of this dream did come true, for Franklin returned a hero. But it was not Galloway who greeted him; rather, Galloway's opponents prepared a warm welcome for the agent and invited Franklin to work closely with them. He was quickly made a delegate to the Second Continental Congress and a member of the Philadelphia Committee of Safety.[18] His adroit political footwork and frequent pro-American pronouncements had paid dividends, in spite of his being absent from the Philadelphia crisis scene. Ironically, Franklin, absent for over ten years, fit right in with Pennsylvania's revolutionary leaders as if he had never been away; Galloway, who rarely ventured far from Philadelphia and Bucks County, was an outcast.

Franklin must have been surprised and dismayed at his old partner's loss of power and at the position he had taken in the *Candid Examination*. Galloway had never expressed such ideas before; he must have appeared to Franklin to have undergone an astounding metamorphosis. In London in early 1775, Franklin had heard rumors that Galloway was becoming an out-and-out royalist and Loyalist, but he could not believe this of his old ally.[19] Now the proof was in print.

18. The *Pennsylvania Packet,* May 8, 1775, greeted the returning hero with suitable verse:

> WELCOME! once more
> To these fair western plains, thy native shore;
> HERE live belov'd, and leave the tools at home,
> To run their length, and finish out their doom;
> HERE lend thine aid, to quench *their* brutal fires,
> Or fan the flame which LIBERTY inspires.

His new appointments were noted in the *Pennsylvania Journal,* May 10, 1775.

19. Franklin had been informed that Galloway transmitted information about the "Popular or Country Party in America" to the minis-

Galloway, although publicly voicing his concern about the "Rights and Freedom of America," had repudiated all that Franklin had recommended and had come out squarely for the subordination of America to Parliament, which Franklin had continually denied.[20] Could partnership and friendship be restored in the face of such polar opposition?

Franklin and Galloway were both anxious to meet to discover if the chasm separating their views was indeed unbridgeable. On May 8 came Galloway's letter asking Franklin to come to Trevose. "I am concern'd at your Resolution of quitting public Life at a time when your Abilities are so much wanted," Franklin replied to Galloway, and he accepted the offer of a carriage to take him to Bucks County.[21] Probably, Franklin had already resolved to make an effort to reconcile both Galloway and William Franklin to the necessity of fighting Britain for American rights. He certainly was not ready to cast them aside as quickly as they had cast aside the Continental Congress. Both were prodigal sons whose return to the family fold was to be sought and welcomed.

The old partners met at Trevose within the week. Franklin must have been startled at Galloway's appearance. The ravages of ill health and ill political fortune had changed his young friend from the vigorous and debonair party leader of 1764 to a prematurely aged, worn out, forty-five-year-old rejected

---

try. To Galloway, February 25, 1775, *Writings*, ed. Smyth, 6 : 311, he expressed his confidence in his old partner's integrity, a trust that the younger man had not betrayed. In the *Pennsylvania Gazette*, May 17, 1775, Galloway denied allegations about his revealing information concerning the First Continental Congress. Nor did Galloway, when he later was in London seeking a parliamentary pension, claim that he had furnished reports for the British. William Franklin, however, wrote the Earl of Dartmouth, September 3, 1774, *N.J.A.*, 1st ser. 10 : 474–75, that he was transmitting secret intelligence received from an informant in the Congress. His source was certainly Galloway, who apparently had not authorized the New Jersey governor to communicate such information.

20. *Pennsylvania Gazette*, May 17, 1775.

21. Franklin to Galloway, May 8, 1775, photostat, Franklin Papers, APS.

politician.[22] The older partner, who, except for some gout, enjoyed surprisingly good health for his sixty-nine years and who basked in the serenity of self-certain rectitude and wide popularity, had hardly changed at all. But ideas had changed more than appearances; it was these the two men met to discuss. Galloway urged Franklin to reconsider the plan of union and to attempt to promote some sort of reconciliation that might incorporate it. Franklin replied that, when in Britain, he had tried everything he knew and could do no more. It was not America that had to conciliate Britain, but the mother country that first had to make amends to her daughters. Franklin then urged Galloway to join with him and the other leaders of revolutionary Pennsylvania, including those against whom the two partners had fought for so long, in the Second Continental Congress. Galloway refused this overture.[23] This first interview proved only that both men were dedicated to their positions and would not easily be swayed.

For five or six weeks, Franklin and Galloway kept apart, probably downcast over their unfruitful meeting and unwilling to repeat the sad experience. Galloway later claimed that during this period Franklin was trying to make up his mind whether to follow or oppose the congress.[24] In actuality, his old partner was already fully cooperating with the revolutionaries. On May 29 he was appointed chairman of a congressional committee to initiate the establishment of a post office. Franklin may have been considering his scheme of union for the colonies by this time; he proposed it in July.[25]

22. Portraits in the Gratz Collection, Old Congress, HSP, show the contrast between the young and the old Galloway.

23. Thomas Hutchinson, *Diary and Letters,* ed. Peter O. Hutchinson (Boston, 1884), 2 : 237. Galloway told the story of his break with Franklin when he met Hutchinson in England in 1779. The account reported by the Massachusetts exile is generally consistent with other accounts Galloway rendered, although it is somewhat more sympathetic to Franklin.

24. Ibid.

25. Edmund C. Burnett, *The Continental Congress* (New York, reprinted 1964), pp. 90–91, 97. Some delegates were suspicious of Frank-

Despite his first failure and his preoccupation with the business of revolution, Franklin still believed that it was worthwhile to attempt to win Galloway over to the American cause. Franklin remembered that about eight years before he had sent part of his journal to William Franklin, who showed it to Galloway, and that Galloway had expressed hearty approval of the agent's efforts in Britain. In June, Franklin brought his journal to Trevose to read to Galloway. He hoped that by relating his more recent strivings for peace and outlining the rebuffs he had received, Galloway would realize how arbitrary and uncompromising Parliament really was; consequently, he would be persuaded that America could gain her rights only by battle. Galloway was already convinced that the Continental Congress was in the wrong; the journal did not change his opinion. When Franklin's reading was interrupted by other business, probably to Galloway's relief, the journal was not continued.[26]

Reluctant to give up his hope of reviving the old partnership, Franklin tried a third time to convince Galloway to join him. In late June or early July, Galloway, Franklin, and William Franklin met at Trevose. After the visitors had enjoyed the hospitality of their host, including the best of his wine cellar, and the hour had grown late, Franklin opened the subject that concerned them all—could they all join in to support the cause of American liberty? Franklin declared for "measures for attaining to Independence: exclaimed against the corruption and dissipation of the Kingdom, and signified his opinion, that from the strength of the Opposition, the want of union in the Ministry, the great resources in the

lin's position. Van Doren, *Franklin,* pp. 527–28, and Jensen, *Founding,* pp. 618–19, think he was slow to make up his mind. But his first meeting with Galloway indicates that he was committed to the cause of the congress. Franklin's *Account of Negotiations,* in *Writings,* ed. Smyth, 6 : 396–98, shows that he was infuriated at the ministry's refusal to compromise and that he was not likely to be timid about rebellion.

26. Hutchinson, *Diary and Letters,* 2 : 237.

Colonies, they would finally prevail. He urged Galloway to come into the Congress again." [27] Galloway was as easily convinced as any belligerent that the foe is mightier than himself. He quickly reminded Franklin that Britain would forget internal quarrels and unite its forces to suppress rebellion.[28] Galloway remembered that after this meeting "the two friends parted as they met, unconverted to the principles of each other." [29] Admiration for British law and authority, fear of social upheaval, and an emotional commitment against the actions of the Continental Congress made Galloway reject his old partner's entreaties.

For about six months Galloway sulked in retirement at Trevose while Franklin, putting aside all thought of his old partner, continued his work in the Continental Congress. Then, in August 1775, came, in response to the Olive Branch Petition, the king's speech declaring that America was in rebellion and aiming for independence; in December Parliament enacted the Prohibitory Act, blockading the American coast and authorizing the British navy to plunder all American shipping. News of these, Franklin recalled in 1781, made Galloway reverse himself again. Although in the summer of 1775 Galloway was not to be moved, "since the King had declared us out of his protection, and the Parliament by an act has

27. Ibid., 2 : 238. Galloway, *Letters from Cicero to Catiline the Second* (London, 1781), p. 47, reported Franklin as saying that *"America would be united,* and always able to draw her powers into exertion, while the British nation, and its public councils, *were, and would be yet more, divided and distracted.* That the *friends to the American cause in Britain, would incessantly maintain and increase that division and distraction, by opposing the measures of government; . . ."* Galloway produced Franklin's sentiments to show that American rebels depended on divisions in British opinion for which "Catiline the Second" (Charles James Fox) was responsible.

28. Galloway, according to *Letters from Cicero to Catiline,* p. 48, reminded Franklin "of the common and apposite fable of the two Bull Dogs tearing each other to pieces, yet, on the appearance of their common enemy, their enmity instantly ceased, and their whole powers became *united, and exerted to reduce him."*

29. Ibid.

made our properties plunder, [Galloway asserted] he would go as far in the defense of his country as any man; and accordingly he had lately, with pleasure, given colours to a regiment of militia, and an entertainment to four hundred of them before his house." Galloway's newfound American patriotism was, however, very shallow. He made no effort to return to politics, probably because he wanted to remain neutral and out of the conflict. Franklin took Galloway's conversion seriously, as it lasted through the Declaration of Independence, when other Loyalists deserted the American cause. In October 1776, when Franklin was preparing to set out on his French mission, he left his papers—twenty years of correspondence—with Galloway, believing that his former partner would keep himself and them out of danger. On November 28, 1776, soon after Franklin's departure, Galloway, who now had to live with a democratic Pennsylvania constitution, a defeated Washington retreating from New York toward Philadelphia, and the Declaration of Independence, found the pressures too great and fled behind the British lines, leaving Franklin's papers to be scattered.[30] At the last he deserted the trust his old partner had placed in him. He discovered that he could not really change the decision he had made in 1775. The indecisive, equivocal Galloway now made his final choice.

The partnership of Franklin and Galloway, born in political crisis, permanently dissolved in the far more serious imperial crisis. This potent political combination had built up a strong party, which for many years had overwhelmed its opposition and driven it to cover, had forced the proprietors to resign some of their privileges, had met wartime emergencies, had

30. Franklin to Richard Bache, September 13, 1781, *Autobiographical Writings*, ed. Van Doren, pp. 509–10. The manuscripts were lost when Galloway's house was plundered. Baldwin, "Galloway, the Loyalist Politician," p. 433, notes a tradition that Galloway left the sooner because he feared that his daughter would elope with a rebel. Writing to Richard Jackson, March 20, 1777, *Facsimiles of Manuscripts in European Archives Relating to America, 1773–1783*, vol. 24, no. 2051, Galloway deplored the political instability of America and expressed confidence that the rebels would soon be defeated.

become supreme in Pennsylvania after the Stamp Act crisis, had begun to come apart during the nonimportation controversy, and collapsed at the outbreak of revolution. The ideological differences springing from the Stamp Act crisis and cultivated by the Townshend Acts crisis finally broke it up. Both partners tried to save it because it had worked so well for them and because it had engendered a firm friendship; but they wished it continued only on terms that suited their opposite, now unchangeable views. Neither admitted after 1776 that he regretted that the partnership was dissolved. Both quickly embarked on new careers.

Franklin had no cause to note the absence of his longtime friend and partner from his side after 1776. His storied career during the years of revolution and constitution-making gives his earlier political activity in association with Galloway a rather dull aspect. Yet as a signer of the Declaration of Independence, statesman, and Founding Father, Franklin never worked with any of the like-minded patriots as closely and as lengthily as he had with Galloway. Politics in Pennsylvania, after the Declaration of Independence, came under the control of new men with new ideas. Franklin kept pace with their revolutionary ideas of democratic and representative government. The famous reforms of the Pennsylvania constitution of 1776 were not of his making, but they were congenial to his principles of representative government and the primacy of the legislature. He never formed close ties with the younger politicians who were attempting to put republican government into practice. Perhaps he was too old for new friends; perhaps he did not try to take a new partner because he could not bear the desertion of the old one. Young men and young men's actions led the revolution; the old leader's career as a political agitator was over.

Franklin's mission to France placed him in a sphere more detached from Pennsylvania issues and Pennsylvania politics than his earlier British mission had. He no longer needed or wanted a partner at home to lead a party that was no longer his. His reputation needed no protection by a Galloway; it

was now secured by his patriotic actions and diplomatic successes. When Franklin returned to Philadelphia in 1785 he
was welcomed as a symbol of unity in a state torn by factional strife.[31] His role in the Constitutional Convention of
1787 was the benign one of promoting unity at critical moments. Clearly, Franklin had reaped all the dividends from
his long association with Galloway. His young partner had
bolstered Franklin's reputation and preserved his career
through trying times, making it possible for the foremost man
of America to earn the accolades of a grateful new nation.

Galloway offhandedly remarked to Thomas Hutchinson
that the main loss accruing to him when the partnership was
finally broken was that he did not get to hear the remaining
part of Franklin's journal, "which probably was the most
interesting." [32] In this callous manner Galloway masked the
true meaning, as it concerned him, of the disruption of the
partnership. Closing up this twenty-year association left the
junior partner with all the liabilities of the business: bitterness and tragedy. He spent the rest of his life trying to live
down and forget both his association with Franklin and his
pro-American pronouncements of 1774–76.

After fleeing to the British, he returned to Philadelphia
with Howe and Clinton as civil administrator of the city in
1777–78; Philadelphia had "royal government" at last, but
only temporarily. When the British army marched back to
New York in 1778, Galloway was with it, leaving his wife
behind to keep possession of her estate. He was attainted a
traitor by the new state, and his property was confiscated.[33]
In late 1778 Galloway went to London, where for about five
years he unsuccessfully pleaded the Loyalist cause. He demanded that Britain make more of an effort to win the war
and use the Loyalists in America more effectively. After the

31. Robert L. Brunhouse, *The Counter-Revolution in Pennsylvania*
(Harrisburg, 1942), pp. 176–77.

32. Hutchinson, *Diary and Letters*, 2 : 238.

33. Grace Galloway to Elizabeth Galloway, October 4, 1779, Galloway
Papers, Library of Congress.

revolution Galloway received a pension for his losses from Parliament, and he retired to near obscurity. Although he fled from his homeland, he still thought of himself as an American, still was deeply concerned for his country's welfare, and dreamed of the day when the empire would be reunited. "I hope my unhappy country has now tasted of the Cup of Bitters, as, to be able to return to its former happiness with real enjoyment," Galloway wrote to his wife during the war. But he never saw his country or his wife again.[34]

Obsessed with the conviction that such a plan as he had proposed in the Continental Congress could yet save the empire, Galloway drafted, between 1778 and 1788, several variations of his original plan for the ministry to consider.[35] They were never employed by Britain as a basis of peace negotiations during the war or as a model for reform of the empire after 1783. Near the end of his life, Galloway turned to politico-religious writing, interpreting history from the Book of Revelation and denouncing revolutionary France as the "beast." [36] He died in 1803, ignored in Britain and disgraced in his native land. Undoubtedly Galloway's richest years were those he had spent as Franklin's partner; after deserting Franklin he lost all inspiration and was incapable of the kind of creative activity which had made him so prominent in prerevolutionary Pennsylvania.[37]

34. Joseph Galloway to Grace Galloway, [July, 1780?], ibid. Grace Galloway died in 1782.

35. Boyd, *Anglo-American Union*, pp. 115–77. For corrections, see W. H. Nelson, "The Last Hopes of the American Loyalists," *Canadian Historical Review* 32 (1951) : 40–43.

36. Galloway's *Brief Commentaries upon such Parts of the Revelation and Other Prophecies as Immediately Refer to the Present Times* (London, 1802; reprinted Trenton, N.J., 1810) are a peculiar mixture of biblical exegesis, numerology, chiliasm, anti-Catholicism, and attacks on "French atheism." Although he neglected to include in this a blast against his old enemies, the Presbyterians, he showed the same sort of distaste for what he considered an unorthodox group stirring up anarchy and revolution.

37. Details of Galloway's later career are summarized by Baldwin, "Galloway," pp. 432–39; by Boyd, *Anglo-American Union*, pp. 51–111; and by Werner, "Galloway," pp. 296–317.

The close connection between the two partners had been blasted so dramatically by the events of 1774–76 that their friendship was perverted into vindictiveness and open hatred. Galloway, in Britain seeking a parliamentary pension, denounced Franklin as heatedly as he had earlier denounced his proprietary enemies. Franklin was the "arch rebel" who was moderately treated in the Hutchinson Letters affair, "when it is considered, that he had surreptitiously obtained confidential correspondence respecting matters of State, and had published it with a design to raise a sedition against the Government, under which he then held an office of trust and by which he and his family had been long maintained." [38] Such was the result of Franklin's careful explanation of the affair to Galloway in 1774. Even more irresponsible was Galloway's claim that his old friend was chief conspirator and chief cause of the revolution. He charged that "the Doctor had been long secretly preparing the way for the present rebellion in America, and that to his intrigues principally, this country and America owe all their present misfortunes." [39] Galloway deliberately fabricated these attacks on Franklin to ingratiate himself with the ministry and arouse British passions against the traitorous American rebels who, in his view, were being treated too leniently. That he would slander Franklin to gain his own ends shows how completely he had deserted his old partner and allowed his vindictive, hot-tempered streak to take control of his actions. That Galloway was one of the losers in the revolution was perhaps undeserved, for he had ability and a plan of union worth trying. That he was a bad loser is unpardonable.

Galloway's defection and slurs helped turn Franklin against all Loyalists. Before the war, several Loyalists had been his friends and one was his son; Franklin soon came to regard

38. Galloway, *Fabricus: or Letters to the People of Great Britain on the Absurdity and Mischiefs of Defensive Operations only in the American War; and on the Causes of the Failure in the Southern Operations* (London, 1782), p. 52. Also see Galloway, *Letters from Cicero to Catiline,* p. 18.

39. Galloway, *Fabricus,* p. 52.

them all as deceitful traitors. As the struggle wore on he became disgusted with the atrocities committed by the Tory raiders. In negotiating the Treaty of Paris of 1783 with the British, Franklin insisted that no definite provision guaranteeing the restoration of Loyalist property be included. He was responsible for the wording of the fifth article of the treaty, which provided that an impotent congress would merely recommend to the states that the confiscated possessions of the Loyalists be restored.[40] Ironically, it was Galloway who broadcast the despair of the Loyalists at the wording of this article. He knew that the states would restore little to the Loyalists and that his own estate was lost to him.[41] By 1783 the old partners became irreconcilably bitter toward each other. Franklin, the successful partner, hurled the last word, the most damaging insult.

Repudiation and recrimination were inappropriate terminations to this long partnership so important for prerevolutionary Pennsylvania. Even if it failed at the last, its achievements over the years were historically significant. The partnership broadened the base of political participation, refined political methods in order to retain its power, upheld the principles of representative government, and left a rich legacy for its political successors. After 1755, when Franklin encouraged neglected groups and persons to enter politics, men of ability, regardless of religious affiliation, were able to take a more active part in the government. The mechanics and small merchants—especially those in the White Oaks club—as well as the Germans gained much more political power. This extension of political participation followed the dictates of the partners' principles and the implications of the Charter of Privileges of 1701. Franklin and Galloway, who

40. Franklin, *Journal of the Negotiations for Peace with Great Britain*, in *Autobiographical Writings*, ed. Van Doren, pp. 562–63. Van Doren, *Franklin*, pp. 690–91.

41. Galloway, *Observations on the Fifth Article of the Treaty with America: and on the Necessity of appointing a Judicial Enquiry into the Merits and Losses of the American Loyalists* (London, 1783), pp. 9–19.

continually termed the voters "the people," had an embryonic Jeffersonian notion that the people would choose their rulers wisely and should have a larger group from which to choose.

Justifiably, Franklin and Galloway called their organization a party. The appelation "party" was opprobrious in the eighteenth century; it generally connoted a faction employing agitation and strife to gain narrow and personal ends. This view of factionalism was changing in America; factions were beginning to be regarded as necessary to the process of protecting and enlarging popular liberties.[42] Franklin, with the aid of Galloway, transformed the preceding Quaker faction into a party committed to this protection and enlargement. It was more like a modern political party than were the amorphous political groups that existed in many of the other colonies or the factions that battled for places in the British House of Commons. The Assembly party was more personalized than a modern party; the two leaders were more important to the organization than were its goals and traditions. Yet, it had meaning and purpose apart from its leaders. The party had members with rather specialized duties, financial dependence on wealthy backers who were not candidates, patronage to dispense, and a standard operating procedure for winning elections. Moreover, the party possessed a self-conscious group identification, a real esprit de corps, for its members thought of themselves as belonging to a worthwhile organization and were anxious to serve it in any way that they could. It proved its durability by surviving the defeat of 1764; that it collapsed in 1770 is no reflection on its organization, for the crisis of that year caused enough discord to destroy any party that combined diverse interests. No party replaced it immediately because Galloway's opponents in Philadelphia were not as competent political operators and because the Speaker tenaciously dominated the Assembly. After 1776 the adherents to and the opponents of the new Pennsylvania constitution built their parties on the traditions

42. Bailyn, *Origins of American Politics*, pp. 125–31.

of political organization established by Franklin and Gallo-way.[43]

One important contribution the partners made to the development of politics was the operation of their political machine. Franklin and Galloway did not invent the methods they employed in persuading assemblymen and constituents and getting out the vote, but they perfected them to a high degree. Shrewd political maneuvering kept the party machine chugging on in the period 1756–70, even when one leader was away in England. By constructing and effectively employing their machine, the partners added to the store of knowledge about political techniques.

Another contribution to political development was made by the partners' struggle to put important principles of government into practice in Pennsylvania. Their efforts to maintain the primacy of the legislature strengthened the tradition of resistance to executive authority. Their attacks on the Penns established in the minds of Pennsylvanians political ideas such as the need for a weak executive, the desirability of appointing judges on good behavior, and the placing of the control of taxation and appropriations chiefly in the hands of the legislature. They also preserved the heritage of political and religious liberty handed down by the founder. In the revolutionary period the ideas of the predominance of the legislature, religious freedom, and political liberty blossomed forth in a democratic constitution that provided for a form of government of which the partners would never have dreamed before 1776; that constitution guaranteed more rights than they had ever considered. By conserving and improving the province's fundamental institutions and political practices, the partnership made possible the changes fashioned after 1776.

The partners' devotion to representative government did not include making it more representative. They were quite

43. William N. Chambers, *Political Parties in a New Nation* (New York, 1963), p. 19, traces a true party system in Pennsylvania back to the 1776 period, but Chambers pushes his search no further into the past.

content that throughout this period the Assembly continued to be composed of the wealthy, well-educated, and demonstrably able. Franklin and Galloway thought it natural and necessary that most political leaders be drawn from the upper levels of society. Generally, they expected that the lower orders would defer to the higher, choosing those whom their betters nominated. For the most part, the lower sort seem to have been content with this situation. Only a few complaints were registered about the "Greatness and Opulence" of the leadership. The backcountry demanded equal representation in 1764 to obtain power for that section, not to institute truly proportional representation; this demand had little overall impact. No one complained that the people lacked the power to turn out an Assembly that oppressed them. Reform was expected to come from the top down; at the same time the Assembly was expected to be very responsive to petitions and other expressions of the popular mood.

Franklin and Galloway generally tried both to reflect and to shape the popular mood. In 1764 they miscalculated, although not irreparably. They failed to comprehend that after 1770 a paternalistic, semi-representative legislature was becoming outmoded. At first during the nonimportation crisis and then in the crisis of 1774, Pennsylvanians began to turn to instruments of policy making and execution outside the Assembly. The final stage of the transition came in the first frantic days of independence when a new group of leaders put democratic ideas into practice. Greater popular participation and proportional representation were the fruits, but not the direct result, of the benevolent, responsive, and effective government under the partners' leadership. Independence made these radical innovations possible.

The partnership's contribution in local matters far surpassed its record in imperial affairs. Franklin, having learned in 1765 not to appear to side with Britain against America, was successful only in encouraging American resistance. Galloway applauded his efforts to state the colonial position in England, but he had no wish to contribute to colonial resistance. Both men were hopeful that some method of reconciling Britain and America would be hit upon, but they were unable to offer anything acceptable to both sides. In preparing plans of union, Galloway did somewhat better than Franklin. The latter's "Hints" failed to take into account, as did the colonial leaders generally, that the British Empire had to meet new challenges in new ways after 1763. The defeat of France and territorial expansion meant new problems, which could be solved neither by parliamentary exertion of centralized authority over the empire nor by returning to pre-1763 principles of administration. Yet the latter alternative was better than the former, which was certain to fail. Galloway's plan was a more constructive proposal designed to make the empire stronger and more defensible. Nevertheless, Franklin made a telling point in arguing that Galloway's plan would force the colonies to follow the British lead too closely. Another defect, pointed out by recent commentators, was that the proposed intercolonial legislature would be remote from the popular will. Despite its drawbacks, Galloway had merit in arguing that his plan was better than bloodshed, and Franklin agreed with him.

Together and separately, however, the partners were unequal to the task of formulating ways to resolve the imperial crisis. Britain frustrated both of them in their attempts to find some settlement. Indeed, Franklin was inflexible in his view that colonial autonomy had to be preserved—a position that led directly to the battlefield. His stand was forced upon him by the constitutional position taken by Parliament. British ministers refused to heed him. His efforts to forestall oppressive revenue and retaliatory schemes were monumental tasks that surpassed the abilities of all American agents and the most capable pro-American British leaders. The measure of Franklin's ambassadorial talents must take into consideration his mission to France after 1776. He proved there that, given some favorable circumstances, he could negotiate ably and effectively.

Notwithstanding the defeat of Galloway's plan in the Continental Congress, its real rejection was by the British ministry. It was given much shorter shrift in Britain than it was in America. Parliamentary approval of it would have placed the responsibility for reconciliation squarely on the rebelling colonials. Then the plan would certainly have gotten a far different reception in America than it did. When it was ignored and scoffed at in Britain, it was dead. Yet Galloway was mainly responsible for his own destiny. His equivocation concerning nonimportation and his *Candid Examination* were gross political errors. It is hard to avoid concluding that, politically, Galloway got about what he deserved.

In surveying the partners' careers over this twenty-year period, one can discern that Franklin and Galloway were basically quite different sorts of persons. Franklin showed that he was temperamentally and intellectually suited to face the problems of his Pennsylvania political endeavors and of his agency. Galloway made him a good partner in Pennsylvania affairs, but he lacked the capacity for sustained effort during the imperial crises. Galloway's legal mind led him to oppose the Penns' government, made him adept at challenging the proprietors in the Assembly, and aided Franklin both in the Philadelphia electoral contests and in England; but it gave him a field of vision too narrow to comprehend the American claims to freedom from parliamentary taxation. Generally, Galloway supported what he thought was the side of law and order. He opposed riotous mobs and ineffective government, for which he thought his political adversaries responsible. He hesitated to resist British policy because he feared that anarchy and mob rule might supplant British authority if moderation did not prevail. As his various twists and turns indicate, the lawyer was never quite certain what his position ought to be, and until 1776 he was reluctant to make a firm, final commitment.

Franklin applied scientific reasoning to political problems, carefully evaluating actions according to their rationality and practicality. The principles he endeavored to uphold—effective representative government, the primacy of the local legislature, the equality of treatment for all citizens of British dominions, the freedom for Americans to engage in whatever economic activities they desired—were to him as fundamental as the laws of gravity and electricity. Political problems could be understood and solved, he thought, by applying scientific analogies. Both Franklin and Galloway had extraordinary intelligence, but Franklin possessed more intellectual consistency and greater reasoning faculties.

Differences in experience, in economic views, and in religious views can also be readily noticed. Wide experience in America and Britain gave Franklin the capacity to judge the meaning of imperial issues more accurately than Galloway could. The younger man was almost as provincial in 1775 as he had been in 1755, and consequently he was unable to understand the manifold implications of complex imperial matters. The Pennsylvania issues—the party and the change of government—loomed too large in Galloway's calculations. Franklin's devotion to the ideas of Poor Richard, that frugality and industry practiced by American producers were the keys to American prosperity, set him off from Galloway. The self-made printer and philosopher saw, after 1768, that America should become more economically independent of Britain. Galloway, scion and heir of wealthy families, did not possess the viewpoint of the producing classes. The existing order, the close economic ties with Britain, had contributed to his prosperity and that of his merchant friends; British restrictions on commerce were to them only minor inconveniences. The religious backgrounds of the two men also pushed them in different directions. Franklin, trained in Calvinist Boston, felt a close affinity to the cause of Massachusetts. His own freethinking position included a belief in liberty of conscience and led him to espouse individual liberty in general. Galloway's Quaker background imparted to him a distaste for war and violence. His fears of "Presbyterian"-led rebellion stemmed from his religious orientation. That he later wrote analyses of Revelation and condemnations of atheists shows that he was more disposed toward upholding higher sources of authority and less self-reliant than his partner. The partners' divergent viewpoints helped to impel Franklin to the American side and Galloway to the Loyalist cause.

Personality differences explain the split as much as do intellectual characteristics. Galloway's career suggests that his personality reinforced his intellect's drift toward Toryism. He prominently displayed traits of arrogance, egotism, and reluctance to compromise. In many ways these traits were serviceable when dealing with inflexible proprietary governors, timid assemblymen, and lowly voters. Galloway's successes in local politics before 1770, especially his recovery after the Stamp Act crisis, reinforced these traits. But his obstinance, haughtiness, and unstable temper were widely noted. Comparatively little harm was done when he had his fistfight with Dickinson at the Statehouse in 1764, or when he raged at Goddard for publishing the "Farmer's Letters," or when he accused Goddard of extortion; a notable figure can lose his temper without suffering complete disaster. But after 1774 Galloway went too far. The *Candid Examination* showed his vengefulness, hotheadedness, and lack of perception of the circumstances. These same personal traits are evident in his Loyalist propaganda written in Britain. Perhaps by about 1790, when all his subsequent plans of union had been ignored by Britain, Galloway realized that not "American demagogues" but an obstinate British government was mainly to blame for the loss of America. More likely, he continued to be as unrealistic, as unfair to his old partner, and as irrational as he had been from 1775 to 1783.

Franklin, no doubt personally affronted and moved to retaliation by the sneering Thomas Penn in 1758, the insults of the Proprietary party in 1764, and the blast of Wedderburn in 1774, never really lost his composure or deviated from his course. Within the limits of his principles he was more flexible, more amenable to compromise, and more adaptable to new situations than was Galloway. His personality never interfered with the business at hand, for his scientific, rational way of thinking prevailed over his emotions. Franklin, personally suited to accommodation and compromise, met firm resistance to all his attempts in Britain. Galloway, in a position where compromise was essential and was sought of him, was unable to make concessions.

The American revolution split many friends apart, although no pair more prominent than Franklin and Galloway. The former was not a typical patriot; the latter was not a typical Loyalist. Franklin, belonging to an earlier generation and fond of life in Britain, had little in common with the younger leaders of the revolution except a devotion to the principles at stake and a deep love of his native land. Unlike most other Loyalist leaders, who were generally connected with Crown or Church, Galloway was a popularly elected official and at times as anti-British as the patriots. One as much as the other was a devoted American, a product of colonial American culture, an admirer of Britain, a popular figure, and a part of the American political system. The careers of Franklin and Galloway illustrate that differences between Loyalists and patriots were not necessarily those of local political partisanship or social standing. For these longtime political partners, and perhaps for other revolutionary Loyalists and patriots, the general determinants of loyalty and patriotism were rooted in their backgrounds, intellectual characteristics, and personalities. These features were complementary during times of little conflict. During very serious and repeated crises, they became the seeds of the partners' tragic split.

A Note on Sources

The largest repository of Franklin manuscripts is the library of the American Philosophical Society in Philadelphia. A number of draft copies of letters written by Franklin are there, but the most valuable contents are the letters to Franklin from Galloway, William Franklin, Isaac Norris, the Whartons, and others of Franklin's party. Letters to William Franklin in this collection are also very informative concerning Pennsylvania politics. I. Minis Hays, *Calendar of the Papers of Benjamin Franklin in the Library of the American Philosophical Society,* 5 vols. (Philadelphia: American Philosophical Society, 1908) is a helpful index to this collection. Yale University Library also has extensive holdings, including important letters from Franklin to Galloway. At Yale is the editorial office of the *Papers of Benjamin Franklin,* which has a card file index, organized chronologically and by subject, referring to all Franklin papers. Most of the useful Franklin material in the Library of Congress has been published in editions of Franklin's papers. The Historical Society of Pennsylvania in Philadelphia has important Franklin manuscripts.

Much of Franklin's significant correspondence and his published works have been collected in *The Works of Benjamin Franklin,* ed. Jared Sparks, 10 vols. (Philadelphia: Childs and Peterson, 1840); *The Works of Benjamin Franklin,* ed. John Bigelow, 12 vols. (New York: G. P. Putnam's Sons, 1904); and *The Writings of Benjamin Franklin,* ed. Albert H. Smyth, 10 vols. (New York: The Macmillan Company, 1905–07). These early editorial projects contain inaccuracies; *The Papers of Benjamin Franklin,* vols. 1–14 edited by Leonard W. Labaree et al., vol. 15 edited by William B. Willcox et al. (New Haven: Yale University Press, 1959–), complete through fifteen volumes, is more authoritative. The Yale edition of the *Auto-biography* (New Haven, 1964), is likewise excellent. Also helpful were the *Letters and Papers of Benjamin Franklin and Richard Jackson,* ed. Carl Van Doren (Philadelphia: American Philosophical Society, 1947); *Benjamin Franklin's Autobiographical Writings,* ed. Carl Van Doren (New York: The Viking Press, 1945); and *Benjamin Franklin's Letters to the Press,* ed. Verner W. Crane (Chapel Hill: University of North Carolina Press, 1950). The latter two were especially pertinent to this study.

There are no large collections of Galloway papers. Material related to Franklin is incorporated in the Franklin papers at the American Philosophical Society, the Yale University Library, and the William L. Clements Library at the University of Michigan. The Ferdinand J. Dreer Collection, the Gratz Collection, and the Society Collection, all parts of the Historical Society of Pennsylvania, contain several Galloway letters and other items connected with Franklin's partner. The Library of Congress has Galloway family letters dated after 1777.

Printed works by Franklin and Galloway, as well as other pamphlets, broadsides, and cartoons spawned by political strife in Pennsylvania are made conveniently accessible in the Early American Imprints series published on microcard by the American Antiquarian Society. Those imprints important for this period are listed chronologically and alphabetically in Charles Evans, *American Bibliography,* 14 vols. (Chicago: Blakeley Press, 1903–59). Franklin's published writings have been republished in more modern editions. Galloway's most important works with American imprints are *A True and Impartial State of the Province of Pennsylvania* (Philadelphia: W. Dunlap, 1759); *The Speech of Joseph Galloway, Esq., in Answer to the Speech of John Dickinson, Esq.* (Philadelphia: W. Dunlap, 1764); and *A Candid Examination of the Mutual Claims of Great Britain, and the Colonies: with a Plan of Accommodation, on Constitutional Principles* (New York: James Rivington, 1775). The polemical tracts that he wrote during his exile are more fugitive. They include *The Examination of Joseph Galloway, Esq., Late Speaker of the House of Assembly of Pennsylvania, Before the House of Commons, in a Committee on the American Papers, with Explanatory Notes* (London: J. Wilkie, 1779); *Historical and Political Reflections on the Rise and Progress of the American Rebellion* (London: G. Wilkie, 1780); *A Reply to the Observations of Lieut. Gen. Sir William Howe, on a Pamphlet Entitled Letters to a Nobleman* (London: G. Wilkie, 1780); *Letters from Cicero to Catiline the Second* (London: J. Bow, 1781); *Fabricus, or Letters to the People of Great Britain on the Absurdity and Mischiefs of Defensive Operations only in the American War; and on the Causes of the Failure in the Southern Operations* (London: G. Wilkie, 1782); and *Observations on the Fifth Article of the Treaty with America: and on the Necessity of appointing a Judicial Enquiry into the Merits and Losses of the American Loyalists* (London: printed by order of the Agents, 1783).

In the American Philosophical Society library and in the Historical Society of Pennsylvania are many manuscript collections of prominent colonial Pennsylvanians. The David Hall Letter Books and the Shippen papers in the former provide much background on the Philadelphia and Pennsylvania scene as well as critical views of Franklin and Galloway. In the Historical Society of Pennsylvania are the extremely important Penn papers, including Thomas Penn's Letter Book, official correspondence, and papers on Indian affairs. Most of these are available on microfilm. The letters contained therein present a uniformly unfavorable view of Franklin and Galloway, which must be tempered by the sifting of both facts and opinions. Indispensable in understanding the viewpoints of the Quakers and the merchants of Philadelphia are the letter books of Thomas Wharton, 1752–59 and 1773–75; the wallpaper letter book of Isaac Norris; Norris' Copybook of Letters beginning June 16, 1756; and the Pemberton papers, correspondence of James Pemberton.

Useful printed collections of letters and papers are *The*

Burd Papers: Extracts from Chief Justice William Allen's Letter Book, ed. Lewis B. Walker (n.p., 1897); *Diary and Letters of His Excellency Thomas Hutchinson, Esq.,* ed. Peter O. Hutchinson, 2 vols. (Boston: Houghton Mifflin Company, 1884); The Adams Papers, series 1, *Diary and Autobiography,* ed. L. H. Butterfield et al., 5 vols. (Cambridge: Harvard University Press, 1961–66); The Adams Papers, series 2, *Adams Family Correspondence,* ed. L. H. Butterfield et al., 2 vols. (Cambridge: Harvard University Press, 1963); *Facsimiles of Manuscripts in European Archives Relating to America, 1773–1783,* ed. B. F. Stevens, 25 vols. (reprinted Wilmington, Del.: Mellifont Press, 1970); and *Historical Manuscripts Commission, Fourteenth Report,* appendix, Part 10: The Manuscripts of the Earl of Dartmouth (London: Her Majesty's Stationery Office, 1895).

The *Pennsylvania Archives* are a mine of material covering political, social, and economic affairs in the prerevolutionary period. Those volumes useful to this study include the *Pennsylvania Archives,* first series, vols. 2–4 (Philadelphia: Joseph Severns and Company, 1853), a compilation of the official correspondence written and received by the governors of Pennsylvania; *Pennsylvania Archives,* second series, vol. 2 (Harrisburg: B. F. Myers, 1876), vol. 3 (Harrisburg: B. F. Myers, 1875), vol. 8 (Harrisburg: Lane S. Hart, 1878); *Pennsylvania Archives,* third series, vol. 2 (Harrisburg: Clarence M. Burch, 1894), vol. 14 (Harrisburg: William S. Ray, 1897); *Pennsylvania Archives,* fourth series, vols. 2–3 (Harrisburg: William S. Ray, 1900), including official papers and messages of the governors; *Pennsylvania Archives,* fifth series, vol. 1 (Harrisburg: Harrisburg Publishing Company, 1906); and *Votes and Proceedings of the House of Representatives of the Province of Pennsylvania, Pennsylvania Archives,* eighth series, vols. 4–5 (Harrisburg, 1931), vols. 6–8 (Harrisburg, 1935). Other important Pennsylvania sources are the *Minutes of the Provincial Council of Pennsylvania,* vols. 7–10 (Harrisburg: Theodore Fenn and Company, 1851–52) and *The Stat-*

utes at Large of Pennsylvania, vols. 5–8 (Harrisburg: William S. Ray, 1898–1900).

Additional useful sources for Pennsylvania politics and the coming of the revolution are the *Journal of the Commissioners for Trade and Plantations from January 1754 to December 1758, from January 1759 to December 1763, from January 1764 to December 1768, from January 1769 to December 1775,* vols. 10–13 (London: His Majesty's Stationery Office, 1933–37); *Acts of the Privy Council, Colonial Series,* vols. 4–6 (London: His Majesty's Stationery Office, 1911–12); *Journals of the Continental Congress, 1774–1789,* ed. Worthington C. Ford, vol. 1 (Washington: Government Printing Office, 1904); and the *New Jersey Archives,* first series, *Documents Relating to the Colonial History of the State of New Jersey,* vol. 10 (Newark: Daily Advertiser Printing Office, 1886).

Philadelphia newspapers of the period give an incomplete view of politics. David Hall's *Pennsylvania Gazette* has much less political news and political controversy than the *Pennsylvania Journal* of William and Thomas Bradford or the short-lived *Pennsylvania Chronicle* of William Goddard. Many of the exciting subjects of the period were discussed in the latter two newspapers, but newspapers were not as important as broadsides and pamphlets for circulating political propaganda, nor did they carry much detail on politicking.

Much of the manuscript material in the Historical Society of Pennsylvania collections has appeared between the covers of the *Pennsylvania Magazine of History and Biography* (hereafter cited as *PMHB*). Important for this study were "Some Letters of Joseph Galloway," *PMHB* 21 (1897) : 477–84; "Correspondence between William Strahan and David Hall," *PMHB* 10 (1886) : 86–99, 217–32; 11 (1887) : 346–57; "Minutes of the Committee of Safety of Bucks County, Pennsylvania, 1774–1776," *PMHB* 15 (1891) : 257–90; "Statement of Benjamin Kite, 1828," *PMHB* 19 (1895): 264–66, a first-hand account of political practices in Philadelphia; "Fragments of a Journal Kept by Samuel Foulk, of Bucks County, While a

Member of the Colonial Assembly of Pennsylvania, 1762–4,"
ed. Howard M. Jenkins, *PMHB* 5 (1881) : 60–73; and "The
Diary of Grace Growden Galloway," ed. Raymond C. Werner,
PMHB 55 (1931) : 32–96; 58 (1934) : 152–92.

Historians generally have been very kind to Franklin. His
major biographers, including James Parton, *Life and Times
of Benjamin Franklin,* 2 vols. (Boston: James R. Osgood and
Company, 1884); Carl Van Doren, *Benjamin Franklin* (New
York: The Viking Press, 1938); and Verner W. Crane, *Benjamin Franklin and a Rising People* (Boston: Little, Brown and
Company, 1954), bring out most sides of Franklin's character.
They tend to slight Franklin's prerevolutionary political activities. Clinton Rossiter's *Six Characters in Search of a Republic: Studies in the Political Thought of the American
Colonies* (New York: Harcourt, Brace, & World, Inc., 1964),
which shows Franklin as a man of strong principles whose
pragmatic approach to social and political problems led him
to a belief in democracy, has been superseded by the brilliant
synthesis of Franklin's political ideas in Paul W. Connor,
*Poor Richard's Politicks: Benjamin Franklin and His New
American Order* (New York: Oxford University Press, 1965).

Several works that deal with Franklin, Pennsylvania politics,
and imperial relations were quite helpful to this study. For
example, Theodore Thayer, *Pennsylvania Politics and the
Growth of Democracy, 1740–1776* (Harrisburg: Pennsylvania
Historical and Museum Commission, 1953) highlights Franklin's political achievements and criticizes his mistakes. Franklin is treated favorably; in Thayer's view his party was really
a people's party, and he contributed greatly to the establishment of a democratic state in 1776. William S. Hanna, *Benjamin Franklin and Pennsylvania Politics* (Stanford: Stanford
University Press, 1964), offers a revisionist opinion. Thomas
Penn is the hero of this book. Hanna argues that Franklin's
political activity was not very successful or noteworthy and
that he did nothing to lead the province toward the political
revolution of 1776. James H. Hutson, "Benjamin Franklin
and Pennsylvania Politics, 1751–1755: A Reappraisal," *PMHB*

93 (1969) : 303–71, challenges Hanna, cites convincing evidence, and returns to the traditional view of a Franklin motivated by principle. Another recent revisionist study, Cecil
B. Currey, *Road to Revolution: Benjamin Franklin in England, 1765–1775* (New York: Doubleday & Company, 1968),
exaggerates Franklin's radicalism and the influence of his
land speculations on his political ideas.

Franklin's biographers do not deal very satisfactorily with
Galloway; they seem to conclude that he was so overshadowed
by Franklin that he was not in himself important. Separate
biographies of Galloway are rare. The fullest account is Raymond C. Werner, "Joseph Galloway, His Life and Times"
(Ph.D. dissertation, State University of Iowa, 1927). Ernest
H. Baldwin, "Joseph Galloway, the Loyalist Politician,"
PMHB 26 (1902) : 161–91, 289–321, 417–42, is also fairly
complete and accurate. The newest account is David L. Jacobson, "John Dickinson and Joseph Galloway 1764–1776: A
Study in Contrasts" (Ph.D. dissertation, Princeton University,
1959), but Jacobson emphasizes Dickinson's achievements more
than Galloway's. Julian P. Boyd, *Anglo-American Union:
Joseph Galloway's Plans to Preserve the British Empire, 1774–
1788* (Philadelphia: University of Pennsylvania Press, 1941)
contains a good brief summary of Galloway's career. His
helplessness and inability to withstand the Whigs is discussed
in William H. Nelson, *The American Tory* (Oxford: The
Clarendon Press, 1961). Robert M. Calhoon, " 'I Have Deduced Your Rights:' Joseph Galloway's Concept of His Role,
1774–1775," *Pennsylvania History* 35 (1968) : 356–78, is a
thorough and close analysis of Galloway during a very critical
period.

Biographical studies of important Pennsylvania associates
of Franklin and Galloway include William H. Mariboe, "The
Life of William Franklin, 1730(1)–1813" (Ph.D. dissertation,
University of Pennsylvania, 1962); William T. Parsons, "Isaac
Norris II, The Speaker" (Ph.D. dissertation, University of
Pennsylvania, 1955); Nicholas B. Wainwright, "William
Denny in Pennsylvania," *PMHB* 81 (1957) : 170–98; David

L. Jacobson, *John Dickinson and the Revolution in Pennsylvania* (Berkeley: University of California Press, 1965); Burton A. Konkle, *George Bryan and the Constitution of Pennsylvania, 1731–1791* (Philadelphia: William J. Campbell, 1922); and Ward L. Miner, *William Goddard, Newspaperman* (Durham: Duke University Press, 1962).

Besides Thayer's book, the following provide insightful treatments of Pennsylvania politics: Dietmar Rothermund, *The Layman's Progress: Religious and Political Experience in Colonial Pennsylvania 1740–1770* (Philadelphia: University of Pennsylvania Press, 1961); David Hawke, *In the Midst of a Revolution* (Philadelphia: University of Pennsylvania Press, 1961); Jack R. Pole, *Political Representation in England and the Origins of the American Republic* (New York: St. Martin's Press, 1966); Bernard Bailyn, *The Origins of American Politics* (New York: Alfred A. Knopf, Inc., 1968); and Lawrence H. Gipson, *The British Empire before the American Revolution,* vols. 6–12 (New York: Alfred A. Knopf, Inc., 1946–65).

Particular studies of the 1755–56 period are Ralph L. Ketcham, "Benjamin Franklin and William Smith: New Light on an Old Philadelphia Quarrel," *PMHB* 88 (1964) : 142–63; Ralph L. Ketcham, "Conscience, War, and Politics in Colonial Pennsylvania," *William and Mary Quarterly,* 3d ser. 20 (1963) : 412–35; and John J. Zimmerman, "Benjamin Franklin and the Quaker Party," *WMQ,* 3d ser. 17 (1960) : 291–313.

Studies of the 1757–63 period include William Smith Mason, "Franklin and Galloway: Some Unpublished Letters," *Proceedings of the American Antiquarian Society,* new series, 34 (1924) : 518–26; Sister Joan de Lourdes Leonard, C.S.J., "Elections in Colonial Pennsylvania," *WMQ,* 3d ser. 11 (1954) : 385–402; Howard M. Jenkins, "The Pennsylvania Assembly in 1761–1762," *PMHB* 7 (1884) : 407–13; G. B. Warden, "The Proprietary Group in Pennsylvania, 1754–1764," *WMQ,* 3d ser. 21 (1964) : 367–89; and Anthony F. C. Wallace, *King of the Delawares: Teedyuscung* (Philadelphia: University of Pennsylvania Press, 1949).

Historians have been attracted to the dramatic events of
1764–66. Important works dealing with politics in this period
include James H. Hutson, "The Campaign to Make Pennsylvania a Royal Province, 1764–1770, Part I," *PMHB* 94 (1970) :
427–63, "Part II," *PMHB* 95 (1971) : 28–49; Brooke Hindle,
"The March of the Paxton Boys," *WMQ,* 3d ser. 3 (1946) :
461–86; James H. Hutson, "An Investigation of the Inarticulate: Philadelphia's White Oaks," *WMQ,* 3d ser. 28 (1971) :
3–25; J. Philip Gleason, "A Scurrilous Colonial Election and
Franklin's Reputation," *WMQ,* 3d ser. 11 (1961) : 68–84;
Glenn Weaver, "Benjamin Franklin and the Pennsylvania
Germans," *WMQ,* 3d ser. 14 (1957) : 539–59; and Benjamin
H. Newcomb, "Effects of the Stamp Act on Colonial Pennsylvania Politics," *WMQ,* 3d ser. 23 (1966) : 257–72. For the
Stamp Act crisis see Verner W. Crane, "Benjamin Franklin
and the Stamp Act," *Colonial Society of Massachusetts, Publications* 22 (1937) : 56–77; and Edmund S. and Helen M. Morgan, *The Stamp Act Crisis: Prologue to Revolution,* new, rev.
ed. (New York: Collier Books, 1963).

Events of the 1767–70 period are discussed in John J. Zim-
merman, "Benjamin Franklin and the *Pennsylvania Chroni-
cle,*" *PMHB* 81 (1957) : 351–64; and Robert L. Brunhouse,
"The Effect of the Townshend Acts in Pennsylvania," *PMHB*
54 (1930) : 355–73. For data on Franklin's involvement in paper
money matters, see Joseph A. Ernst, "Genesis of the Currency
Act of 1764: Virginia Paper Money and the Protection of
British Investments," *WMQ,* 3d ser. 22 (1965) : 33–74; Joseph
E. Ernst, "The Currency Act Repeal Movement: A Study in
Imperial Politics and Revolutionary Crisis, 1764–1767,"
WMQ, 3d ser. 25 (1968) : 177–211; and Jack M. Sosin, "Im-
perial Regulation of Colonial Paper Money," *PMHB* 88
(1964) : 174–98.

Works that give much attention to Franklin's activities in
Britain after 1767 include: Michael G. Kammen, *A Rope of
Sand: The Colonial Agents, British Politics, and the American
Revolution* (Ithaca: Cornell University Press, 1968); Jack M.
Sosin, *Agents and Merchants: British Colonial Policy and the*

Origins of the American Revolution, 1763–1775 (Lincoln: University of Nebraska Press, 1965); Charles R. Ritcheson, *British Politics and the American Revolution* (Norman: University of Oklahoma Press, 1954); Bernard Donoughue, *British Politics and the American Revolution: The Path to War, 1773–1775* (New York: St. Martin's Press, 1964); and B. D. Bargar, *Lord Dartmouth and the American Revolution* (Columbia: University of South Carolina Press, 1965).

Useful background studies for the 1763–76 period are Arthur M. Schlesinger, *The Colonial Merchants and the American Revolution* (New York: Frederick Ungar Publishing Company, 1957); Arthur M. Schlesinger, *Prelude to Independence: The Newspaper War on Britain, 1764–1776* (New York: Alfred M. Knopf, Inc., 1958); John C. Miller, *Origins of the American Revolution* (Boston: Little, Brown and Company, 1943); Lawrence H. Gipson, *The Coming of the Revolution, 1763–1775* (New York: Harper & Row, Inc., 1962); Edmund C. Burnett, *The Continental Congress* (New York: W. W. Norton & Company, 1964); and Merrill Jensen, *The Founding of a Nation: A History of the American Revolution, 1763–1776* (New York: Oxford University Press, 1968).

Index

Franklin, Benjamin (*continued*)
sents New Jersey, 205; represents
Massachusetts, 228–29, 230, 235,
238; needed in London, 228, 230–
31; problems, 229, 234, 269, 270;
significance, 294
—alliance with Galloway, 35, 68,
69, 102–03, 132, 134, 162, 236,
285–86, 287, 290–93, 298; aims,
1; beginnings, 5, 6, 10; intellectual comparison, 7, 130–31, 212,
234–35, 280, 295–98; chooses, 40,
41; supported by Galloway, 41,
138, 139, 141, 155, 157, 159, 206–
07, 234, 286–87; makes plans, 71;
speech, 83; works on propaganda,
87; mutual trust, 102, 236; reports to Galloway, 112, 171; split
develops, 130–31, 142, 159, 162,
183, 190–91, 200, 206, 234, 266,
271, 286; congratulates Galloway,
132; directs Galloway, 134; understanding of Galloway, 143–44; on
Galloway as Speaker, 146; con-
soles Galloway, 147; friendship
for Galloway, 159, 207, 234, 236;
on paper money, 169, 178; patriotism used by Galloway, 189–
90, 195, 201–02, 227; and Galloway's moderation, 182, 189, 196,
200; and interest in Galloway's
activities, 204, 207, 259–60, 281;
and attacks on Galloway, 226;
and Galloway's retirement, 226,
227; and Tea Act, 238–39; and
reconciliation of partners, 269–70,
279, 280, 281–84; papers deposited
with Galloway, 285; and betrayal
by Galloway, 285, 289
—economic ideas, 128, 197, 203;
industry and frugality, 177, 188,
266, 296; American manufacturing, 203; Poor Richard, 204, 296
—and paper money, 107, 149;

scheme, 108, 109–10, 129, 165,
166, 167, 173; in Pennsylvania,
169, 170; repeal of prohibition,
169, 171, 172, 174, 175, 176; cooperation of merchants, 171–72;
end of quest, 176; changes mind
on paper money, 177
—as person, 8, 9, 10, 212, 297; ambition, 12, 80, 81, 158; homesick,
60, 228; man of reaction, 74, 81;
wealth, 80; optimism, 98, 138,
230, 233, 260; and moderation,
113–14, 115, 130, 160, 178, 182;
sarcasm, 127, 128, 197, 238; confidence, 138; conciliation, 160,
178, 240, 270; caution, 180;
health, 282; rationality, 297
—and political activities, 26, 34, 35,
37, 38, 41, 42, 69, 90, 91, 99–100,
101, 129, 227; control of Philadephia, 38; leads Assembly, 40,
42, 68, 88, 91, 100–01; as Speaker,
90–91, 108; disassociation, 227;
significance, 291–92
—political ideas, 40, 41, 42, 105,
106, 107, 127; and science, 8, 14,
71, 83, 152, 187*n*, 295–96; and
law, 12; doing good, 13; Whig
view of history, 15; on British
constitution, 15, 16; on factionalism, 28, 29, 30, 36, 291; and
American rights, 79–80, 82, 84,
131, 156, 159, 185, 200, 203, 205,
207, 227, 262–63, 264, 280, 292,
296; and representative assembly,
80–81, 286, 290; and parliamentary privilege, 81, 283; on authority of Parliament, 106, 107,
126, 128, 135, 140, 141, 143, 163,
181, 186, 187, 208, 229, 264, 273,
294; and primacy of assembly,
127, 131, 158, 163, 181, 187, 208,
286, 292, 295–96; and imperial
constitution, 136–37, 143, 161, 162,

253–54, 255; predicts struggle with France, 254, 288; presents plan of union, 254; signs petition to king, 257; signs Continental Association, 257; revises minutes, 257; unseated as Speaker, 258; in New York, 259, 271; attacks Continental Congress, 272, 274, 275, 278, 283; reverses position, 271, 274, 277; and *Candid Examination*, 272; opposes Association, 272; and Loyalists, 272, 274–75, 279; opposes anti-British leaders, 273–74, 276; and petitioning separate from Congress, 275, 276–77; political career ends, 278–79; on outbreak of war, 279; as temporary patriot, 284–85; as Loyalist, 285, 287, 289, 290, 298; civil administrator of Philadelphia, 287; on British war effort, 287, 289; attainted, 287; separated from wife, 288; death, 288; and results of revolution, 289; evaluation of, 295

—in alliance with Franklin. See Franklin, Benjamin

—as person, 34, 93, 121, 146, 202; legal mind, 5, 8, 12, 168, 227, 273, 295; personality, 9, 10, 42, 212, 297; ambition, 12, 80, 81, 139; temper, 54, 89, 214–15, 221, 271, 275, 276, 278, 297; man of reaction, 74, 81; wealth, 80; character change, 137, 235; vanity, 147, 268, 297; caution, 170, 180, 210; illness, 202–03, 207, 210, 225, 278, 281; arrogance, 216, 275, 297; lacks initiative, 221–22, 225, 235, 242, 243, 246, 250; despondent and resigned, 225; need for prestige, 246; confusion, 257–58; vengeful, 274; inconsistent, 274, 277, 295; changed appearance, 281

—political attitudes and ideas, 40, 103, 107, 147, 184, 191, 216–17, 226; on public service, 13; on British constitution, 14, 15, 16, 248; and Whig view of history, 15; on legislatures, 67, 80, 81, 117, 131, 163, 182–83, 252, 290, 292; and American rights, 79–80, 82, 116, 117, 137, 139–40, 141, 182, 190, 200, 210, 215, 221, 250–51, 252, 273, 275, 281, 292; on royal government, 82; on British imperial policy, 107, 117, 193, 235; on moderation, 115, 116, 117, 125, 131, 134, 137, 160, 178, 193, 196, 201, 223, 235, 244, 246, 248, 249, 250, 256, 274, 275, 295; on parliamentary authority, 116, 124, 131, 135, 143, 163, 251, 273, 274, 278–79, 281, 296; fear of violence, 116, 124, 131, 192, 242, 256, 284, 295; and imperial constitution, 117, 162, 189; desires conciliation, 160, 178, 247; on colonial constitution, 179; on American representation in Parliament, 274; and freedom of the press, 220; on independence, 271, 272–73, 274, 279; on republicanism, 271–72; on contract theory of government, 273; on union of king and Parliament, 273; on political participation, 290–91, 292, 293

—as politician, 13; strategy, 42, 47, 78, 82–83, 100, 144, 147, 151, 183, 190, 192, 194, 195–98, 202, 218, 246, 247, 248–49, 253, 254, 272, 276, 290; party leader, 57, 71, 90, 91, 99–100, 124, 138, 197; Assembly leader, 88, 91, 100–01, 258–59, 277, 291; electioneering, 99, 100, 122, 199; machine politics, 124, 217–18; significance, 291–92

—on union with Britain, 132, 163,